John Man has written widely in the fields of history, anthropology and travel. A long-standing interest in Mongolia led him to write *Gobi: Tracking the Desert*, which is to be followed by a history of the Mongol Empire. His other books include *The Penguin Atlas of D-Day*, *The Survival of Jan Little* and *Jungle Nomads of Ecuador: The Waorani*. He devised and presented BBC Radio 4's *Survivors* series (1994 – 7).

For Jonathan, Tom, Emily, Will and Dushka

HARVARD UNIVERSITY PRESS
CAMBRIDGE, MASSACHUSETTS
1999

Atlas

of the Year 1000

930
940
950
960
970
980
990
1000
1010
1020

JOHN MAN

First United Kingdom publication by Penguin Books Ltd, 1999

ISBN 0-674-54187-1
Library of Congress Catalog Card Number: 99-61774

JACKET (FRONT)
(also facing page):

*Map of the World, late
10th or early 11th century,
from Macrobius,*
Commentary on the
'Somnium Scipionis',
*in the Bodleian Library,
University of Oxford
[MS. D'Orville fol. 100r].*

JACKET (BACK)
(clockwise from bottom left):

*Viking silver pendant,
10th century, in the Statens
Historiska Museum,
Stockholm (photo: Werner
Forman).*

*St Vladimir, from Russian
cloisonné pendant, 12th
century, in the Hermitage,
St Petersburg (photo:
Bridgeman Art Library).*

*Stone figure of Hoa Haka
Nana Ia, from Easter Island,
in the British Museum
(photo: C. M. Dixon).*

*Nigerian bronze pendant,
10th century, courtesy
National Commission for
Museums & Monuments,
Lagos (photo: Dirk Bakker).*

*Somaskanda, Chola bronze
figure, in the National
Museum of India, New
Delhi (photo: Bridgeman
Art Library).*

*Head of Christ, stained
glass, c. 1070, in the Musée
de l'Œuvre de Notre Dame,
Strasbourg (photo: Bridgeman Art Library).*

*Toltec Atalante statue from
Tula (photo: Tony Morrison /
South American Pictures).*

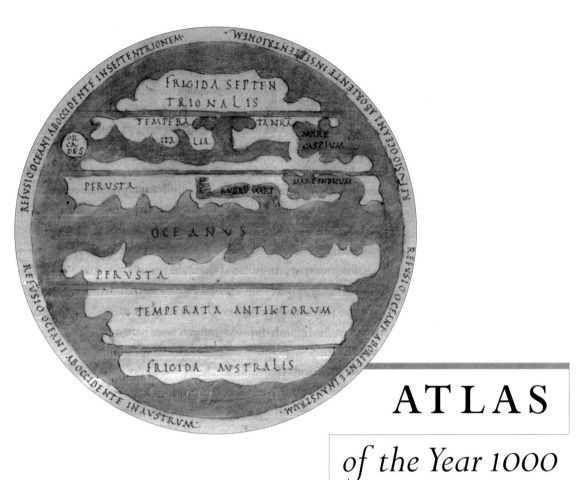

ATLAS

of the Year 1000

Contents

Introduction

One World in the Making 8

The Americas

Isolated Cultures Brought to Light by Archaeology 12

1 *The Enigma of Tiahuanaco* 16
2 *The Toltecs' Brief Heyday* 18
3 *Cahokia: Capital of the Eastern Woodlands* 20
4 *The South-West: A Cultural Bloom in a Harsh Land* 22
5 *Bison Hunters and Farmers of the Prairies* 24
6 *A Tapestry of Cultures on the West Coast* 26
7 *The Far North: The Coming of the Thule People* 28
8 *The Vikings in Vinland* 30

Europe

A Benighted Continent on the Brink of a New Dawn 32

1 *The Reach of Rome* 36
2 *The Viking Heartland* 38
3 *New-found Lands in Iceland and Greenland* 40
4 *England: A Nation on Its Knees* 42
5 *The Celtic World* 44
6 *France: Powerful Dukes, an Embattled King* 48
7 *Viking + Greek = Russian Orthodox* 52
8 *Otto III's Teenage Dreams of Imperial Grandeur* 54
9 *The Coming of the Ashkenazim* 58
10 *The Emergence of Hungary* 60
11 *Byzantium: Fighting to Preserve the Glory* 62

Africa

Early States and Proto-Empires 108

1 *Islam's Peaceful Trade with Realms of Gold* 112
2 *The Rich Land of the Great Lakes* 116
3 *Ethiopia: A World Apart* 118
4 *The South: The Golden Meadows of Zimbabwe's First Capital* 120

Asia

Two Suns and Their Planets 84

1 China: The Success of the Sung 88
2 Tibet's Dark Age 92
3 The Liao: A Challenge from the North 94
4 Hsi-hsia: 'The Great State of White and High' 96
5 Korea: Struggle for Unity, Wealth and Independence 98
6 Japan: The Rise and Rise of Michinaga 100
7 The Khmers: The First of Angkor's Wonders 102
8 India: Fleeting Power, Enduring Glory 104
9 Indonesia: Two Empires Built on Spices 106

The World of Islam

A Political Patchwork, a Cultural Unity 66

1 Baghdād: The Heart of Islam 70
2 The Slaves of Islam 72
3 The Fatimids: Ambition, Power and Madness 74
4 Islamic Spain: Glory and Egomania 76
5 Central Asia: The Coming of the Turks 78
6 Mahmud, Scourge of Northern India 80
7 Judaism: A Faith Toughened by Trials 82

Oceania

Remote Worlds Linked by Polynesian Voyages 122

1 The Moth-Eaters of the Australian Alps 128
2 Colonists of the 'Long White Cloud' 130
3 Easter Island: The Message of the Statues 132

Appendix

A Millennial Gazetteer 135
Bibliography 137
Acknowledgements 138
Index 139

INTRODUCTION

One World in the Making

It is often said that the year 1000 has no 'real' importance, that it acquires significance only from its zeroes, from our determination to read significance into birthdays and big numbers. Far from it: the time has a real historical significance, rooted in the way human society developed, from scattered diversity to today's 'one world'.

The significance is this: by pure coincidence, the year 1000, or thereabouts, marked the first time in human history that it was possible to pass an object, or a message, right around the world. This had, of course, been almost possible for a long time. Although no culture knew what the world looked like, and few had any idea of its size, almost every habitable region had been peopled for thousands of years, and almost every culture had a neighbour or two. Messages and artefacts had been passed between neighbours, across continents and between continents. Such messages – pottery styles, agricultural techniques, new technologies, religions – are the stuff of cultural diffusion. But there were gaps. Even in 900, no human being had visited New Zealand. No one had crossed from Europe to the Americas. If any New Guineans were commuting to Australia across the Torres Strait, there is no sign of it in the archaeological record.

A hundred years later, however, these gaps were tenuously bridged, and this invites a thought experiment. Imagine a vital piece of information despatched by word of mouth from, say, the heart of the Islamic world, the civilization with the most cross-cultural links. The word is passed across cultural borders from messenger to messenger whose task in each case is to transmit it to neighbouring cultures. Ignore all practical problems. Assume peaceful progress, perfect translation, a steady pace.

In 1000, Islam derives slaves and gold from sub-Saharan Africa. The message heads quickly south, across the Sahara and down the Nile, being carried on through the continent by Bantu farmers and herders, until it reaches the Khoisan in the Kalahari Desert. Islam also trades with Byzantium, which is in close touch with proto-Russia, for reasons of commerce, politics and religion, for Russia is just now in the process of adopting Byzantium's Orthodox Christianity. The Rus, dominating the north–south trade routes along the major rivers, still have close dealings with their ancestral Viking culture. Not only are the Vikings everywhere around Europe's coasts – this message would echo round Europe like a gunshot in the Grand Canyon – but they also commute regularly to Iceland. Icelanders have recently colonized Greenland. Greenland Vikings are at this moment doing their best to establish a colony in Newfoundland, and are trading, as well as fighting, with Inuit from northern Canada. Here the message divides. One route heads south, through the cultures of the eastern woodlands, through the arid south-west via the town-dwellers of Chaco Canyon, to central America, and thence to the Andes and down the Amazon. In the north, the Inuit of the Thule culture, who are spread across the Canadian Arctic, pass the word along to their relatives in Alaska, who paddle it across the Bering Strait to north-east Siberia. Inuit there obtain iron from the borders between Siberia and China. In China comes another division. The message flows east through Korea, or directly with Chinese traders, to Japan; and west, following long-established Silk Road routes to Central Asia, then down through India, where the expansive Chola Empire transmits it to Sri Lanka. Meanwhile, messengers are advancing southward through south-east Asia, via the Khmer Empire of ancient Cambodia. Offshore, two local trade kingdoms, linked by Arab, Chinese and Indian traders, create alternative routes by land and sea through the Indonesian archipelago. There is a hesitation, perhaps, about the penetration of New Guinea. But then comes a sudden impetus as the word passes along Pacific island chains to the Polynesian frontier, even being carried with the very first settlers to the virgin land of New Zealand. Back to the north and west, on the coast of northern Australia, traders are just beginning to exploit sausage-like marine creatures, bêches-de-mer (also known as sea cucumbers, or trepang), much prized as a delicacy in China, then as now. From the bases set up by sea cucumber gatherers in Arnhem Land, Australian Aboriginals carry the message across the continent. Meanwhile, north of the Hindu Kush, where we left one of our Silk Road messengers, it is a small step through Muslim Afghanistan back into the heart of the Muslim world.

Imagine all this to have occurred at walking pace, 24 hours a day. Our message has covered 35,000 miles in one year, right around the world plus another 10,000 miles for the twists and turns. If we allow for our path to divide and radiate at crucial points, a year or two would be enough for global diffusion. There would be hardly a community left out: Easter Islanders, cut off centuries earlier after their arrival on their remote home, must remain in ignorance, and so perhaps must the inhabitants of Tierra del Fuego, and some Amazonian tribesmen, and numerous tiny isolated communities, in Siberia, the Himalayas, the Philippines. But to all intents and purposes, the world is one already.

This is, of course, a fantasy. No culture could have initiated such an experiment, no message could have diffused with such speed. But there is a sort of reality

A Year Like Any Other

The millennium as it would have been recorded in the calendars of selected cultures.

Mesoamerica
10 baktuns, 8 katuns, 1 tun from start of Mayan Long Count (3114 BC).

Judaism
3761 AM – Anno Mundi (Latin for 'In the year of the World' – from the Creation.)

Islam
378 AH – Anno Hegirae (Latin, from the Arabic Hajra: 'In the Year of the Emigration' – of Muhammad to Medina.)

India
3102 of Kali Era, 752 of the Kalakurikedi Era, 682 of the Gupta Era, 1058 of the Vikrama Era, 922 of the Saka Era.

Nepal
4095 of the Thakuri Dynasty.

China
40th year of Sung Dynasty, 3rd year of reign of Emperor Chen Tsung.

Japan
2nd year of Choho, the 5th year-period of reign of Emperor Ichijo.

embedded in the fantasy. The links were real, and there was a theoretical window of opportunity.

Nor was it a fleeting one. The links endured, being snapped only briefly. In the late 14th century, Greenlanders ceased visiting the American coast because they and their colony were frozen out of existence, just a century before Columbus's voyage of re-discovery. It does not seem too fanciful to look for the roots of today's 'one world' in the world of 1,000 years ago.

There is something else special about the time, something other than the briefly formed interconnections – something special not about the year, but the era. It is this: on a scale recording the advance of civilization from tribal isolation to international-ism, from nature-dependency to urbanized control, the world of 1,000 years ago was evenly balanced.

In half the world – the four continental interiors of North America, South America, Africa and Australia – most people lived, as they had for unrecorded cen-turies, in conformity with the dictates of nature and their own ancient behaviour patterns. Migrations and cultural change left only shadowy records, to be deduced from folklore or retrieved by archaeologists.

In the other half, China and India already had 2,000 years of recorded history behind them, while the Middle East was dominated by a religious newcomer: Islam, a splintering empire politically, but with a cultural reach – from the Pyrenees to the Hindu Kush – not seen since the fall of Rome, 600 years before. Part of Europe – now Turkey, then the Byzantine Empire – laid dubious claim to the glory that had been Rome's.

On this spectrum, northern Europe occupied a pivotal position, in the middle ground. Though most people lived out their lives dominated by clan and tribe, strong leaders imposed wider loyalties, foreshadowing nation states. Pillagers were turning into citizens, citizens fought off pillagers. Trade and agricultural innovation were building a foundation for future wealth, and the continent's political hotchpotch was steadily acquiring an identity of its own, as Christendom. A monk could travel from Scotland to Constantinople and find himself on familiar ground at every stage, if he chose his route carefully.

The cross-section through time cut by this book depends on many different discip-lines. Traditionally, historians give pride of place to the written record. China had millennia of records built up by its ancient bureaucracies, Islam vast libraries record-ing its recent rise. Europe may have been a backwater, but it was acquiring an impressive weight of documents, thanks to those institutions with an interest in records: the church, royalty, aristocracy.

But even in these societies much remained hidden, for ordinary people left few written records. Elsewhere, many regions had none at all. There, great events left traces only in the memories of men and women, and in the ground. Much was lost for ever. But these areas, which would otherwise be utter blanks except for the unreliable testimony of folklore, now offer some of the most fruitful areas of research. Scientists of diverse disciplines – ethnology, botany, archaeology, geology, climatology – summon lost worlds from a forgotten past, and find explanations for what was once mysterious. In doing so, they reveal more of the ways in which human beings fumbled from tribalism towards ever larger social units: clans, chiefdoms, nations, empires.

When was the Last Millennium, Anyway?

AD **2000**. The start of the third millennium. We all know what that means, or think we do. 'Anno Domini' – Latin for 'in the year of our lord'. 2,000 years from the birth of Christ.

But wait. Why should the world at large take the birth of Christ as a baseline? What is there in that date that is of significance for Muslims, Hindus, Buddhists and Jews, for Australian Aboriginals and native Americans? There is no sense, within their own cultures, in which Jesus was their lord.

These cultures (and many others) had their own historical baselines. The Chinese dated events from the beginning of a new reign, Buddhists from the death of Buddha, the Romans from the foundation of Rome, Muslims from Muhammad's flight to Medina, Greeks from the first Olympiad, Mayans in Mexico from their date for the creation of the world. Even Christians had a number of systems – the creation, or the accession of

the Emperor Constantine, or the Year of Christ's death – until the 15th century.

But all systems had their problems. No one knew exactly how months related to years, or how long a year was to the exact hour and minute. Each culture found its own local, short-term solutions, but as cultures interlinked, and as the need for accuracy increased, the underlying disorder was revealed.

The need for a universal standard arose first in the West. Western chronology was Roman. But the Romans counted a year as 355 days, and their dating became steadily more confused. Julius Caesar reformed it in the 1st century BC, defining the year as 365.25 days, inserting a leap year every four years to account for the extra quarter. The changes reduced the previous dating system to chaos, because there was still no agreed baseline. In the 6th century, a Greek monk, Dionysius Exiguus, had another try. He opted for the year of Christ's birth (actually, from his conception: Day One was March 25) as a baseline, which he called AD 1, for the new era.

But this was no complete solution. As it happened, Dionysius got it wrong. Depending which Gospel

is the more accurate, the Christian Era 'really' began either in the last year of Herod the Great (now dated at 4 BC) or the year of the first Roman census in Judaea (6–7 BC).

A baseline error was compounded by a flaw in the Julian reform. 365.25 days is just over 11 minutes too long. By the 13th century, the calendar and the sun were out of step by over a week.

Again chaos was countered, by further reforms under Pope Gregory XIII in the 16th century. But reform was a slow process. Catholic states followed suit, but Protestant and Orthodox nations lagged behind. For a while, if you timed your journey right, you could leave Calais in early January and arrive in Dover the preceding December. Britain finally switched in 1752, when 2 September was followed by 14 September (inspiring riots by people who thought they had 'lost' 11 days). Russia did not change from the so-called Old Style to New until 1917, and anyone reading Russian history has to wrestle with both: the October Revolution was in November, in today's New Style.

Our present solution derived from a combination

of European power, scientific advance and practicality. European domination carried Christianity and its chronology around the world. Historians, bureaucrats and scientists followed, borne on the wave of European supremacy. By the time that supremacy started to fade, it was too late to backtrack.

And it worked, after a fashion, because in the end the baseline is less important than agreement and accuracy. Now, even Islamic and Chinese historians refer to the Christian chronology as well as their own.

But perfect accuracy remains illusory, whether you work backwards or forwards. If you work forwards, remember there was no Year Zero – the Christian Era begins with AD 1. So, even if the supposed baseline were real, the millennium began on New Year's Day in the year 1001. But what is the 'real' baseline if the year AD 1 was actually 4, or 6, or 7 BC? Perhaps the year 1000 was 'actually' some time in the mid-990s. Counting backwards, you could be sure of getting it right – but only from today's perspective. By popular acclaim, that baseline is the dawn of the year 2000. Technically, though – recalling that there was

no Year Zero – it should be 2001. Our current obsession is dictated by the emotional impact of the initial '2.' Whichever, a time traveller zooming back exactly 1,000 years would find nothing much to celebrate on arrival.

The closer the analysis, the more elusive the answer. Actually, there isn't one. The best that can be done (as in this book) is to adopt the New Style, and hope to spot any significant discrepancies between it, the Old Style, and the alternative systems. Since many of these are still in use – especially in deeply religious cultures like Judaism and Islam – some historians, in an attempt to escape Eurocentrism, choose to replace AD with CE, for 'Common Era' and BC with BCE, 'Before the Common Era.' This decision asserts politically correct thinking, but is no solution. Rather than be mired in paradox, most historians concentrate on their prime task, which is to record and try to explain events by analysing causes and effects.

THE AMERICAS

Isolated Cultures Brought to Light by Archaeology

For hunter-gatherers, both North and South America were cornucopias. But the south had more potential for settled societies. Around 1000, the north was beginning to feel its way towards a similar urbanized complexity. Its late start poses unique social and historical problems.

A cursory glance at the Americas in 1000 reveals a peculiarity about the continent: large-scale civilizations in the south and centre, nothing comparable in the north. All indigenous Americans shared a similar genetic inheritance. All must have been equally intelligent, talented and motivated. Why the difference?

A similar question arises after comparing Old World and New: why did great civilizations emerge so much earlier in Eurasia than in the Americas? The answer is the same in both cases: access to the right sort of crops and animals. With domesticated crops and animals, people can settle, intensify food production, make cities, create wealth, fund armies and bureaucracies and libraries. But what the right ones are no one knows in advance. It takes centuries of experimentation to discover, for the answers involve a whole package of crops, animals, tools and behaviour patterns.

In the New World there was wealth enough for hunter-gatherers, but the central and southern parts of the continent possessed a better combination of domesticable food sources – corn, beans and squash, all of which can be planted and weeded with no more than pointed sticks. And the south also had a family of camel-related herbivores, the llama, and its cousin the alpaca, which could turn grass into food, wool and muscle-power. A suitable package of crops and animals emerged in about 3000 BC, underpinning settled civilizations which had no need of the ploughed-field systems of Europe and Asia. In the north, nuts and berries were no substitute for Old World cereals, and dogs could not do the job of llamas, let alone horses and cattle. Quite simply, the north lacked hardware. The software – the ingenuity that allowed others to develop agriculture – never had a chance.

Chance came only when something of the south's domestic package began to spread north, crawling over the barriers of terrain and climate – the tropical isthmus of Darien, the deserts of Mexico, the cooler lands to the north – at an average rate of a mere 550 metres (600 yards) a year. This snail's-pace process did not involve a complete package. Central America, for instance, apparently had no need for pack animals, relying very effectively on human muscle-power.

Hand-stones and mortars, like these found in a south-western cave, were used for grinding maize, productive varieties of which had spread through the arid south-west to the eastern woodlands by around the turn of the millennium.

For the north, there was a particular reason for the slowness. It had taken millennia to make the tiny, hard ancestral corn (maize) into something nutritious, large and cookable. Even then, it remained a tropical plant, of little use north of the Mexican deserts. Corn of a sort was known in the eastern United States by AD 200, but it took another 700 years to breed suitable species. Only then could large-scale settled cultures evolve (though this is not necessarily an ideal — the West Coast peoples lived so well on game, fish and fruit that it seems they felt no urge to build towns). Once the triple package of corn, beans and squash was in place, northern cultures changed — urbanites would say 'advanced' — even though they still lacked suitable domestic animals. By about 1000, two significant cultures were evolving fast, as the remains in Cahokia, Illinois and Chaco Canyon show. Given the lack of cattle and horses, of the wheel and of iron-working, these were astonishing achievements.

Of all this the outside world knew nothing. The only non-Americans to have first-hand experience of the Americas — sub-Arctic America, for Inuit occasionally made the 80 km (50-mile) paddle across the Bering Straits — were the Vikings, who briefly set up a base in Newfoundland in 1000. Their adventures left few traces. There were rumours of Norsemen journeying across the icy northern ocean and reaching a land of wine and good grazing, but no one in Eurasia (except Inuit-related peoples in Siberia) knew anything for sure about the inhabitants. Possibly the great 12th-century Arab geographer al-Idrisi was writing of the Inuit and their use of whale-bones when he wrote of people living at the limits of the known world, people who shared their land with 'animals of such enormous size that [they] use their bones and vertebrae in place of wood in constructing houses'. Even this reference may have been to Greenland, not mainland America. No one else tried to make the journey, and this world was left to its inhabitants until the 15th century.

Thereafter ancient ways vanished fast, with important effects both on the awareness of America's past and on the business of discovering more about it — effects more apparent in the north, which lacked the south's massive architecture and records. First came colonization, destroying native cultures and the evidence for them. For information on these cultures, researchers have relied on the records of first contacts and the most obvious relics: the ruins of Pueblo towns, for example, or the great burial mounds of the eastern woodlands. This was a minor area of study, full of rumour and speculation. Since northern indigenous cultures left no written records, they were deemed to be outside history. This was a useful opinion: it allowed a culture busily seizing land to avoid self-criticism. In pursuit of her Manifest

Destiny of coast-to-coast nationhood, young America readily consigned its victims to non-existence.

But in the last four decades new techniques and theories in archaeology, overlapping numerous other disciplines, have steadily provided histories, of a sort. This is very different from history as written in Europe, China or the Islamic world, where the story of the past is in large measure rooted in human character – history as narrative. In the American drama, this element is missing. This section of the *Atlas*, like other sections on non-literate cultures, necessarily has a wide focus. There are few incidents, few individuals – in all of North America around 1000, there was no native American whose name has survived.

The archaeologists who serve as historians for these cultures have no option but to deal with the fundamentals of behaviour, ecological change, cultural adaptation. They have a formidable range of approaches. Different dating techniques, oral histories, mathematical and statistical analyses, experiments with artefacts and seeds, immersion in ancient ways of life surviving today – all these and more have combined to turn researchers into detectives skilled at resurrecting vanished peoples from what little remains of where they lived and what they used.

Since these are virtually the only ways of researching the past, and since they are young fields, the history of native America is, to say the least, lively, fraught with controversies and academic spats. It is controversial in two other ways as well, because so many sites are threatened by development, and because such research impinges on the interests of native Americans today. Seeing their identities at stake, many claim rights to ancestral lands, and to their own names for their communities and cultures. The Pueblo people prefer to call their ancestors Hisatsinom rather than Anasazi, a pejorative Navajo term. Eskimos become Inuit. Native Americans resent the loss of sites, artefacts and remains to scientific institutions – some 600,000 native American human skeletons are thus stored. Are these 'ancestors' or 'evidence'? Group A's 'scientific research' is 'vandalism' to Group B. Between the three competitors – history, development and ethnicity – there is no easy peace.

History, at least, has been served. We now know, for instance, why the Vikings were wise to make their retreat. The conditions that allowed them to settle in Newfoundland – the Medieval Warm Period that had made Greenland habitable – brought them into contact with two other groups: Inuit from the far north, and Beothuk, forest-dwellers who came to the coasts for the summer. In their different ways, both were expert at exploiting their harsh lands. They had a hinterland of resources, territory, reinforcements. If it came to violence, the Vikings had no chance.

So neither they nor any other outsiders learned anything of the worlds beyond the forests and hills of Newfoundland: the hundreds of peoples and languages; the mosaics of forest, river, mountain, plain, desert, canyon and coast; the embryonic civilizations then thriving in the eastern woodlands and the south-west, the powerful empires of Central America and Peru.

None of these indigenous cultures had an overview of their continent, either. But at least they knew of their neighbours. Those in the middle knew of several. Many more were linked indirectly by trade, and by the slow flow of cultural change. If northern Europe was progressing along the scale from barbarism to sophistication, so too were Cahokia and Chaco, two city-based states that were unwittingly creating in the north what had long ago been achieved in the south.

South and north, there is no telling how far or fast indigenous Americans would have developed had the Europeans not arrived.

The Enigma of Tiahuanaco

Around 1000, the Andean highlands and arid coastal regions were under the influence of two linked cities, Wari and Tiahuanaco. They would not last much longer. But between them they ran an empire foreshadowing that of the Incas.

Tiahuanaco in Bolivia has always amazed visitors. It is a massive temple complex of finely hewn stone. It is about a kilometre long with huge gateways and enigmatic statues, and some of its stone blocks weigh over 100 tonnes. At first sight, its very existence is an enigma. It stands 30 km (20 miles) from the shore of Lake Titicaca, the world's highest navigable lake, in a bleak, chilly landscape. Who built it? Why?

The mystery once encouraged wild speculation. Some claimed it must be immeasurably old, or the source of all American civilization, or that it was founded on an island that was lifted into its present position when the Andes were created. But there is no need to evoke magic. The truth, such as it is now known, is astonishing enough.

Tiahuanaco (or Tiwanaku, as it is also spelt) did not exist in isolation. Nor was the city itself new – it was founded in about 200. By 1000, Andean peoples from Columbia to Peru and Bolivia had a tradition of settled civilization – of religion, pottery, weaving, metallurgy, city life – stretching back some 1,700 years. For all that time, Andeans possessed the keys to the door of social complexity: corn, beans, squash, potatoes, quinoa (a grain crop), cotton, pack animals. Since successive cultures never developed writing, there was no formal history. But ways of life endured, and so did traditions. Any traveller in the latter part of the first millennium – a chief, a rich man, a trader – would have seen something of the ruins, canals and terracing that told of past greatness. A structure like the great Moche pyramid near Trujillo – 140 million adobe blocks forming a rectangle 230 metres (250 yards) long and 18 metres (60 feet) high – pointed to a complex, tightly run society. One culture, Paracas, produced exquisite weavings, others wonderful pottery, and one – Pucara, just north of Lake Titicaca – was a religious centre to which Tiahuanaco owed a debt. On the stone-dry coastal desert of southern Peru, our hardy traveller would have been as baffled as modern researchers by the gigantic geometrical markings now known as the Nazca Lines.

At 3,850 metres (almost 13,000 feet) on the bleak and windy plateau, Tiahuanaco is the highest city in the Americas, and one of the highest in the world. Several kilometres from the lakeside, the site looks bleak indeed today. Yet it was a good place to build a city, especially for a religious community. The 8,000-square-kilometre (3,000-square-mile) lake, which then lapped the site, had long been a focus for settlement. Its inhabitants, perhaps the ancestors of today's Aymara, fished its waters and grew potatoes on its marshy shores in a sophisticated system of long earth platforms. The site was well positioned to control the flow of hallucinogens, used in religious ceremonies, from the eastern jungles to the highlands and the coasts. To the east lay the snow-capped Cordillera Real, a focus for reverence, as was the lake.

So, some time after AD 300 the Andeans, whoever they were, cut large stone blocks from local quarries. One source was the other side of the lake, across which the blocks were shipped in reed boats. On site, they were shaped and fitted snugly. Canals led lake-water into a surrounding moat, making a natural clasp for this architectural jewel. Around a core of religious buildings, a city of adobe houses arose, eventually housing up to 40,000 people.

No one knows who built this pre-Inca cathedral city. No carvings depict their ceremonies or way of life. There are no names, no language. Their successors, the Incas, made no reference to them. Researchers must be detectives, drawing conclusions from ceramics, carving, weaving, architecture and surviving behaviour patterns (the Aymara have recently revived the ancient art of growing potatoes on raised platforms).

The religious centre of Tiahuanaco was a wonder, covering almost 400 hectares. Massive stones

Tiahuanaco and Wari (Huari)

- Tiahuanaco state
- area under Tiahuanaco influence
- • Tiahuanaco site
- Wari (Huari)

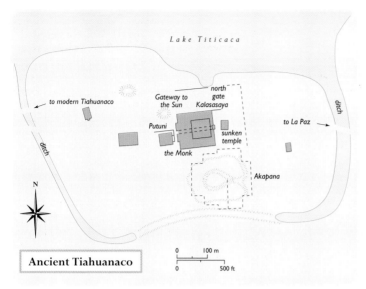

Ancient Tiahuanaco

Lake Titicaca

to modern Tiahuanaco
Gateway to the Sun
north gate
Kalasasaya
ditch
to La Paz
Putuni
sunken temple
the Monk
Akapana
ditch

N

0   100 m
0   500 ft

The Gateway of the Sun commemorates a god, possibly Viracocha the Creator, or Thunupa, a weather deity. The arch is carved from a single block of andesite, quarried from across Lake Titicaca.

were carved into four-square gateways leading to two main structures – a pyramid and a raised temple precinct – and several lesser ones.

The pyramid, the Akapana, is in the shape of an irregular, stubby 'T,' 210 metres (almost 700 feet) long. It originally had seven terraces, surmounted by two stairways. Its flat summit held a sunken courtyard lined and paved with stone and flanked by rooms, possibly priestly quarters. Nearby stood a second, smaller T-shaped shrine of superbly finished masonry, in which was found a 7-metre (24-foot) statue that now stands in a La Paz plaza.

The precinct, the Kalasasaya, 135 by 130 metres (445 by 425 feet), was once surrounded by a wall punctuated by monoliths, making the ceremonial heart of the site. The interior was raised, with steps leading down into a sunken courtyard. It was always open to the skies. Its gateway still frames a monolith carved in Tiahuanaco's typically cubic style, with mask-like face and geometrical limbs. If later beliefs are anything to go by, he could be Thunupa, the god of thunder, holding what may be a spear-thrower and spears. Nearby stands a single 10-tonne block of andesite cut into an arch known as the Gateway of the Sun, with a lintel on which are carved 48 figures running inwards towards a god, possibly Viracocha, the Creator.

This centre grew into a capital, with outlying provinces and subsidiary temples. Its greatest sister-culture was Wari (Huari), which lies in a high, arid valley 650 km (400 miles) to the north-west. It matched Tiahuanaco in size (probably: it has not yet been much excavated), and shared similar religious and artistic traditions. But the relationship between the two is speculative. Perhaps they were rivals; perhaps allies and

co-imperialists; perhaps both at different times.

Whatever its centre, this civilization expanded in the later part of the first millennium, its influence reaching along all the coast of Peru and up into the highlands, 150–300 km (100–200 miles) inland. One Wari outpost was Pachacamac, which around 1000 was a famous pilgrimage centre and one of the most revered of Andean religious sites. At a score of strategic places, people built solid walls, streets, plazas, huge buildings for civil and military administration. Some historians have suggested that the Wari–Tiahuanaco 'empire' was a patchwork of minor nations, reminiscent of medieval Europe. But these were well-planned projects, the expression of orderly minds and large, centrally controlled workforces. There are hints here of a dedicated efficiency reminiscent of ancient Rome.

Though little-known because of its lack of a written history, this culture (if Tiahuanaco and Wari are counted as one) had influenced, and perhaps in part ruled, a stretch of land 1,500 km (1,000 miles) long for around 750 years – a startling achievement by the standards of any continent. It vanished around 1000, for reasons that can only be guessed at. Researchers point to a decrease in rainfall from 950 onwards that could have led to prolonged drought. Perhaps Lake Titicaca retreated, the river dried up, the people fled, the pilgrims ceased coming. With its religious heart stilled, the empire died.

But its traditions were remembered, for it was on them that later Peruvian empires drew. First came the Chimu, who arose around 1300 to dominate an area that overlapped Wari–Tiahuanaco, and then the Incas, who from 1400 onwards built an empire that took in all their predecessors' sites.

2 The Toltecs' Brief Heyday

*The Toltec capital,
Tula, was a city that
seemed to have
sought security in
religious fervour.
It was undermined
by its own success,
but found new
expression further
east in Chichén
Itzá.*

History offers many examples of the Law of
Unforeseen Consequences. Some of those consequences are on view an hour's drive north-west
of Mexico City. On an L-shaped ridge overlooking
the Río Tula stands a mound topped by a line of
what look like stone totem poles. These sturdy,
expressionless figures, standing as if at attention,
are grim replicas of a warrior god, armed with a
javelin-thrower and a sheaf of short javelins, protected by padding and a round shield. On their
heads, pillbox fashion, are headdresses of feathers.

The mound is the remains of a pyramid,
built some time after 950 by people known as
Toltecs to venerate their god, Queztalcóatl. The

rectangular statues are probably of Quetzalcóatl
personified as Venus, the Morning Star. They are
not simply statues – they were pillars carved to
hold the roof-beams of a temple. Together, pyramid and temple formed the northern side of a
great plaza. A kilometre and a half (a mile) away
stand the remains of another temple, one of several that once dominated the city.

This was a rich culture, but not a charming one
by modern standards. The city – Tollan, sometimes
known as Tula after today's nearby town – was
arrayed with stylized reliefs and friezes of armed
warriors, predatory animals with their jaws full of
gory human hearts, serpents swallowing bodies.
The images seem to express a mix of strength and
insecurity – knowledge of the past, fear of the
immediate future.

By the year 1000, Mexico's civilized roots
reached back two millennia, during which its
cultures shared many common features – maize-
based agriculture, ceremonial cult sites, human
sacrifice, ritual ball-games, hieroglyphic writing
and complex calendars. The huge city-state of
Teotihuacán, which is awesome even today, with
its two giant pyramids and rows of temple platforms, had dominated central Mexico for almost
1,000 years. Its influence, like that of Mexico's
other great urban complexes, seems to have been
undermined when its trees were used up and its
soil exhausted. With its economy in ruins, it was
open to attack. In about 750 the city was sacked,
perhaps by 'barbarian' invaders, much as Rome
had fallen three centuries before. And, as after the
fall of Rome, the destruction of Teotihuacán left
chaos, a residue of knowledge and an ideal of
civilization.

In his version of Mexico's pre-conquest history,
the 16th-century chronicler Fray Bernadino de
Sahagún described how a great darkness fell. The
wise men of Teotihuacán 'carried off the
writings, the books, the paintings;
they carried away all the
crafts, the castings of
metal.' When they

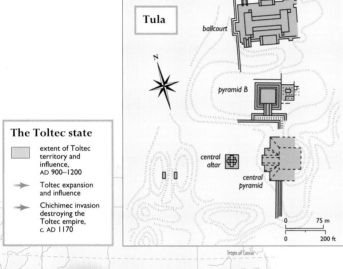

The Toltec state

- extent of Toltec territory and influence, AD 900–1200
- Toltec expansion and influence
- Chichimec invasion destroying the Toltec empire, c. AD 1170

Tula

ballcourt

pyramid B

central altar

central pyramid

0   75 m

0   200 ft

Tropic of Cancer

La Quemada

Tamuán

Morelos

Sierra Madre Oriental

CHICHIMECS

HUAXTECS

Tula

L. Texcoco Teotihuacán

Tenochtitlán

Malinalco Tlaxcala

Xochicalco Cholula

Tehuacán

Veracruz

MATLATZINCAS

Balsas

Sierra Madre del Sur

Monte Albán

Yagul

Isthmus of Tehuantepec

Gulf of Mexico

Xicalanco

Chiapa de Corzo

Sierra Madre de Chiapas

Izamal Chichén Itzá Coba

Mayapán Tulum

Santa Rita

PACIFIC OCEAN

0   200 km

0   200 miles

went, the gods gathered in the darkness of the fallen city, immolated themselves and re-emerged as the sun and moon in a phoenix-like renewal.

Renewal would, 600 years later, lead to the rise of the Aztecs. But between Teotihuacán and Tenochtitlán, between the Olmec heritage and the Aztec Empire, lay several related cultures of which the two greatest, both of them highly militaristic, were the Toltec, centred on Tula; and the Maya, centred on Chichén Itzá.

Tula, like the Toltec kingdom itself, was short-lived, flourishing for 200 years between 950 and 1150. The Toltecs' history, interfused with legend, was recorded only after the Spanish invasion in the 16th century, but much has been revealed by their surviving art and by archaeological research.

Their origins are obscure: legends suggest that the first Toltecs contributed to the fall of Teotihuacán and that their kingdom was founded by a prince known as Topiltzin. But Toltec names are confusing – Topiltzin means 'our prince', and the term was perhaps a title. Confusingly, it applied to the last as well as the first ruler.

The Toltecs seem to have felt themselves to be a people under threat both from less civilized nomads of the arid north-west and from the foundations of their own lives. Drought or a sudden assault from beyond the shifting frontiers of civilization could bring disaster. In addition, they, like their predecessors, undermined their own security by overcropping and tree-felling.

Living with insecurity, oppressed by the knowledge that former empires had vanished, the Toltecs were obsessed with war and the seizure of tribute. But mere power does not create a sense of security. Gods, too, had to be appeased. Their obsession was symbolized and sanctified by Quetzalcóatl, the 'green-feather serpent' or 'plumed serpent', who infused the Toltecs' spiritual life. He was creator, the morning star, the evening star, the god of wind, and the namesake of Toltec priest-rulers. Like their predecessors, the Toltecs sought divine protection in grisly cults of human sacrifice.

With a core population of only some 120,000, Tula won a kingdom some 250 km (150 miles) across, reaching to the rich southern lowlands of Morelos. The Toltecs even had close trade, social and artistic links with the much older Maya city of Chichén Itzá in Yucatán, 1,200 km (750 miles) to the east (though theories that their empire stretched that far are now discounted). Soon after the kingdom's foundation, one Toltec ruler was forced to flee. Either he or a successor ended up in Maya lands, there he became known as Kukulcan, Maya for Quetzalcóatl, and set about building a city to match, and eventually succeed, Tula. Today, Chichén Itzá's most impressive remains are as much Toltec as Maya.

At its height, Tula was both a vast religious campus and a city. Its ceremonial centre, which had no network of streets, was the focal point for a community of villages. Private houses were of adobe blocks, not stone, making cubby-hole rooms for farmers who grew maize, beans and chillis when they were not serving as soldiers. Economic life was underpinned by weaving, and by the working of obsidian, a dark volcanic glass which served as the local equivalent of flint. The Toltec artisans obtained it, as preceding cultures had, from the mines in Pachuca, north-east of Mexico City, and then made it into tools and weapons, and traded it widely. Either by trade or force of arms, they acquired from the tropical lowlands the iridescent plumes of the trogon bird (*Pharomachrus mocinno*), or quetzal, which were used as regalia by their priest-kings.

Tula had no sooner reached its peak than it collapsed. According to the accounts, in which history and legend are mixed, internal strife and the threat of invasion undermined the state. Possibly, the expansion of the deserts of the American south-west were forcing Chichimec nomads from northern Mexico southwards. Possibly, also, like their predecessors, the Toltecs had undermined the basis of their own economy by exhausting their soil and using up their sources of timber.

Whatever the causes, they forced the last Quetzalcóatl-king, another Topiltzin, to flee. According to legend, he went in procession to the 'heavenly edge of the divine water' – the east coast – immolated himself, and on the eighth day reappeared as the morning star. Either that, or (as another account says) he vanished across the sea on a raft of serpents. Whatever happened, he left behind a belief that he would one day return.

So it came about that a religion flowering around the turn of the millennium had a crucial effect 500 years later. Some two centuries after Topiltzin's death, the legend of the Quetzalcóatl's second coming became central to Aztec beliefs. Quetzalcóatl became a chief Aztec deity; Tula, a cult centre, and Topiltzin the once and future god-king.

When the Spanish under Hernándo Cortés arrived in 1519, his astonishing appearance – bearded, covered in armour, apparently at one with his unknown four-legged mount, able to kill at a distance with explosive sticks – could be explained only if he were the returning Quetzalcóatl. Cortés, of course, had the advantages of gunpowder, steel and horses. But it helped to have divine status. For that, Cortés had the Toltecs to thank. By forging their own link in the chain of Mexican belief, they played a role in undermining the civilization they had so obsessively sought to dominate.

These figures on top of Tula's truncated Pyramid B represent Toltec militiamen. They wear the same back-shields as the noblemen below, and the same headdresses, but without the upper-class quetzal feathers. Made of four pieces of basalt, the figures originally supported the roof.

A Toltec pot portrays two noblemen in full regalia, complete with headdresses topped by feathers from quetzals, a species of trogon whose iridescent green plumage was prized as a symbol of aristocracy in all Middle America.

3 Cahokia: Capital of the Eastern Woodlands

In south-western Illinois stands an immense mound that is a memorial to North America's most advanced and influential culture.

Driving east from St Louis across the Mississippi along Interstate 55–70, you find yourself in the American Bottom, a pocket of floodplain washed flat by the ancient meanderings of the Mississippi and Missouri, which run together a few kilometres to the north. In the distance, you see a surprising sight – a 30-metre (100-foot) hill that should not be there, looming out of the plain. It is Monks Mound, the largest precolonial structure in North America.

After the mound was first described in 1810, some historians speculated that it was the work of a mysterious civilization of Mound Builders – pre-Columbian Europeans, perhaps, since native Americans were deemed incapable of building such a structure. In fact, this mound, and the other smaller ones that surround it, were made by local people – though who they were no one knows. In the year 1000 it was well on its way to completion, and was the focal point for the densest population north of the Mexican border.

Unique in size, it and its surrounding site – Cahokia – was an expression of a culture that was one among many. All across the forested lands of the Mid-West and south-east, from the Great Lakes to the Gulf of Mexico, a complex patchwork of chiefdoms had emerged. They formed one of North America's most brilliant and diverse cultures, known now as the Mississippian. It arose along river valleys and floodplains rich in game, fruits and nuts, with fertile, easily cultivated soils that required no irrigation. As the cultivation of

new strains of corn spread, around the turn of the millennium, the population began to rise.

But climate was arbitrary, floods frequent, and every decade or so starvation was a threat. For this reason, extended families would have several gardens in different areas to minimize risk, and maintained communal granaries with a bank of grain which would be topped up in times of plenty and drawn on in adversity.

Such communal activity needed discipline, exercised by a chief through an elitist hierarchy. Locally, he would perhaps have combined roles that included those of priest, bank manager and prime minister, supervising income, expenditure and dividend payments – ceremonies at which surpluses were handed out. He would also have had a diplomatic role, ensuring good links with neighbouring communities, offering gifts in times of plenty, negotiating help in times of adversity.

Eastern Woodlanders gradually built a network of support and exchange over huge areas. As rewards for loyalty or payment for trade goods, Mississippians used exotic and impractical objects like shells made into cups or ornamented with engravings. These were communities of non-specialists in which everyone looked after their own needs, planting, gathering, hunting, manufacturing. Only in two products does there seem to have been a degree of specialization – in the mining of a flint-like rock known as chert, used to make hoes, and in the production of salt, vital to supplement the diet of farmers who could not go looking for salt on their own account.

Across this huge region, most communities were ephemeral, rising, falling, changing with the ambitions and talents of their chiefs. But some formed lasting complexes that almost qualify for statehood. The most famous of these is Cahokia, named last century after a local tribe (as was the nearby town of the same name).

By 1000, after a century of growth, Cahokia covered 1,500 hectares (3,500 acres) and housed 10,000–20,000 people, with cultivated areas reaching out over 13 square kilometres (5 square miles). Along the ridge on which Cahokia sat were dozens of mounds, most in or around open areas. They were tombs, boundary markers and bases for public buildings or the houses of high-ranking Cahokians. Eventually, Cahokia had 120 mounds, of which 68 are now preserved.

The largest is Monks Mound, named after Trappist monks who were growing crops on it when it was first described in the early 19th century. The mound dominated the 15-hectare (40-acre) Grand Plaza, which was protected by an immense 3-kilometre (2-mile) stockade constructed from an estimated 20,000 logs. The mound is a rectangle with a flat top on which

The Secrets of Mound 72

In or shortly after 1000, one of Cahokia's leaders died. Aged about 40, he was a rich man, and was buried in style. He was placed on a bed of 20,000 marine shells laid out in the shape of a bird. Nearby were caches of possessions: 800 new arrowheads made hundreds of kilometres away, a metre-long roll of copper which may have been a ceremonial staff, 15 polished stone discs

used in a spear-throwing game. Several other bodies lie nearby, perhaps those of servants or relatives buried with him in a tomb about 15 metres across.

This was just one among 280 corpses which were buried along with funereal objects, and excavated in 1967 – 71. Some were the remains of women aged between 15 and 25, 50 of them stacked two or three deep in two rows. Another 19 women lay in a pit, with a trove of 36,000 marine-shell beads. Four men were found, with their heads and hands cut off.

Perhaps they were all sacrificed when their leader died, either as victims, or – as the Natchez used to do in early colonial times – as volunteers who offered themselves for sacrifice to raise their status, and that of their families.

Perhaps the three mounds that covered these bodies all related to the same chief or his family, for some time after they were made all three were capped by a single massive earth-ridge – Mound 72, 40 metres (140 feet) long, 20 metres (70 feet) across and 2 metres (6 feet) high.

posts (12 multiplied by 2, 3, 4, 5 and 6). Probably, from a central observation point individual posts aligned with the sun and moon rising and setting, and thus pinpointed important dates for festivals.

Cahokia was the centre of a far-reaching economic empire. To the west, where East St Louis's factories and vacant lots now straggle, was another mass of mounds marking a satellite town (45 mounds were still there in 1810, 15 in the 1860s; today there are only a few archaeological sites). St Louis itself used to have 26 mounds, which once gave it the nickname 'Mound City'. All across the American Bottom were other settlements – nine villages with mounds, 40 smaller communities. Local pottery and chert found its way along trade routes in every direction for several hundred kilometres, while in Cahokia itself archaeologists have found copper from Lake Superior, mica from the Appalachians, and shells from the Atlantic and the Gulf of Mexico.

Possibly in the end Cahokia was too large for its own good. The stockade round the central plaza would have needed replacing regularly, as would the houses. The surrounding forest would have been cut back, exposing the soil to erosion, making the area more susceptible to flooding. The climate turned colder. There is some evidence of increasing warfare. Whatever the reasons, the city that had endured for 500 years was abandoned around 1400. Its inhabitants scattered, and vanished. Though the Natchez of southern Mississippi kept a Mississippian lifestyle alive until the 16th century, no tribe has ever claimed to have its roots in Cahokia, North America's grandest culture.

stood a 30- by 35- metre (100- by 50-foot) building, perhaps a temple, chief's residence and seat of government all in one.

The mound is an immense structure. The 5.5-hectare (14-acre) base underlying its four stages is larger than that of the Great Pyramid in Egypt. According to one estimate, it would have taken 19 million man-hours to complete – 1,000 men working every day for 6.5 years to carry and dump the mound's 600,000 cubic metres (22 million cubic feet) of earth. Put in this way, it sounds an astonishing effort. But it was not built all at once. It was an expression not of a single burst of activity, but of an idea of community, worship and government steadily held for over three centuries (c. 900–1200). A few hundred people working one day a week would have been enough to build it. Its four terraces arose in fits and starts – drillings have identified up to 14 separate stages – perhaps with the palace-temple on top being rebuilt at each stage.

Scattered round the outside of the Grand Plaza were collections of single-family pole-and-thatch houses grouped around their own small plazas. Communal houses included granaries, meetinghouses and 'sweat lodges' – saunas – where people took steam baths, probably as part of cleansing rituals.

This was a culture which, like numerous others elsewhere in the world, seems to have been centred on the sun, moon and seasons. Postholes suggest that Cahokians built wooden 'henges', five successive circles each more complex than the last, with 24, 36, 48, 60 and 72

An overview of Cahokia at its peak shows Monks Mound in its stockaded plaza. The town includes dozens of subsidiary mounds, a 'woodhenge' solar calendar (FAR LEFT), maize gardens, and flooded quarries excavated for mound-building materials.

The South-West: A Cultural Bloom in a Harsh Land

4

The south-west was the unlikely home of several related cultures whose people traded far and wide. One in particular was so successful and so puzzling that its prime site has been termed the 'Chaco phenomenon'.

In north-west New Mexico, at the end of 30 km (20 miles) of dirt road, lies a mystery: a once-thriving imperial capital in the depths of a dry-as-a-bone canyon. This is Pueblo Bonito in Chaco Canyon, the remnants of a four-storeyed honey-comb of rooms and houses that in 1000 held sway over at least 65,000 square kilometres (25,000 square miles), an area the size of Scotland. Nor was this the only township. Along the canyon runs a line of 13 communities, each clustering round a central plaza. The concentration of people prompts a cascade of questions. Where did the people come from? Why did they settle here? How did they live? How did they achieve their outreach?

Some answers remain controversial. Others have their roots in the wider culture of the south-west. In this mesa-and-canyon land, the local people had bred drought-resistant forms of maize, that together with beans and squash can provide a foundation for settled lifestyles. In a slow and complex series of changes, single-room pithouses gave way to adobe houses with several rooms. Once committed to a base, householders turned to making pots, building storehouses, and elaborating their milling and cooking techniques. To conserve heat, buildings tended to be attached, growing like cells into pueblos. As populations rose, families split off and formed other villages. By 1000, three main village-based cultures had developed in the south-west: Anasazi, Mogollon, and Hohokam, each with its own building styles, ceramics, local variants and trade links.

The best known of these are the Anasazi, ancestors of today's Pueblos who now live mainly on the Rio Grande. Incidentally, they object to the use of the name Anasazi, a pejorative term meaning 'enemy ancestors' in Navajo. They use the Hopi word Hisatsinom — ancestors, or 'the Old Ones'. In the 10th century, the Anasazi dominated the Four Corners region where Utah, Colorado, Arizona and New Mexico join. They lived in some 150 villages scattered along dozens of canyons, many of which are on today's tourist trails: Mesa Verde, Colorado; Monument Valley and Canyon de Chelly in Arizona. The greatest of these villages, or great houses, lay in Chaco Canyon.

And the greatest of them all, the hub of the Anasazi trade empire, the second largest town and probably the most sophisticated in north America in 1000, was Pueblo Bonito. Here, in the mid 9th century, the Anasazi started to build, making a capital of over 800 rooms, home to an estimated 5,000–10,000 people. Tile-veneered stonework finished with plaster formed airy rooms on four levels, with flat roofs serving as balconies. The rooms were grouped in a giant D-shape around a

Pueblo Bonito today is like an X-ray of its ancient self, with its three dozen circular kivas and bee-hive rooms exposed. Originally, entry was by ladder, over the outer wall.

Chaco Canyon

N

Escavada

Chaco Wash

Penasco Blanco

Atlatl

New Alto

Casa Chiquita
Kin Kletso

Pueblo Alto

Pueblo del Arroyo

Chetro Ketl

Pueblo Bonito

Casa Rinconiada

Hungo Pavi

Werlto's Rincón

Tsin Kletzin

Kin Nahasbas
Una Vida

Wijiji

Kin Klitzin

Marcia's Rincón

0   2 km

0   2 miles

Shabik'eshchee Village

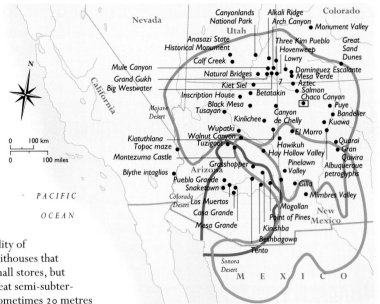

plaza, giving equality of access to kivas – pithouses that were originally small stores, but developed into great semi-subterranean temples, sometimes 20 metres (more than 60 feet) across, with 3-metre (10-foot) walls and roofs supported by pine-beams. From Chaco's 40 storehouse kivas grew several temple-kivas, three of which have been restored.

The harshness of the conditions and highly variable rainfall inspired great ingenuity. The Chacoans seem to have developed three strategies. First, they built other 'great houses' upstream and downstream, which perhaps served as food storage areas. Second, they went into the art business, specializing in ritual objects like vases and incense burners, and turquoise ornaments made from raw turquoise imported from the great mine in Mount Chalchihuitl, just south of Santa Fe, about 150 km (100 miles) to the east (the same mine from which the Aztecs later derived their turquoise). Third, they traded. A network of roads linked other Chaco pueblos – in 1000, there were over 20 major ones within a 250-km (150-mile) radius. Beyond this, the trade network reached indirectly from coast to coast, bringing in abalone from the Pacific coast, seashells from the Gulf of Mexico, copper and live macaws – highly prized for ceremonial purposes – from Mexico.

The roads, some of them as straight as Roman roads and up to 10 metres (30 feet) wide, pose a mystery. The Chaco people had no vehicles or beasts of burden. Why such highways? Perhaps they eased the way for armies, or labourers – or pilgrims, for some some archaeologists suggest that Chaco was a religious centre, a sort of Anasazi Mecca with a small number of residents boosted by an influx for annual ceremonies. This suggestion is supported by a nearby site, Pueblo Alto, where archaeologists have found 150,000 pot-

sherds, far more than would have been left by the few residents. And Pueblo Alto's refuse tips are oddly layered, as if built up intermittently.

But the dynamics of the Chaco phenomenon are much disputed. Perhaps the outlying villages arose as a burgeoning population spilled outwards; or perhaps they arose independently and were drawn into Chaco's imperial web.

As a centre for religion and trade, Chaco was assumed to have been a place of tranquillity. But there is some intriguing evidence that this was not so. Christy Turner of Arizona State University has gathered bones which show signs familiar to any cook: pulverization, abrasion, boiling. The bones are from some 300 human corpses found next to villages. He concludes that the Chacoans indulged in cannibalism. If so – and the matter is highly controversial – it was almost certainly not done for food, but more likely for a social purpose, like the ritual execution of supposed evil-doers.

Pueblo Bonito was abandoned around 1200, perhaps because the climate turned against the Chacoans, who were driven to internecine warfare in a struggle for diminishing resources. Villages built in ever more inaccessible places (like the cliff dwellings of Mesa Verde and Canyon de Chelly) support the idea. By the end of the century, the Anasazi had left all their villages.

Why they finally went is a mystery. Researchers suggest that the growth of a new religion to the south-east – beliefs to which today's Pueblos still hold – drew the Hisatsinom, the Old Ones, away, never to return.

Bison Hunters and Farmers of the Prairies

*The rich grasslands
of the Mid-West are
remembered as
bison-country.
It was that – and
much more besides.*

A century ago, anthropologists thought that America's Mid-Western heartland, the Great Plains, became inhabited only after the Spaniards had introduced the horse. To outsiders, these look harsh lands, with searing summers, brutal winters, vicious winds, unpredictable rains and no shelter. In fact, as archaeologists discovered in the 1920s, people had been living on these 2 million square kilometres (800,000 square miles) for some 10,000 years, for underfoot was a wonderful resource: grass. And across the grass roamed wealth, in the form of bison, which, together with other animals and seasonal plants, could provide almost everything people needed: food, clothing, shelter, weapons. From before the 6th millennium BC, native Americans moved into the plains and became bison hunters.

By 1000, the plains dwellers had had bows and arrows for over four centuries, a more convenient and safer weapon for hunting than spears, though no more effective. They therefore retained a dependence on bison-jumps, managing the prairies like a vast ranch, combining in large groups to drive herds over cliffs. The bison-jumps had been used for the purpose for centuries, and in some cases for millennia. This spectacular event, which would leave hundreds of beasts dead, could be repeated only once every generation or so. It depended on the herds reaching a critical density. Then, restless for new grass, the herds could be encouraged into gathering areas, and stampeded along drive lanes – both natural

and artificial – which led towards a cliff. These places – like Head-Smashed-In, Alberta, or Gull Lake in Saskatchewan – would become a scene of mass slaughter, with a vast campsite and processing area to butcher the meat and process the hides. Head-Smashed-In, named after a 19th-century Blackfoot who was unfortunate enough to find himself at the foot of the 10-metre (30-foot) cliff when a herd of bison came off the top, was used over a period of 7,000 years up to the late 19th century.

Since bison-jumps were rare events, routine kills were made in corrals, like the one in Wardell, in the basin of Wyoming's Green River. Here, a steep cliff and slopes create a natural enclosure where bison on the move could be herded and then killed with bows and arrows. The meat was then dried on site for use through the winter.

At the time this was a way of life that was kept in balance by the difficulties of hunting on foot. Only later, when native Americans acquired horses, and especially when they and the white colonists brought guns, did the scales swing irrevocably against the bison.

Bison-hunting was not the only lifestyle open to plains dwellers, for the grasslands are only one of the varied landscapes and ecologies. River valleys, particularly in the upper Missouri, offered opportunities for farming, for the wooded valleys provided protection against frost. Around 900, at the start of the 350-year warm period that affected both North America and Europe, farmers learned to grow maize, breeding tough strains that could cope with the short growing season and unreliable rainfall. Along the major river systems, like the

*In a museum diorama,
terrified bison gallop to
their death (left) over a
bison-jump like the one at
Head-Smashed-In, Alberta
(right).*

Missouri, Custer, Washita and Republican, people adopted a semi-nomadic life, combining farming with fishing and hunting. Villages arose, usually on bluffs overlooking valleys and lakes, with trails used by the inhabitants when they went off for seasonal bison hunts or to trade with full-time bison-hunters out on the plains and woodlanders further east. Life would probably have been organized by leaders who by tradition possessed spiritual authority and wealth.

If later patterns of life were inherited from this period, as anthropologist Preston Holder argued in a 1970 study, village life would have been focused by the leader's sacred 'bundle', a portable 'ceremonial centre', a tribal or clan equivalent of the Ark of the Covenant containing ritual objects. Since only the owner understood how to use these objects, they conferred power. They symbolized political and religious continuity, and their loss could have meant a loss of identity, dissolution, death. The bundle and its revered priestly owner would have been at the centre of the network of authority controlling the young men, whose daily life would have been devoted to fighting, gambling and dancing. It was the bundle and the chief who focused the great annual ceremonies marking bison-hunts and harvests.

Around 1000, a typical group of 'Plains Village' peoples (as they are known) lived on the fertile and well-wooded tributaries of the Upper Republican River in present-day Nebraska. Living in scattered villages of some 50–75 people, they built substantial square houses, about 8 metres (25 feet) square, with post walls holding up roofs of poles, grass and sod. Every house had underground storage pits for maize and beans, and everyone used hoes made of bison shoulder-blades to cultivate the valley bottoms. They apparently lived in relative peace, feeling no need to fortify their houses, and trading with neighbours as far afield as Colorado, Wyoming and Texas.

This was never an easy life. Rivers would flood, rains would fail, and village fought village for land, even if there was no large-scale warfare. Sites would often be abandoned after the harvest, and abandoned completely as the inhabitants took to bison-hunting, especially when the climate became harsher again after about 1250. Yet a tradition of village life centred on agriculture endured. These farmers were possibly the ancestors of the village-dwelling Wichita, Pawnee and Arikara described by the first European explorers.

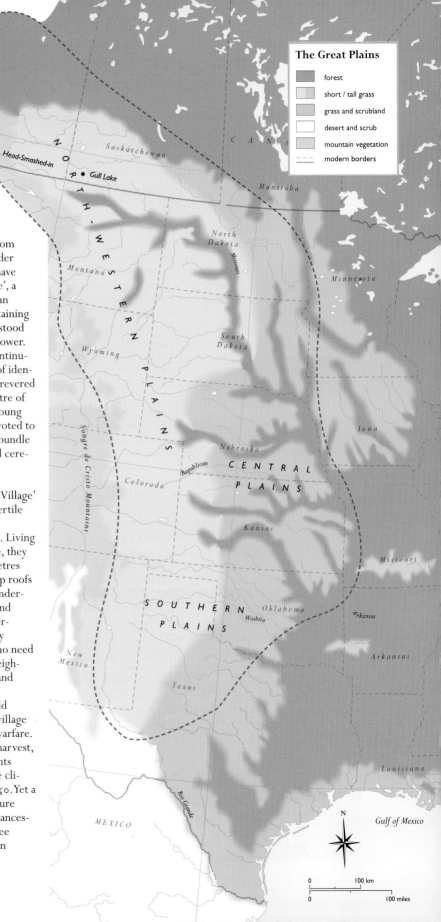

The Great Plains

- forest
- short / tall grass
- grass and scrubland
- desert and scrub
- mountain vegetation
- modern borders

Saskatchewan

CANADA

Manitoba

Head-Smashed-in

Gull Lake

NORTH-WESTERN PLAINS

Montana

North Dakota

Missouri

Minnesota

Wyoming

South Dakota

Sangre de Cristo Mountains

Nebraska

Iowa

CENTRAL PLAINS

Republican

Colorado

Kansas

Missouri

SOUTHERN PLAINS

Oklahoma

Washita

Arkansas

New Mexico

Arkansas

Texas

Louisiana

Rio Grande

MEXICO

Gulf of Mexico

N

0   100 km
0   100 miles

6 A Tapestry of Cultures on the West Coast

No area has such a wealth of societies as California and the north-west, and none such a frustrating combination of change and continuity.

For archaeologists and historians, the West Coast is both a nightmare and a blessing. The natural riches of the forests, rivers and oceans had long made the whole strip, from southern California to south-west Alaska, an Eden for hunter-gatherers. Local tribes had it so good here that there seems to have been no lasting pressure to evolve new technologies, develop large and complex societies, migrate, or seek additional security by taking over neighbours.

Not that these were static societies fixed within static ecologies. El Niños warmed the seas and delivered storms, while droughts periodically ravaged the south. Lean periods drove tribes to attack their neighbours – bows and arrows had reached California some 500 years previously. The Medieval Warm Period had as much effect here as elsewhere, warming the centuries either side of the millennium.

But the changes were not enough to upset underlying patterns of life. The result was a shifting chequerboard of localized cultures. Archaeologists are spoilt for choice: 500 small tribal groups, who spoke 100 separate languages in five main language-groups. Reference points are few, change is hard to document, and narrative history is an impossibility.

There is nothing here that focuses attention specifically on the century spanning 1000, for what can be said about that time might equally apply 500 years before or after, right up to the coming of Europeans. At Friendly Cove on Vancouver Island, for instance, Nootka-speaking peoples seem to have lived much the same sort of life, hunting sea mammals and fishing and weaving baskets, for 2,000 years. They would go on doing so until their ways were disrupted by contact with Europeans.

Coastal peoples – Tlingit, Salish, Nootka, Suquamish, Makah, Kwakiutl – lived mainly by fishing. They formed large villages and village-

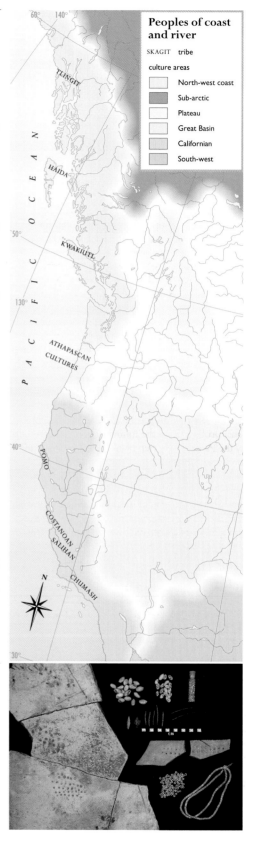

Peoples of coast and river

SKAGIT tribe

culture areas

- North-west coast
- Sub-arctic
- Plateau
- Great Basin
- Californian
- South-west

The variety of Chumash beads, used both as money and decoration, is evidence of a hunter-gatherer society more sophisticated and complex than many supposedly more advanced farming and urban cultures. The indentations on the stone slabs were used to hold beads while holes were drilled through them.

The Salish people of Scowlitz controlled this forested promontory where the clear waters of the Harrison meet the turbid Fraser River.

Pacific Ocean

N

The coast Salish

/// Salish area

SKAGIT other tribe

0 — 150 miles

groups, fortified against attack from neighbours. Presumably they were already elaborating the skills and behaviour for which some tribes would become famous: the statuary, the giant houses, the elaborate potlatch ceremonies that proclaimed status through ritualized generosity. Presumably: from 1,000 years ago virtually nothing survives to provide evidence.

In southern California, at some point around the turn of the millennium, Chumash peoples developed a more complex culture that involved the extensive use of shells as money. Originally shells had been used as ornaments, then – like Rolexes or diamond necklaces today – to mark status. Some Chumash lived on the coast as fishers, others inland as hunters. Those on the coast profited from the immense bounty served up by the Pacific – the rich planktonic soup that fed food-chains of sea mammals, fish and birds.

Along the Oregon and Washington coasts, villagers invested in plank-built houses, large structures that suggest stability and social complexity. Trade was extensive. Probably, the villages were under the control of chiefs who dominated the acquisition and distribution of food. Sometimes, villagers would set up camp on the seashore to fish. In a rock-shelter at the mouth of the Hoko River on the Olympic Peninsula first used around 1000, archaeologists have found evidence that its inhabitants were expert at catching cod, salmon and halibut.

Inland, many tribes relied on salmon runs, particularly on the Fraser River, which flows from the Rockies down to Vancouver. At the confluence of the Harrison and Fraser, 150 km (100 miles) upriver from Vancouver, a Salish village on the edge of the Scowlitz Reserve has begun to emerge from the past. Since 1993, the site has been excavated and mapped by archaeologists, principally from the local Coast Salish band (the Scowlitz), Simon Fraser University and the University of British Columbia.

The village, first occupied in about 500 BC, runs along a narrow river terrace facing the fertile plains and distant snow-capped mountains of the Fraser river valley. For over 1,000 years, the ancestors of today's Scowlitz people used the site to hunt, gather and fish, rebuilding and extending their village over the years. It was a good spot. The river was a highway into the interior, so the villagers had a stranglehold on trade. Forests were rich in berries, roots and cedars, which provided wood for houses and canoes, and fibre for baskets, mats and clothing. Fish, attracting seal and waterfowl, made the river a rich source of food. In particular, as bone analysis has shown, half a dozen salmon species provided the Salish with 65–90 per cent of their protein. As the Salish still say today, 'Our bones are made of fish.'

Around AD 500, the Scowlitz lifestyle underwent a change. They began to build earthen mounds and rock cairns in which to bury their dead. The Salish of the Fraser river and nearby Vancouver Island were the only known northwestern people to bury their dead in this way, and untouched mounds are a rarity – uncounted numbers have been destroyed by development. So far at Scowlitz, over 50 mounds and cairns have been mapped, most of them intact. They range from little more than body-sized up to one measuring 11.5 metres (38 feet) long and 3.5 metres (11 feet) high, one of the largest recorded on the north-west coast. The size and contents of the mounds reflected status – the largest mound, with an elaborate stone overlay, was that of a wealthy man of 30–35, who was buried covered with dentalia shells, copper ornaments and beads.

There is a mystery here. The mounds are part of a wider 'burial-mound' culture – a mortuary complex – that seems to end about 1000. Why did the culture emerge? Why did it end? Were the burial mounds part of the village, or was the site used as a cemetery? The search for answers, and the answers themselves, if found, are of more than academic interest – they would contribute to the local Salish sense of identity. In the words of those working on the project, 'Scowlitz is a place and a community; the two are inseparable. The Scowlitz people have embraced the archaeological project as a window onto the world of their ancestors.'

The Far North: The Coming of the Thule People

Around the turn of the millennium, Inuits whose Thule culture originated in Alaska were spreading eastwards, slowly superseding the less sophisticated ways of the Dorset people.

At first glance, it is surprising that people ever colonized this harsh immensity. From the Alaskan mountains east to the Greenland ice cap, from the Arctic Ocean archipelago south to the first scattering of trees, these barrens are larger than all the United States. Trees can begin to find a precarious hold only where the temperature averages 10°C (50°F) in July, one of the three frost-free months. In high summer, permafrost is a foundation for mud. Midwinter averages −32°C (−26°F), colder than a domestic freezer. Windchill can drive it down to below −70°C (−94°F). Yet life thrives. Lichens, sedges, insects and plankton nurture food-chains running up through hares and lemmings, to foxes, wolves, polar bears, caribou, musk ox. Plankton-rich seas teem with fish, whales, seals, walruses. This environment imposed harsh rules, but hunter-gatherers discovered how to obey them from the time they first moved across the Bering Strait untold thousands of years ago.

The people of the Arctic are now known by their own term as Inuit – 'people' – the older 'Eskimo' being a pejorative native American word meaning 'eaters of raw meat'. Though Arctic archaeology has been a thriving field since the 1920s, the Inuit are of unknown origin from somewhere in Siberia, separate by blood group, language and looks from native Americans to the south. Outsiders tend to lump all Inuit together, but they form a group of cultures, speaking half a dozen related languages, with many differences in lifestyle. There could never have been many of them. With no possibililty of agriculture, they remained hunter-gatherers in isolated groups, numbering at most some 70,000. The Arctic was always a continent with the population of a town.

In 1000, the Aleutian islanders (whose relationship to the Inuit is controversial) were still living as they had for three millennia, in large houses dug into the ground, covered with poles and earth, with doors in the roof.

Farther north, Inuit on both sides of the Bering Strait had become experts at hunting sea mammals – whale, seal, walrus. Local communities preferred their own style of kayak design and ornamentation, for the people of this tradition, known as Thule (pronounced 'Tu-leh'), were artists who loved to decorate their intricate, toggled harpoons. For 1,000 years they had had treasured iron tools, acquired by trade across the Bering Strait with Siberian Inuit who in turn got

them by trade from their origins 3,000 km (2,000 miles) farther west and south, on the borders between Siberia and China. With their dog-sleds, the Thule people could range widely in pursuit of herds. Depending on resources, they built either semi-subterranean houses of driftwood, stone or whalebone, or igloos. Both were wonderful conservers of heat, with entrance tunnels below floor level, allowing cold air to form a sink apart from the warmer interiors (though warmer is a relative term: the interior of an igloo hardly reaches zero, but this is 'warm' compared to outside temperatures which could plunge to below −40°C (−40°F)). Coast-dwellers would venture out on to the ice to harpoon seals as they rose to breath through air-holes, or take to the sea in kayaks and larger umiaks, which acted as stable harpoon platforms, to kill whales. The rewards of whaling were high. One whale could keep a community in food, fuel and bone for a whole winter.

It was a successful and flexible way of life that, towards the end of the first millennium, allowed the Thule people to expand eastwards, with their sophisticated range of tools: bone and driftwood bows, stone-tipped arrows, tiny stone blades. More specialized ways developed: caribou hunting inland, seal- and whale-hunting round the coasts, each with their range of bone tools and artefacts.

Why did they move? There are several possible reasons: population pressure or tribal warfare on the Bering Strait, or the warm spell that made travel easier and encouraged whale migration, or an increase in the whale population, or a combination of all these. In any event, Thule people spread across the far north towards Greenland.

There, around 1000, an earlier Inuit tradition was reaching its high point. These people, named

An ivory comb decorated with a face hints at the talent for carving developed by the Inuit of the Dorset culture.

after a site on Cape Dorset, Baffin Island, seem to have been less well equipped. Lacking dog-sleds, bow-drills, and bows and arrows, they hunted caribou, seal, walrus, whale and sometimes even polar bear with nothing but spears and harpoons with toggled heads that slipped off and lodged firmly once they were plunged into an animal. This way of life demanded tremendous skill and bravery – a hunter had to stalk prey and kill from in close. It was enough not only to ensure survival, but also to create the freedom to develop a tradition of carving in antler, bone, ivory, soapstone and driftwood that ranks as one of the finest in prehistoric North America.

As the climate warmed, the Thule people moved in. The more ancient Dorset culture began

Thule whale-hunters built this whale-bone framework for a skin-covered house as they island-hopped eastwards off Canada's north coast. Using the original bones, the framework was rebuilt in the 1990s as part of an archaeological site outside Resolute Bay.

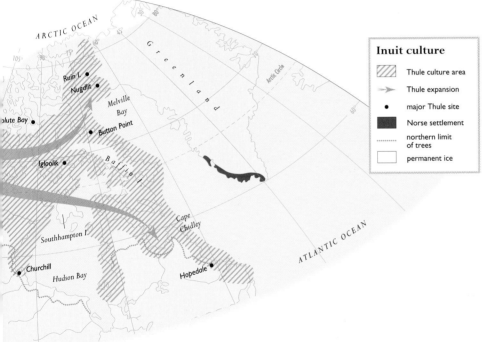

Inuit culture

- Thule culture area
- Thule expansion
- major Thule site
- Norse settlement
- northern limit of trees
- permanent ice

to die back into isolated areas of Greenland and Labrador in the face of competition from the more sophisticated, wider-ranging, whale-hunting westerners. This was not a matter of direct confrontation. From the archaeological evidence, the two traditions existed side by side, sometimes for centuries. But greater efficiency won. Thule people were teamplayers who cooperated in the use of dog-sleds and boats, with which they could follow migrating herds, or large sea mammals, like seals and whales. Especially whales. With the higher temperatures, the pack ice would have retreated northwards, allowing whales more room. Teamwork afloat would have paid dividends.

Exactly when these changes occurred is uncer-

tain. Many archaeologists accept that Thule culture was establishing itself 'around 1000' on the basis of radiocarbon dates. But dating is confused by the discovery of Thule house-sites in north Greenland and Ellesmere Island which contained Viking artefacts. Since the Norse did not arrive until 1000, their artefacts should not have been so far north so early. No one knows yet which to trust, the radiocarbon dates or the artefacts.

Whatever the dates, sometime early in the new millennium eastern Thule culture began to develop into a highly sophisticated form, with an astonishing range of ingenious tools. With these, the Thule Inuit dominated the high Arctic, helping to limit Norse influence, until the climate turned against both cultures in the 15th century.

The Vikings in Vinland

The first European to sight the North American coast did so by mistake. The consequence – an attempted colonization, which ended in warfare with local inhabitants – leaves one of history's great 'what-ifs'. What if the Vikings had stayed on? What if they, rather than their seafaring successors, the Spanish, Portuguese and English, had won control of the continent's eastern seaboard, creating an American Normandy? Their success would have set the histories of both North America and Europe on entirely different courses.

The wanderer was Bjarni Herjolfsson, a descendant of those who had colonized Iceland over a century before. After spending a winter in Norway, he returned to Iceland in the summer of 986 with a full cargo, intending to meet up again with his father. To his surprise, he found that his father had sailed westward, to Greenland, as part of Erik the Red's colonizing expedition (p. 41). Somehow re-inspiring his tired crew of 35, he set off in pursuit.

Three days out, winds pushed his boat south beneath a blanket of fog. Several days later the weather cleared, revealing a line of low, forested hills. This was definitely not Greenland. The trees were proof that Bjarni was way to the south, and since there were no other islands south of Greenland, well to the west as well. For two days Bjarni tracked the coast northwards, then swung away to the east. Four days later he arrived safely on the western tip of Greenland.

For 14 years, the

Greenlanders did nothing about Bjarni's discovery. They had their work cut out establishing their new homesteads. But they were a community under pressure, isolated from their original homeland, yet dependent upon it for timber. News of fresh pastures and a new source of wood was bound to lure them eventually.

It was Erik's son, Leif the Lucky, who took on the task of exploration. In 1000 he bought Bjarni's boat and made the 3,000-km (2,000-mile), two-week voyage in reverse, back to the unexplored coast. He made three landings. The first was in a grim, treeless place which was probably southern Baffin Island. His next stop further south, across the Hudson Strait, brought him south of the tree-line, to 'Markland' (Wood Land), the flat, forested coast south of today's Nain, where white-sand beaches shelve gently into the Atlantic.

Finally, he beached at the place he called Vinland, where he spent the winter. It was a terrific spot, and he had no need to explore further. He returned to Greenland the following spring, full of praise for Vinland's riches. The sagas mention grass,

The western voyages of the Norsemen

→ Norse voyages of exploration and settlement

▨ Norse settlement in Greenland

grapes, wild wheat, timber and salmon. In addition, the shallow bay caught quantities of driftwood, and its bogs were rich in iron ore, which could be refined to produce tools and weapons. Greenlanders could not have asked for more.

Now Leif's brother, Thorvald, assumed the role of explorer. From Vinland he sent a crew to probe westwards, while he sailed north, turning into a big inlet where he encountered local tribesmen, *skraelings* (a pejorative word perhaps meaning 'screechers' or 'uglies'). These *skraelings* were almost certainly Beothuk, a people who lived on elk, moose and caribou in the winter and came to the coast in the summer to fish and gather. In a skirmish, Thorvald was killed by an arrow. His crew returned to Vinland, spent the winter there, and sailed back to Greenland with their sad news.

Next to make the journey, in about 1018, was another man close to Erik, Thorfinn Karlsefni, who had married Erik's daughter-in-law Gudrid. Karlsefni planned a colony, and persuaded perhaps 60, perhaps as many as 160 men (sources vary) to accompany him, with their families and livestock. They arrived in Vinland, built houses of wood and turf, set up a smithy, and settled for the winter.

Come the spring, more *skraelings* appeared, this time a mass of them paddling in skin-boats. They were probably Inuit. At first, contacts were peaceful, with the two sides trading, the Inuit offering skins, the Vikings meat, cloth and milk. Relations turned sour, however, when the Inuit demanded the Vikings' weapons. The Vikings refused. A local who tried to steal a weapon was killed. When the *skraelings* returned, there was a battle in which two Vikings and four *skraelings* were killed.

It was the outbreak of violence that was crucial. In a clash, the locals, whether Beothuk or Inuit, would clearly have the upper hand eventually. They had good food sources, and could flee to their homes and call on reinforcements. The Vikings had no such freedom. After a couple of years, probably in 1020, Karlsefni decided to pull out.

The wealth of Vinland was still an attraction, though. One further venture was organized by Freydis, Leif and Thorvald's illegitimate sister. The aim of the mixed team of Greenlanders and Icelanders was to acquire local produce, not colonize. Freydis seems to have been a fearful harridan, and the colony collapsed into atrocious violence, with Freydis turning Greenlanders against Icelanders and herself murdering five Icelandic women. Freydis and the other survivors fled for home.

Thereafter, Norsemen never returned to settle, only making occasional forays from Greenland for timber and furs, before their colony vanished from history in the mid 14th century.

Vinland's Would-be Capital

The identity of 'Vinland' has been the subject of passionate debate, intensified by the discrepancies between the two sagas which are the chief sources. Down the years, many commentators, struck by the mention of grapes, went along with the sagas, assuming that Vinland meant 'Wine Land'. Certainly, that was what the saga-writers intended, for in their epics grapes and wine become a sort of Holy Grail sought by their heroes. Since grapes did not grow that far north, the name's supposed meaning inspired speculation that the Vikings ventured further south, even as far as Florida. Other researchers have tried to cast Newfoundland plants — wild cranberries, lyme grass — in the role of vines and wheat.

In fact, the references to grapes, wine and wheat are almost certainly spurious. The confusion seems to have been sown in the late 11th century by a geographer-monk, Adam of Bremen, who equated Vinland with a mythical place referred to by Latin authors as Insulae Fortunatae, the Fortunate Isles, where all good things abounded. Deceived by the name, Adam transferred the attributes of the Fortunate Isles, where 'vines grow wild, yielding the most excellent wine', to Vinland. Unaware that the drift-ice, fog banks and bitter waters of the Labrador Current would never have allowed for grapes of any sort, the saga-writers a century later seized on this seemingly authoritative source

to present Vinland as a paradise, a suitable find for heroes of old.

The most likely explanation is simpler than the myth. As well as meaning 'wine', 'vin' is also Old Norse for 'pasture'. Norway still has some 1,000 place-names with 'vin' as a compound. All Leif Eriksson was claiming, rightly, was that Vinland was as suitable for colonization as Greenland.

Much wild speculation about Vinland began to fade in 1960, when the Norwegian archaeologist Helge Ingstad, searching the coast for Vinland, arrived at the north coast of Newfoundland. He was at once reminded of the description of Vinland in the Greenlanders' Saga: a land 'not mountainous, covered with forest, with low hills'. He was drawn to a great grassy plain — L'Anse aux Meadows, an Anglo-French name meaning 'Meadow-Bay'. In a small fishing village, he asked a 60-year-old, George Decker, about ruins in the vicinity.

'He said, yes, and asked me to follow him,' wrote Ingstad. 'We walked along a path leading westwards over a great plain, where some sheep and cows were grazing. Soon we came to a bay, Epaves Bay, where a small river, Black Duck Brook, ran out, sparkling as it wound its way through the landscape, between heather, willows and

grass. Not far from the head of the bay, an ancient marine terrace extended towards the river, about 4 metres (13 feet) high. This was it.'

In the next few years, Helge Ingstad and his wife Annie excavated nine turf houses, enough to protect some 100 people. They identified hearths, cooking-pots, boat-houses, a bronze Viking pin, a soapstone spindle-whorl, outdoor cooking-pits, an anvil and a forge. Clearly the Norsemen had brought with them the Norse art of making iron from 'bog-ore', easily dug from a nearby swamp. Charcoal provided radiocarbon dates of around 1000. Nearby were several cairns, probably raised so that those in the community could tell the time by comparing the sun's position against the cairns. All in all, the finds match similar ones in Greenland and Iceland, as well as the information in the sagas.

Karlsefni would still recognize the site. Though there is no woodland there now, for most of it has been cut down, there are still spruce groves further round the coast. Black Duck Brook still has salmon, as it did in Karlsefni's day. Few now doubt that 'Meadow Bay' is indeed Leif Erikson's Vinland, or at least the gateway to it.

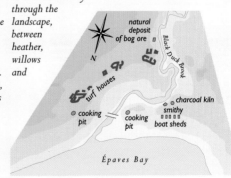

2

EUROPE

A Benighted Continent on the Brink of a New Dawn

Though no one could have seen the significance of the slow changes, Europe at the turn of the millennium was emerging from a long night of barbarism.

In the spring of 1000, an optimistic European astrologer wishing to foresee greatness for his continent could have taken heart from two unconnected events. In the American north-east, Vikings set up a base which would, they hoped, act as a foundation for colonization (p. 30). In Europe, a young German emperor, Otto III, made a pilgrimage to the tomb of of the Frankish ruler Charlemagne in Aachen seeking inspiration to realize a grand dream: to restore Charlemagne's continent-wide empire, and to link it with Christendom's other half, Byzantium.

With this scanty evidence, our crystal-gazer might have predicted an imminent wonder: Europe and Byzantium united, the Roman Empire reincarnated as a Greater Christendom, an empire reaching from present-day Iran to Spain, from the Urals to the Atlantic, and then on across the northern seas to a thrusting young nation of Christianized Vikings making a new world for Europeans in an empty land.

Now look at Europe in the year 1000 from the point of view of an imaginary Islamic intellectual. A civilized Europe? Impossible. Byzantium, though still a glory, was under constant threat. Europe – certainly Europe north of the Alps – was an insignificant region of peasants and embattled warlords. Pirates and nomads raided its flanks and heartland at will. The wonder that had been Rome was a distant memory, sustained by ruined villas, stark monuments and roads that led nowhere. The empire of Charlemagne, Rome's pale reflection, was shattered. Allegiance was to tribe, clan, or at best regional ruler. No northern city could match Córdoba, Damascus, Baghdād or Bukhara.

After the end of the Roman Empire, Europe north of the Alps had become an economic and cultural backwater. Towns declined, trade goods were rare, barter replaced coinage, and people in the countryside survived on what they could grow. They were caught in a cycle of deprivation. The only way of increasing yields was to use animal manure and break new ground. But animals lacked fodder. There was no surplus of energy, time, animal products or manufactured goods to make life for ordinary men and women anything but nasty, brutish and short.

This was a world of communities separated by gulfs of space and time. Northern Europe was still largely forested. 'Towns' would seem no more than villages today, clusters of hovels lining evil-smelling alleys. Europe's population was perhaps about 36–40 million, not much more than it had been for centuries. North of the Alps, centres of over 5,000 people were rarities. Travel was at walking-pace along tracks that were often impassable. Wolves roamed the forests, and brown bears, though recently extinct in England, were still common on the European mainland. Forests, a source of new life when cut – arable land, timber, firewood, honey, acorns for pigs – still exuded a fairy-tale menace.

Christendom was broken in two, with Rome and northern Europe cut from their Greek, eastern Mediterranean roots. Though the Roman west and the Orthodox Byzantine east often spoke of the need for unity, they were in fact rivals. Each saw itself as the only true church. Each believed that unity meant superiority on its own terms.

The rivalry, which often appeared as theological debates of baffling subtlety, was as much about power as religion. Each side sought to extend its reach into pagan lands wherever it could. Rome, which had long since founded outposts in the farthest corners of Ireland and Scotland, looked north-east to Scandinavia and east to Poland. Constantinople looked to the Slavs, who were not only pagan but a constant threat, and needed taming. A hundred years before, two great missionary-saints, Cyril and Methodius, had opened the way, adapting Greek to unwritten Slavonic languages by devising a new script, named Cyrillic after its inventor. They failed in Moravia (today's Czech Republic), where German missionaries beat them to it, but inspired success in Serbia and Bulgaria (whose example was later followed by Russia). The rift in eastern Europe still endures.

To our imaginary Arab, the idea that Europe, divided from its Byzantine roots, might amount to anything would have seemed ludicrous. It would have come as no surprise to see the dreams of Vikings and the Emperor Otto come to nothing.

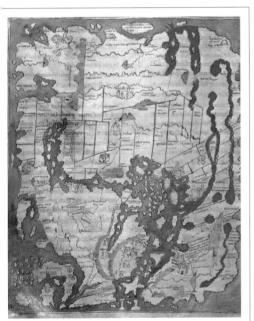

An early-medieval European world map of Eurasia places Jerusalem roughly at the centre. Britain is bottom left. The Mediterranean, with its scattering of Greek islands, vaguely connects the Black Sea, the Volga and the Danube. The shapes of Asia (top) and Africa (bottom right) are fanciful, dictated by the need to design a rectangle bordered by ocean.

Yet both Islamic intellectual and European crystal-gazer would have had a point. It was a question of timing. Europe, particularly northern Europe, was a benighted place; but the foundations were there for nationhood, for peace, even for a new continental identity.

In part the foundations were laid by climatic change. Possibly, increased solar

The Myth of the Great Fear

Popular histories still speak of the Great Fear that supposedly attended the approach of the second millennium. Did the Book of Revelation not prophesy that an angel shall bind the Devil for 1,000 years, and that Christ would reign with his martyrs, and that the Devil would then be loosed, and that he would then be cast into the lake of fire and brimstone, and a new heaven and a new earth come into being? Had not Christ bound Satan 1,000 years before, as St Augustine assumed? As 1000 approached, did not people foresee the imminence of the Second Coming, the Last Judgement, the world's end?

Yes, and no. There had always been 'millenarians', Christians who believed in the imminence of the Second Coming. And there were indeed those who feared the end of the millennium, especially in France, where social unrest inspired doom-laden dread. Some proclaimed world-weariness, literally – mundus senescit, 'the world grows tired', became a catch-phrase. In mid 10th-century France – a divided, anarchic and fearful land – sermons were preached, rumours spread, significance seen in famines and plagues and comets. A feeling grew of something awful pending.

Against this vague fear, mainstream millenarians continued to base themselves on the Book of Revelations, and believed that the crucial 1,000 years had yet to start. Real doomsday would lie another 1,000 years beyond. The Roman Church adopted a pragmatic view. Since it was not given to mere man to second-guess the mind of God, and since nothing undermines faith like a failure to predict doomsday, the Church, unlike St Augustine, refused to commit to a schedule for the Second Coming.

Good sense prevailed. As the millennium entered its last two decades, the rumours of doomsday faded. They had, in any event, only touched part of France. The year itself passed without particular forboding. In the words of the historian Henri Focillon, 'the decisive moment, it would seem, left men indifferent'.

Centuries later, though, there arose the notion that there had been a Great Fear, for it suited the humanists of the Renaissance to believe so. If their age was enlightened, as they knew it to be, its light glowed the brighter if the past could be seen as darker. As one historian has put it, this was a 'historical mirage' that suited the times: 'At the centre of medieval darkness, the Year One Thousand, antithesis of the Renaissance, presented the spectacle of death and abject submission.'

By hindsight, looking back at both the year itself and the beliefs about it, the whole issue of millennial fear was a mirage.

activity made for global warming. Certainly, there was a *regional* warming in Europe. Climatologists debate the temperature rise that defined this so-called Medieval Warm Period – probably only a degree or two at most – but it was enough. Swiss glaciers were on the retreat, and seas were rising – in the early 11th century, Bruges (Brugge), once 15 km (10 miles) from the North Sea (as it is again today), became a port.

A slow revolution was under way. There had been no major plagues for 200 years. From the 8th century, population had been on the increase. As numbers rose, people drew together in villages, building on hills, around manors. New monasteries acted as seeds of stability. Slowly growing wealth and security went hand in hand. Both flowed from the land. Kings and nobles seized it, married into it, inherited it, bargained with it. Landowners needed workers, workers needed protection. There arose the system deriving from the Germanic notion of a *feohu*, a gift that conferred an obligation. Originally the gift was land, given by many to a powerful individual in exchange for protection. The system that evolved, feudalism, was made hugely complex by overlapping and conflicting pressures, but in theory the serf provided service, with loyalty; the lord provided protection, with justice.

These changes were joined by another in the round of toil. For generations, the only hope of an easier life had been in the ownership of slaves. The opening of new lands to the east by the Franks brought contact with Slavs – and the flow of captive Slavs gave several European languages their word for 'slave.' But slaves themselves needed food. In Europe (though not in Muslim lands) they were an expression of wealth for the few, not creators of it for the many. Escape from the round of toil could come only from technological change.

In north-east France during the 9th century, farmers had discovered that crops were better if grown in sequence, using three fields in a three-year cycle, which included one fallow year. 'Three-field rotation' was a practice that, around 1000, was spreading steadily to the rest of Europe (it would take another 300 years before a second revolution – the use of legumes to replace nitrogen in depleted soils – increased productivity further).

Taming Northern Europe

—— border c. 1000

···· main trade routes

→ Viking trade routes

▨ forests

Christendom Divided by Three Words

A major controversy dividing Rome and Constantinople concerned the nature of the Trinity — God-in-Three-Persons (Father, Son and Holy Spirit). The difficulty of defining a God seen as both one and three had always spun off into mysticism and paradox. Were the three equal, or should they be ranked? The question had been controversial for centuries. In the answer, it was felt, must lie the truth about God's nature, the essence of Christianity's uniqueness.

In 1000, East and West had come to different conclusions, and were about to find the differences irreconcilable. In Orthodox dogma, the Holy Spirit proceeded 'from the Father', and thus through the Son. In Roman dogma, the Spirit proceeded 'from the Father and the Son' (filioque, in Latin). Introduced from the 6th century, the Filioque Clause became an official part of the Catholic Creed in 1020. It has remained there ever since.

The division would lead to formal schism in 1054. A thousand years later, it has not been healed.

In addition, farmers were increasingly using a new sort of plough. The earliest ploughs were simply enlarged digging sticks dragged by an ox or two. They made a furrow, but did not turn the soil and left a ridge of earth untouched between furrows. The new 'heavy' plough consisted of two wheels to guide and support the weight, an iron-sheathed blade, and a mouldboard to turn the sod over. It took two oxen to pull it, but it increased productivity enough to pay its way and allowed the opening of new areas for cultivation.

These were part of a whole spectrum of causes and effects, much debated by historians because all interacted in slow motion on one another – greater productivity, colonization of marginal lands, more animals, less work, more wealth, increased specialization, less dependence on the soil, higher emigration to towns, greater wealth for nobility and clergy. A few, like young Otto, could dream not just of empire, but of civilization renewed. Rome and Christianity together floated an ideal of once and future greatness before the eyes of a few ambitious leaders and churchmen. Christian missionaries probed north and east, creating a spiritual counterweight to Byzantium. In Normandy and Scandinavia, men whose ancestors were piratical Norsemen settled into citizenship. In the continental heartland, a nascent Germany quelled the onrush of nomadic Magyars, and settlers began to push into Poland. Tiny enclaves of Jews provided trade links with Islam and Asia.

Though they could not be aware of it, the peoples of Europe had hit rock-bottom and were on the way up. In 1000, they faced a future that was rosier, or at least less dismal, than their past.

I

The Reach of Rome

As Christianity spread north and east, it built a network that gave Europe the beginnings of its new identity.

In 1000, Latinized Christianity, the Church of Rome, lay at the heart of Europe's civilization. It had preserved the continent's Christian heritage from the ravages of six centuries of barbarian invasion. From Italy to Scotland, monks, most notably the followers of the 6th-century St Benedict, had made copies of the Bible and other Christian texts, work that received a tremendous boost under Charlemagne. At a time when few wrote, only the clergy ran schools. Virtually all art was rooted in religion. Everyday life was governed by it. From the cradle to the grave, the Church was there for peasant and ruler alike, a super-state whose servants, the soldiers of Christ, fought the Devil on earth and guarded the doors to heaven and hell (there was no purgatory yet). This was a super-state with clout, continuously strengthened by those who sought bliss in the next world through generosity in this.

In 900, Latin Christendom was limited to Italy, France, northern Spain, Germany's heartland and Britain. Half a century later, Otto I, German ruler of what was shortly to become the newly reconstituted Holy Roman Empire, opened his eastern and northern borderlands to Christianity. From there missionaries spread north into Scandinavia. Beyond the Elbe, there were seven bishoprics by 1000. Another in Skara (Sweden) followed in about 1014. Where missions came, buildings followed. In the words of a Burgundian monk, Radulf (also known as Raoul or Rodolfus) Glaber: 'The world then shook off the dust from its old vestments, and the earth was covered in a white robe of churches.'

The Reach of Rome

- extent of Catholicism
- ⚑ archbishoprics

Why exactly Latin Christianity, with its foreign liturgy and dead language, should have been so successful is much debated. Prelates in Rome had their own agenda, of course – to spread their version of the Word, and to forestall their Byzantine rivals from Constantinople spreading theirs. But at first sight, there is no reason why peasant communities in the Baltic and the borderlands of Rus should accept a Roman creed.

The reasons overlap those that underlie the new mood of Europe north of the Alps. With a monopoly on sanctifying rituals, the Church held the keys to peace, stability, prosperity and education, and upheld its faith with all the force it could muster. Warriors, traders and churchmen informally agreed on its benefits, absorbing the rituals and beliefs along with the economic and political advantages. Peasants had no choice but to tag along.

In some ways, Church and civil administration marched hand in hand; in others, the Church acted on its own account. The Pope granted bishoprics, bishops created abbeys. But bishops also worked with local rulers. Both had their estates, their power structures, their economies. From top to bottom, Europe was an interfusion of Church and state, each with its own agenda, each relying on, using and opposing the other.

Such conflicts led to paradox – a Church corrupted by materialism, a laity infused with spirituality. Locally, bishops were often happy to secure power and wealth by dispensing land to henchmen, forcing monks into beggary. Clergy were notoriously corrupt, happily using their power and wealth to live an easy life, often setting up house with a woman who was a wife in all but name, scandalizing those who were keen to assert Catholic chastity. As Atto, Bishop of Verceil, put it around 950, 'A number of you are so enslaved by passion that they allow obscene courtesans to live in their dwellings, to share their food, to appear with them in public.'

Corruption was lodged in the Church's very heart. Popes were pawns in the hands of Roman aristocrats, which made it a high-risk job. One pope was suffocated on the orders of the wife of a local lord. She then had her son appointed – an illegitimate son, conceived with a previous pope. Pope John XII (955–63) was a teenager who devoted himself to wine, women, song and hunting. Since the papacy still claimed that its incumbent had to approve a secular ruler, rulers had an interest in ensuring a compliant pope. Around the turn of the millennium, might was right in Rome: whoever could dominate the Italian aristocrats could make and break popes. It was only in the late 11th century that the papacy would find its way again, under the aegis of Pope Gregory VII.

The Rule of Cluny

In Christendom's splintered world – corrupt papacy, weak kings, grasping nobles – many longed for a life of Christian austerity, as expressed by the 6th-century father of monasticism, St Benedict. In 1000, hundreds were able to live out that ideal, thanks to two men, a Burgundian monk, Berno, and William, Count of Auvergne and Duke of Aquitaine.

In 909, William – 'the Pious', as he was known – gave Berno the villa of Cluny, just north of Mâcon, on the River Grosne. Here, the two established a monastery independent of temporal power, owing loyalty only to the Pope. Other princes followed suit, and Cluny became the heart of Christian revival in France. In Cluny, wrote the monk Radulf Glaber, 'the life-giving sacrifice was celebrated so continuously that not a day passed when such celebration did not snatch souls from the Devil's grip.'

Soon, Cluny was at the head of a growing order of monasteries, many of them established ones reformed from within by Cluniac 'cells'. These were the arks to be stocked against the floods of anarchy and materialism by doing God's works – performing the disciplined, uniform rituals as laid down by the Rule of St Benedict. Cluny's clarity of vision was sustained by centralized authority and stable rule – in 200 years it had only five abbots. In 1000 the abbot was Odilo, who increased the number of Cluniac monasteries from 37 to 65, with hundreds of 'cells' in established monasteries.

Though Cluny was supposedly dedicated to spiritual matters, it wielded great political power. Its abbot was one of Europe's most significant figures, wielding influence with kings as well as the Pope. Its new church, started in 1090, was the to be the largest in Christendom until the building of St Peter's in Rome. At heart a French organization, it steadily infiltrated every other European region. By the end of the 11th century it had over 1100 cells – 815 in France, 105 in Germany, 23 in Spain, 52 in Italy, 43 in Britain, even a few in Poland and the Holy Land. Eventually it would exercise direct control over some 300 monasteries, inevitably accruing wealth against which later monastic movements would revolt in the everlasting struggle to restore austerity.

Christ feeds the 5,000 in an 11th-century gospel illustration made for the monastery in Echternach, on the border between present-day Luxembourg and Germany. Echternach was a base for missionaries eager to bring Europe's north-east into the Christian fold.

Christ's head was a continent-wide symbol of Christianity. This one is part of a stained glass window from the church of SS Peter and Paul, Wissembourg, eastern France.

The Viking Heartland

For a life that captured the essence of the times, nothing could rival that of Olaf Tryggvason of Norway. He was the exemplar of a culture that combined strong roots and foreign adventure, ferocity with heroism, paganism with Christianity. The greatest hero of his day, he is still seen as father of the nation.

He was, of course, a Viking, one of those who for 200 years had been venturing away from their *viks* (creeks) to pillage the coasts of northern Europe. Their *vikings* (raids) gave them their name and their fearsome reputation.

But pirating was just one facet of a culture that linked all three main Scandinavian peoples, from the lakes, bogs, forests and meadows of Denmark in the south, up through Norway, with its backbone of mountains, and eastwards to the lowlands of Sweden. These proto-nations of powerful *jarls* (earls) were held together by kings, but boundaries were forever fluctuating as *jarls* combined and fought for wealth, security and power. Medieval Scandinavian history is a compendium of sagas, stories of heroes with caricature nicknames designed to instill fear and admiration. Norway, its offshore islands guarding the 'North Way', favoured seafarers, Denmark and southern Sweden were more for farmers. In these areas of pastoral wealth the first Scandinavian towns arose. The largest, Hedeby, was little more than a village, but safe behind defensive walls and ditches its 1,500 inhabitants minted coins, and produced metal and glass. By 1000, another nine major centres had arisen, including Oslo, all of them administrative and ecclesiastical bases.

All three areas inspired foreign adventure. Two

centuries before, when Charlemagne's empire pressed in from the south across Saxon lands, Scandinavians had honed their seafaring skills, and looked outwards. Danes and Norwegians were drawn west to the coasts and islands of northern Europe. Swedes – 'Rus' in Finnish – looked east and south, across the Baltic. Any of them might be drawn to, or forced into, *viking*. For some it was a way of life, for others an occasional distraction.

The lands across the Baltic had been left to the 'Rus'. By 900, the Rus had navigated the Volga and the Dnieper, and founded Novgorod and Kiev. Soon thereafter, they controlled a state that reached almost to the Black Sea. Drawn by the long-established flow of silver from the Middle East, they traded with the Byzantine Empire, whose inhabitants called them Varangians, probably from the Norse for 'confederates'. When, around 965, the flow of silver dried up, the Scandinavians again turned westwards, going off *viking* in search of easier pickings in England.

This was the world Olaf was born into, a world of shifting rivalries and allegiances between kings, would-be kings and *jarls*. Norway had been held by a succession of rulers – Erik Bloodaxe, Hakon the Good, Harald Greycloak – leading in 995 to Olaf's succession. To the south, Denmark was a bridge to, and defence from, the rich lands of Saxony. The Danish king Harald Bluetooth (950–85) had became the first Scandinavian ruler to accept Christianity, a move that helped secure his southern border from attack by co-religionists. His ambitious son, Svein Forkbeard, cast hungry eyes on Norway.

Olaf, Harald Greycloak's great-grandson, was born in about 968. He had grown to manhood in Russia, where he had an uncle in the court of Vladimir. He allied himself to Svein Forkbeard, and fought in England, where, after raiding Maldon in 991 (p. 43) and London in 994, he was handed vast amounts of silver in Danegeld, on the understanding that he would go away. In 995, to back his promise, he converted to Christianity, being confirmed at a great ceremony in Andover. At some point he married the daughter of Boleslaw the Brave of Poland (a relationship complicated when he later married one of Boleslaw's former wives, Thyri). He then returned in triumph to Norway, determined to take it as his birthright and bring it into the Christian fold. It proved something of a vain ambition. Though little is certain about his reign, Olaf seems not to have exercised power over much more than the coast.

But he was strong enough to be a threat to his former colleague, Svein, England's future conqueror. By now, after two centuries of maritime warfare, the Danes and Norwegians could sum-

This lion's-head bedpost, one of many other fine examples of Norse artistry, was buried in a queen's grave in Oseberg, southwest of Oslo, in the 9th century.

A model of a timber-and-earthwork fortress at Trelleborg, near Slegelse, 50 miles west of Copenhagen. It dominated the inland area and the coast, providing shelter for shipping.

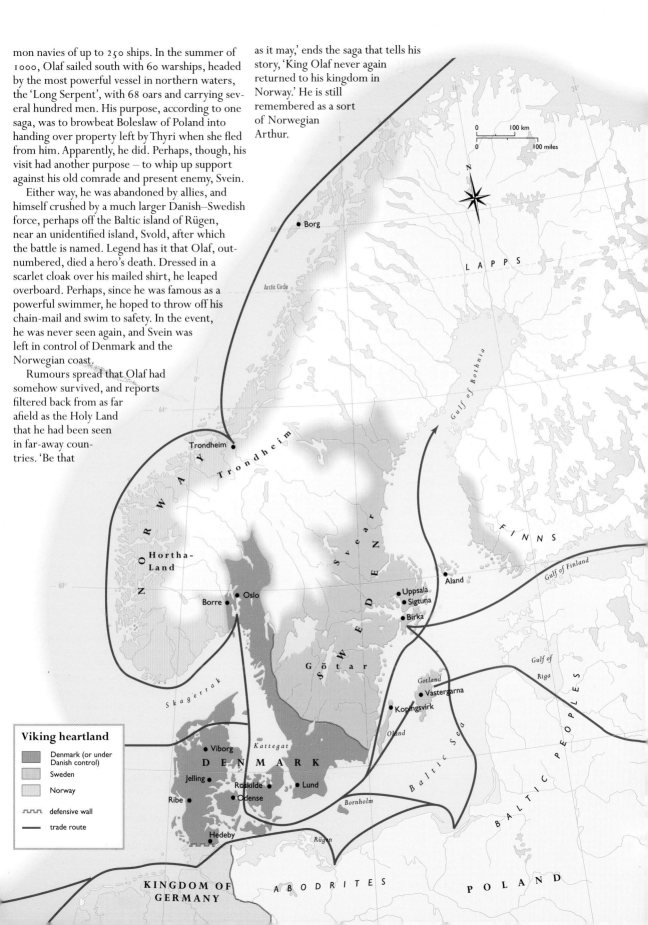

mon navies of up to 250 ships. In the summer of 1000, Olaf sailed south with 60 warships, headed by the most powerful vessel in northern waters, the 'Long Serpent', with 68 oars and carrying several hundred men. His purpose, according to one saga, was to browbeat Boleslaw of Poland into handing over property left by Thyri when she fled from him. Apparently, he did. Perhaps, though, his visit had another purpose – to whip up support against his old comrade and present enemy, Svein.

Either way, he was abandoned by allies, and himself crushed by a much larger Danish–Swedish force, perhaps off the Baltic island of Rügen, near an unidentified island, Svold, after which the battle is named. Legend has it that Olaf, outnumbered, died a hero's death. Dressed in a scarlet cloak over his mailed shirt, he leaped overboard. Perhaps, since he was famous as a powerful swimmer, he hoped to throw off his chain-mail and swim to safety. In the event, he was never seen again, and Svein was left in control of Denmark and the Norwegian coast.

Rumours spread that Olaf had somehow survived, and reports filtered back from as far afield as the Holy Land that he had been seen in far-away countries. 'Be that

as it may,' ends the saga that tells his story, 'King Olaf never again returned to his kingdom in Norway.' He is still remembered as a sort of Norwegian Arthur.

Viking heartland

- Denmark (or under Danish control)
- Sweden
- Norway
- ⌁⌁⌁ defensive wall
- —— trade route

3

New-found Lands in Iceland and Greenland

Across the northern seas, Norsemen created the foundations of a new nation, a successful colony, a sturdy form of self-government and an enduring literature.

In the 10th century, Norsemen island-hopping from bases in the Shetlands, the Orkneys and the Hebrides had begun to settle Iceland. Here the colonists, possibly losers in the intensifying struggle for land in Scandinavia, found good grazing, and formed a rough frontier society. The settlers, having escaped the rule of kings, were all kings in their own right, squabbling over their estates, using Irish and English slaves for labour. But in 930, tired of blood-feuds, the 36 *godar* – 'godly ones', as the leaders termed themselves – combined to form an all-Iceland parliament, the Althing. They sent off one of their number to Norway to research a constitution and elected a president, a Lawspeaker, who held office for three years, at which point he would be sacked or reconfirmed. The system became more sophisticated in 965, when the country was divided into four, each quarter holding several local assemblies each year. The Althing divided into legislative and judicial sections. Each quarter acquired a court. Later, a court of appeal was formed.

The greatest achievement of this system of aristocratic democracy was the peaceful adoption of Christianity, which probably occurred in 1000. According to the main source, Ari Thorgilsson, writing over a century later, the motive force was Olaf Tryggvason of Norway – the ruler who had been baptized in England. In 995, he sent a German missionary, Thangbrand, who met with little success. Olaf was displeased. Icelanders must have become uncomfortably aware that Olaf could well decide to impose his will on the distant colony. Perhaps the threat, like an impending execution, concentrated their minds, bringing to their attention arguments for Christianity: literacy, contact with Latin culture, trade links. Anyway, one of the most powerful of the *godar*, Gizur the White, converted. Two others did the same. There followed a confrontation in the Althing, with Christian and heathen swearing they could not live by the same set of laws. The Lawspeaker, Thorgeir, who had already held the office for 12 years, faced a crisis.

In Ari's words, 'Later, when men had returned to their booths, Thorgeir lay down and spread his cloak over him, and lay quiet all that day and the night following, and spoke never a word. But the next morning he sat up and announced that men should proceed to the Law Rock. And when men had made their way there he began his speech.'

He told them that it would be disastrous if they did not have the same law. 'It will prove true,' he said, in a phrase that gains in translation, 'that, if

The remains of Erik the Red's farm, Brattahlid, part of Greenland's 'Eastern Settlement' in 1000, still preside over the stretch of water named after him – Eiriksfjord.

we break the law in pieces, we break the peace in pieces too.' Then, with the *godar* behind him, Thorgeir sprang his surprise. He was not himself a Christian, but seeing where Iceland's interests lay, he decreed that all should be baptized into the Christian faith.

Thus one man decided the destiny of the nation, if Ari is to be believed. However it happened, the effects were dramatic. Instead of remaining a despised and barbaric outpost of heathendom, Iceland joined Europe's community of Christian nations. Priests came, bringing Roman script, literacy, trade. Gizur's son Isleif became Iceland's first native bishop. Within a century, scholars were writing Iceland's history, in both Latin and Icelandic, making the first contributions to the body of literature which, over the next 200 years, gave the country its pride of place in history, poetry and language.

Further west, other Norsemen were already building another outpost. From reports by storm-driven sailors, the Icelanders knew of land some 280 km (175 miles) to the west almost as soon as they settled in their new country. It was a

Epic Histories in Verse and Prose

The strangest, and many say greatest glory of early Iceland was its literature. Poetry was a national industry, and poets a major export, travelling from Iceland to the Swedish, Norwegian and Danish courts. From the 960s, the poet laureate of Norway was traditionally an Icelander.

The literature spanned three centuries, but was written down only from the 13th century. It is in both verse and prose. Anonymous lays from a collection known as the Edda tell tales of ancient heroes and Norse gods. One great Eddic poem, Völuspa (The Sybil's Prophecy), composed in Iceland around 1000, tells the history of the world and its gods, men, and monsters, from the time of the 'great void' until the Ragnarok, the Doom (or Twilight) of the Gods.

Skaldic verses by court poets (skalds) commemorate royal patrons in lines rich in elaborate alliteration. One warrior-skald, Egill Skallagrimsson (c. 910–90), composed a poem in honour of the notoriously violent Erik Bloodaxe, king of the Norwegian colony of York. He wrote it overnight, with the best possible incentive: he was Erik's captive, and was due for execution the next morning. The threat focused his mind wonderfully. 'Head Ransom,' flattering Erik for his bravery and generosity, saved his life.

The 120 surviving sagas in verse and prose typically tell of blood feuds over many generations, providing a unique insight into pre-Christian northern European society. They also contain accounts of the families, feuds and alliances that founded Iceland, though the balance of fact and fiction is hard, sometimes impossible to determine. Writers mined their past, but like historical novelists they reformed it to suit their own artistic purposes.

Their artistry has always been admired. Men like Thorarin the Black, Viga-Glum and Einar Jingle-scale gave their country an eminence in literature and history out of all proportion to their country's few inhabitants. Moreover, these tales, sharing much with early English and Germanic mythology, echo today in works from Wagner's Ring Cycle — Siegfried is the Norse hero Sigurd — to Tolkien's Lord of the Rings.

Norwegian outlaw who found it was fit for habitation.

Erik (or Eric, or Eirik) Thorvaldsson, nicknamed Erik the Red, was not a man to cross. He had been brought to Iceland by his father, who had been outlawed from his native Norway for murder. Erik clearly inherited his father's violent tendencies. So dedicated was he to feuding – he had his slaves engineer a landslide to flatten a neighbour's farm – that he was himself outlawed for three years. He decided to explore the unknown icy land to the west.

As it turned out, it was rather less icebound than it is today. Erik rounded the point now known as Cape Farewell in 983, and to his astonishment discovered fjords, kept ice-free in spring and summer by a finger of the Gulf Stream current. Here were grassy slopes, bears, foxes, caribou, fish – and no inhabitants. The place was his for the taking. For three years, he and his crew explored.

Returning, he painted a glorious picture of a place ripe for colonization. To enhance its appeal, he called it Greenland. This was good news for his countrymen, for they had just come through ten years of famine, and in any case their habitable patches were all occupied.

In 986, 25 ships set out for the new land. It was a rough trip. Only 14 survived the journey, landing some 350 people around today's Julianehåb, the area they would soon call the Eastern Settlement. Here Erik and his wife and three sons settled in a fjord named after him, on his farm Brattahlid.

By 1000, some Norsemen had pushed 500 km (300 miles) north to today's Godthåb (the Western Settlement) and grown to some 1,000 strong. The two communities were exporting furs, hides, woollens, and narwhal and walrus tusk in exchange for corn, iron, timber and clothes they needed from Iceland and Norway.

This was the beginning for the communities that would eventually have outposts another 650 km (400 miles) to the north. They were to live well for over 200 years. But then the climate turned harsher, crops failed, ice increasingly hemmed them, and hostile Inuit moved southwards. When one last ship called in 1540, the crew found only deserted farms, and one unburied body.

4 England: A Nation on Its Knees

For some years, England was ruined by Danish backmail and pillage. Briefly, it became a Danish kingdom.

In 980, the Vikings returned to southern England. The last of their previous provinces, York, had been overthrown by Wessex in 954, leaving the country united for the first time. But to the two rivals for power in Scandinavia, Olaf and Svein, England was a constant lure and challenge, a source of cash to fund their ambitions.

Their policy was simple: blackmail. A century before, in King Alfred's day, raiding Vikings had

extorted cash, in effect a bribe to go away. Now the potential was far greater. England had been at peace for 30 years. Coffers were full. But conquest, even if possible, would be expensive. Better to threaten mayhem, and be mollified with cash. Besides, control was now vested in a single king. If the point of attack was well chosen, a successful invading army could hold the whole country to ransom, rather than one small area. Besides, the king was the ineffectual Ethelred, not the 'Unready' of schoolbooks, but *unraede* – 'the ill-advised'. He was not the man to withstand professional racketeers like the Vikings.

This medieval extortion, Danegeld ('Dane's

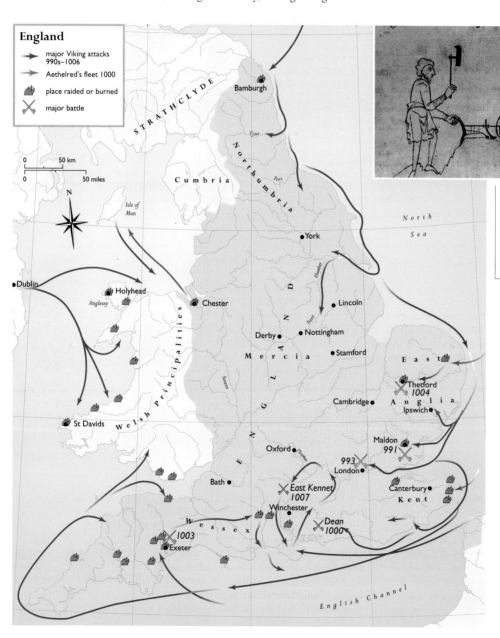

England

→ major Viking attacks 990s–1006

→ Aethelred's fleet 1000

🔥 place raided or burned

✗ major battle

In a rough sketch, an Anglo-Saxon farmer shows off his two prize possessions, an axe and a new style heavy plough drawn by two oxen with shoulder-harnesses.

An Ideal to Die For

In 991 a Viking force raided Ipswich, then sailed up the River Blackwater towards the town of Maldon. The battle that followed was more famous than most because it was commemorated around the year 1000 in one of the greatest of early English poems, The Battle of Maldon, *which captures the essence of the ideal that held these little societies together: loyalty to a lord.*

The Viking leader, Anlaf – almost certainly the Norwegian king Olaf Tryggvason – disembarked his men on Northey Island. It was a good base to escape from at high tide, but not much use for an assault, because the island, then as now, was surrounded by tidal flats and linked to the mainland only by a narrow causeway. Even this was under water at high tide.

At the other end of the causeway stood the local leader, Bryhtnoth, Earl of Essex, leader of the East Saxon army, who had been tracking the Viking fleet for days. Olaf's spokesman yelled across the inlet, demanding a deal – 'We need not meet if you can meet our needs!' Bryhtnoth refused. There seemed nothing the Vikings could do about it. The causeway, now emerging from the falling tide, could easily be held by a few men. Deadlock threatened, inspiring the Vikings to crave 'leave to fare over the footpath'.

To this, Bryhtnoth made an astonishing response. He agreed that the Vikings should come over while the Saxons held back, so that the two sides could fight it out fair and square. In the light of what happened next, historians have assumed this was a foolhardy gesture. But Bryhtnoth was an experienced commander. He would not have courted disaster without good reason. More likely, he calculated that he had better gamble on victory now than have the Vikings retreat unscathed, only to attack again in some undefended spot.

The Vikings accepted, for present victory would lead to easy pickings in the future. As the tide went out, they filed across, and lined up. The battle started, with Bryhtnoth leading the attack. From the start, the Saxons were outclassed. A spear shattered against Bryhtnoth's shield and he drove his spear into a Viking's heart, but then he was cut down. Defeat was imminent. Some Saxons fled, one of them on Bryhtnoth's horse, giving the impression that the leader himself was fleeing the battlefield. But others rallied, reminding one another of their duty: loyalty to their lord, even beyond death, even in the face of certain defeat.

One ageing warrior, Bryhtwold, is given ringing words that summon up the ideals of heroism and loyalty:

Courage shall grow keener, clearer the will,
The heart fiercer, as our force faileth.
Here our lord lies levelled in the dust,
The man all marred: he shall mourn to the end
Who thinks to wend off from this war-play now.
Though I am white with winters, I will not away,
For I think to lodge me alongside my dear one,
Lay me down by my lord's right hand.

(translation by Michael Alexander)

All in vain. The remaining Anglo-Saxons died bravely. The Vikings bore Bryhtnoth's head away in triumph. It was no great victory, for the Vikings had suffered too much to capitalize on their win that day, but in the long run the Vikings benefited hugely. Bryhtnoth's decision led directly to defeat, and the payment of an immense sum to Olaf in Danegeld.

But rather than castigate Bryhtnoth for incompetence, the anonymous author of The Battle of Maldon turned defeat into a cause for celebration. Here were men determined to forge the bonds of nationhood with high ideals: heroic leadership matched by death-defying loyalty.

---

money') as it was called, started in 991, when, after the Battle of Maldon, Olaf was bought off with treasure – 10 tonnes of silver. This immense sum – coins, plates, goblets, brooches, ingots, and arm-rings wrought by smiths across the country – was snatched from churches and landholders, many of whom were ruined. For Britain, this was a suicidal policy: though it might buy peace in the short term, all it did in the long term was to finance the invaders to strike again.

Two years later, Olaf returned, this time in alliance with Svein. Again, the threat worked. But back home the two piratical rivals fell out. It was Svein who emerged victorious at the Battle of Svolt (p. 39). In 1002, after Olaf's death, he returned to England and collected another 10 tonnes of silver.

Ethelred's response was that of a weak monarch. Unable to guarantee security from foreign invasion, and fearful of conspiracy and revolution, he turned on the Danish settlers living in England. On 13 November 1002, he had hundreds of them murdered. One of those killed was Gunnhild, Svein's sister.

There followed a disastrous time for England. The vengeful Svein ravaged south-west England in 1003 and East Anglia the following year. In 1005, another scourge took its toll: famine. In 1006 Svein was back, this time making off with 16 tonnes of loot. In 1010 the Danes burned Oxford, Ipswich, Cambridge. Danegeld mounted: in total, the Vikings took an estimated 70 tonnes in silver.

By 1012, English morale had collapsed. After Canterbury fell to another raider, Thorkell the Tall, a kidnapped bishop who refused to pay a ransom was pelted with bones until he was put out of his misery with an axe. Svein sailed up the Humber, then swept southwards in a figure-of-eight via Oxford, Winchester and Bath. Ethelred fled to Normandy. Svein took over, founding a dynasty that ruled Norway, Sweden, Denmark and England. But this was no conquest by mass migration. Svein's officers came for Danegeld, and most departed for home again.

Fortunately for England, this was almost the last gasp of the Viking Age. Svein's successor, Cnut (anglicized as Canute), never ruled a united empire. England reverted to native rule. When the Norwegian king tried to restake a claim in 1066, the English proved too strong – only to fall to the armies of another claimant with Viking blood, William of Normandy. But by now Normans were

Ethelred's head on a silver penny suggests that he exercised a firm grip over England until the Norse invasions.

5

The Celtic World

With its intricate panels, the damaged and eroded West Cross is the tallest of three so-called High Crosses carved in Monaster-boice, Louth, probably in the 10th century.

For Irish schoolchildren, Brian Boru is the founder. He was the one who 'united Ireland', they are told, and 'saved us from the Danes'. To go deeper than this is to enter the murky borderland of Celtic myth and history. Yet from the shaky evidence of Gaelic chronicles, something firm can be discerned.

For two centuries, the Vikings had gnawed at Ireland's flanks, seizing the best harbours for settlement, undermining a land and culture once known for art and learning. Against them, the Irish were impotent. The rival clans were roughly di-vided among Ireland's five rival kingdoms – Ulster, Connaught, Meath, Munster and Leinster. True, there was an idea of unity, based on the tradition that whoever held the Hill of Tara in Meath could claim to be Árd-rí – 'High King' – of all Ireland. For centuries, that honour had been held by the O'Neills (Uí Néill in Gaelic), a vast and powerful dynastic group who dominated the north and east. But by the mid-900's, Tara had been long aban-doned, and High Kingship was a mere title. Rivalries precluded nationhood. The Vikings came at will, probing rivers for unwary monasteries.

This was a complex, shifting world. Dynastic chiefs paid reluctant tribute to local kings if they had to, gaining security and wealth if they were lucky. Kings, too, paid and profited and fought. Every ruler wanted more, employing every means possible: war, cattle-raiding, diplomacy, tribute-taking, hostage-holding, intermarriage, betrayal, the maiming or blinding of rivals. Borders were elastic.

These ambitions could be played upon by the Norsemen, who could negotiate, trade and farm as well as fight. Some 150 years before, the Norse had seized a ford on the River Liffey known as Dubh Linn, 'the black pool'. The town had flour-ished. As the millennium approached, Dublin was the wealthy centre of a county-sized kingdom of Norse smallholders. Elsewhere the Norse held a dozen enclaves, notably Limerick, Waterford, Cork and Wexford.

But in the south-west, events threw up sturdier opposition in the form of Brian, the younger son of the ruling clan of northern Munster. By tradition, Brian (pronounced 'bre-an') was born in about 941 to a ruling line, the Dalcassians (Dal Cais in Gaelic, pronounced 'dawl gosh') at Kincora (Ceann Coradh), a palace now lost beneath the town of Killaloe. Possibly, he came from Beal Boramha or Boroimhe (pronounced 'boroo'), 'the fort of the tribute', a pallisade just north of Killaloe, commanding the Shannon, where it

emerges at the southern end of Lough Derg. It was this fort that gave him his nickname, anglicized as it sounded – Boru.

Brian, raised with tales of Celtic heroism and Christian scholarship, must have harboured ambi-tions to reclaim Celtic lands from the Norse intruders. Under the aegis of Munster's king, his elder brother Mathgamain (pronounced 'mohun'), he became a guerrilla fighter against the Norsemen, and in 968 the brothers drove them from Limerick. Two years later, Mathgamain was murdered by rivals. Brian, now about 35, had his revenge in battle in 979, and was crowned in Cashel, Munster's capital. To secure his eastern borders, he then seized neighbouring Leinster.

Next, his attention turned to Meath, whose leader Maoil Seachlainn (pronounced 'mail-shachlin') held Tara and was thus High King. Before Meath and Munster could fight, chance made them allies. Sitric 'Silkenbeard', Norse king of Dublin, joined the king of Leinster, Maol Mordha (pro-nounced 'mwal mora'). Munster and Meath united against this common enemy. In 999, the armies met at Glenn Mama, an unidentified site near Dublin. Though there are no details of the battle, the Munster–Meath coalition won. Maol Mordha hid in a yew tree until captured by Brian's eldest son, Murchadh.

Brian, the dominant partner in the alliance, cemented his position with new family ties. He married Gormfhlaith, daughter of a leading Leinster family and mother of Sitric, while Sitric himself was married to Brian's daughter, who became queen of Dublin.

Rapidly the unnatural Munster–Meath alliance collapsed. Brian demanded the surrender of Meath's king, who duly abdicated. Brian was now High King, the ruler of Tara, but Tara had no palace. Brian returned home to Cashel for his coronation in 1002.

With old age approaching – he was now about 60 – Brian revealed other talents. Ireland, almost a nation, underwent a brief renaissance. Acknow-ledged by the O'Neills of Ulster as well, Brian confirmed Armagh as Ireland's spiritual head-quarters. In his palace in Kincora, its double moat fed by the Shannon, he held lavish banquets for his subservient princes. Schools and monasteries thrived. He ordered local rulers and priests to record their histories. Young men were sent off to study in the courts of Europe. Roads were up-graded and bridges built, allowing Brian's army quick access to trouble spots. His six sons were loyal, and marriages increased the network of alliance – three daughters were queens, in Dublin, Desmond (roughly, present-day Kerry and Cork) and Scotland. But lesser kings fretted at the tributes they were forced to pay – Leinster's in particular. One demand, for three large ship's

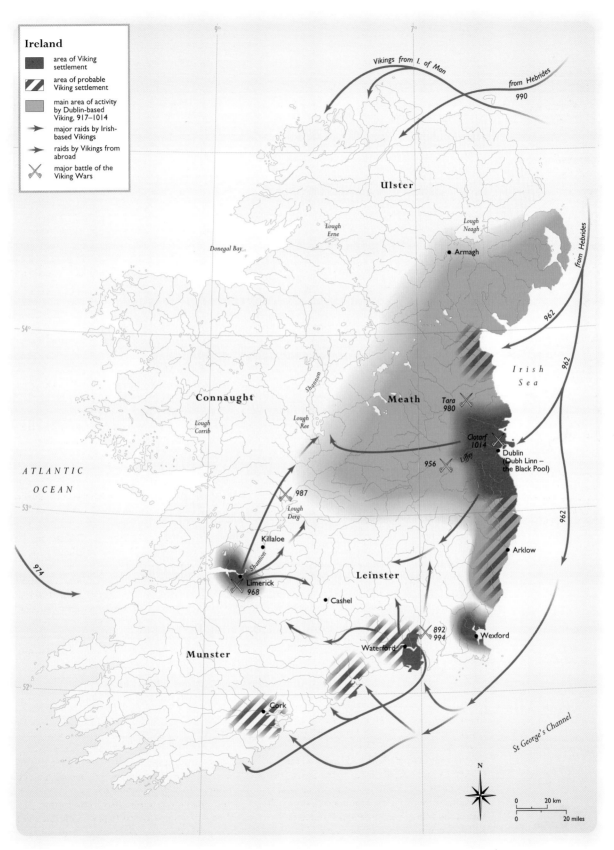

Ireland

- ◼ area of Viking settlement
- ▨ area of probable Viking settlement
- ▨ main area of activity by Dublin-based Viking, 917–1014
- → major raids by Irish-based Vikings
- → raids by Vikings from abroad
- ✕ major battle of the Viking Wars

Ulster

Vikings *from I. of Man*

from Hebrides
990

from Hebrides

962

962

Irish Sea

Lough Erne

Lough Neagh

Donegal Bay

● Armagh

Connaught

Shannon

Lough Ree

Meath

Tara
980 ✕

Lough Corrib

✕ *956*

Liffey

Clotarf
1014 ✕

● Dublin
(Dubh Linn —
the Black Pool)

ATLANTIC
OCEAN

✕ *987*

Lough Derg

● Killaloe

Shannon

Leinster

● Arklow

962

974

Limerick ✕
968

● Cashel

● Wexford

✕ *892*
994

Waterford

Munster

● Cork

St George's Channel

N

0   20 km

0   20 miles

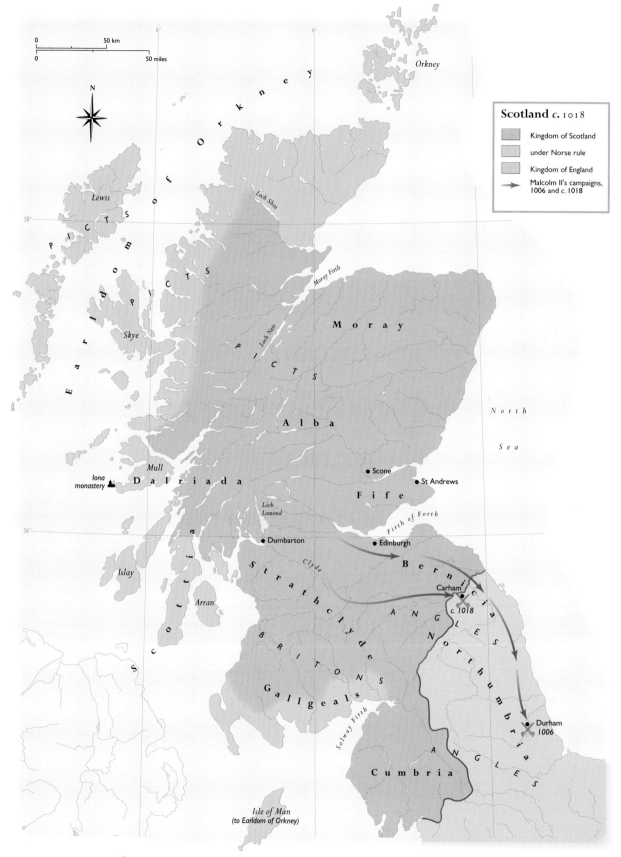

Scotland c. 1018

Kingdom of Scotland

under Norse rule

Kingdom of England

Malcolm II's campaigns, 1006 and c. 1018

Orkney

E a r l d o m   o f   O r k n e y

Lewis

P I C T S

Skye

Loch Shin

Moray Firth

M o r a y

Loch Ness

P I C T S

A l b a

N o r t h

S e a

Mull

Iona
monastery

D a l r i a d a

Scone

St Andrews

F i f e

Loch
Lomond

Firth of Forth

S c o t t i a

Dumbarton

Edinburgh

Islay

B e r n i c i a

Arran

S t r a t h c l y d e

Clyde

Carham
c. 1018

A N G L E S

B R I T O N S

N o r t h u m b r i a

G a l l g e a l s

Solway Firth

A N G L E S

Durham
1006

Cumbria

Isle of Man
(to Earldom of Orkney)

masts, brought high drama, according to the main Irish–Gaelic account.

The chief character was Maol Mordha, Leinster's king, the one who had been defeated with the Danes in 999, and then ignominiously dragged from a yew tree by Murchadh. On his arrival with the masts, Maol Mordha was reviled for cowardice by his kinswoman, Brian's wife Gormfhlaith. That evening, watching Murchadh play chess, Maol Mordha suggested a move that lost Murchadh the game.

'That', muttered Murchadh, 'was like the advice you gave the Danes at Glenn Mama!'

Maol Mordha's suppressed anger boiled over. He'd advise the Danes again, and this time 'they shall not be defeated!'

Murchadh sneered. 'Then you had better remind them to have a yew tree ready for your reception!'

Humiliated beyond endurance, Maol Mordha stormed out, declared war, and threw the whole south into disarray. Some rulers joined him, while others remained loyal to Brian.

With chaos threatening, Brian sent an army across Leinster and blockaded Dublin. Sitric, still Dublin's ruler, sent for help, from Sigurd the Stout, Norse ruler of the Orkneys, and from two notorious pirates. Brian, now over 70, summoned help from Meath. Old opponents faced each other again – Munster and Meath against Leinster and Dublin.

The two sides met on Good Friday, 1014, in Clontarf, a level area on the north of the Liffey, on the outskirts of present-day Dublin. An estimated 8,000 men fought it out that day, the greatest battle in Ireland to date. Sigurd fell, after wrapping himself in the raven banner of Odin, Norse god of war. Maol Mordha fell – no yew to hide in this time. Leinster men and Norsemen retreated, to the sea, and into it, many of them drowning. Sitric watched from inside Dublin, with his wife, Brian's daughter, beside him. When she made a sharp comment about his 'foreigners' fleeing into the sea, he 'dealt her a rude blow, which knocked out one of her teeth'.

On Munster's side, Murchadh also perished. Then Brian, praying by his pavilion, and exposed by the advance of his troops, was spotted by one of the piratical Norsemen, Brodar. Brodar cut his way to the old king, and struck him down with an axe. The victorious Munstermen took a horrible revenge. They seized Brodar, cut him open, and wound his entrails round a tree. Brian's body was carried to Armagh, and buried beside the cathedral he had restored. A plaque on the cathedral's modern replacement records his resting place.

The battle has widely been seen as a national struggle, Norse *v.* Irish, with the Irish coming out on top. Certainly, Norse influence declined, but

The Forging of Scotland

In the Celtic world, Scotland was unique – a nation in embryo. This was surprising, given that when the Vikings came in the 8th century, inland Scotland was a vague patchwork of four peoples – Irish, Britons, Angles and the aboriginal Picts. A century later, the Irish – 'Scotti' as their ancestors had called themselves – and Picts had merged. Perhaps they were hammered together by the Vikings, who drove a wedge between the Scots and their original homeland, and both Norse and Anglo-Saxons in the south. In any event, under joint Scottish-Pictish influence, all four recognized a single king. All were linked by a Church that had been a force for spiritual unity for over 400 years. All had in some sense become part of 'Scotia' (also known by the early Celtic term for England, 'Alba').

Within this context, details are non-existent, obscure or contradictory. Much has to be deduced or guessed. Since the days of the first king, Kenneth mac Alpin in the mid 9th century, kings ruled according to 'alternating succession',

a power-sharing arrangement that in theory balanced the ambitions of rival sub-dynasties. This system broke down in the 990s in a spate of killings which left three rival factions. Only with the accession of Malcolm II, who slew his way to the throne in 1005, does the murk lift a little.

Scottish identity, though only vaguely glimpsed in surviving documents, must have been clear enough at the time. Certainly, other leaders recognized the Scottish king as an equal, for many sought and accepted marital alliances. One of Brian Boru's daughters was married to Malcolm II long before he became king. Later, Malcolm married his daughter to Sigurd, King of the Orkneys (the one who was killed in Clontarf).

For Malcolm, there was little to be gained by confronting the Norse, who were almost as much family as the Irish. It was in the south that the problems lay. There, the Scottish-controlled Strathclyde, and Northumbria with its ancient legacy of Christian learning, had been buffer states between the Scots and the Norse in York. The defeat of the notorious exile, Erik Bloodaxe, by the Anglo-Saxons in 954

had opened the way for direct Scottish–English confrontation.

In 1006 Malcolm advanced south, raiding for cattle, treasure and, perhaps, slaves. He got as far as Durham, seizing the treasure of St Cuthbert from the newly founded cathedral, before he was forced out by a local Anglo-Saxon earl, Uhtred. He returned again ten years later (c. 1018), allied himself with Owen the Bald, ruler of Strathclyde, and trounced Uhtred at Carham, 30 km (20 miles) up the Tweed from Berwick. (Uhtred was summoned south by his overlord, Canute, and assassinated.)

Malcolm went on to rule his feud-ridden kingdom until 1034, when he was murdered in Glamis – a murder shifted to his successor Duncan (who ruled 1034–40) by Shakespeare in his version of the events leading up to Macbeth's accession in 1040.

Though the Scottish throne remained steeped in blood, Malcolm's successes were never reversed. He had carried the Scottish frontier south to the Tweed, where it remained. As the historian Alfred Smyth writes, 'the Scots had established the most stable and successful monarchy in Britain prior to the Norman invasion.'

mainly because they became Irish. Clontarf also marked a moment at which the possibility of nationhood gave way again to petty rivalry. Brian's descendants, the O'Brien dynasty, were no more than local rulers. Tara remained a grassy knoll, its enigmatic mounds reminding shepherds of vanished glories. Ireland returned to internecine strife and cattle-raiding. The way was open for another, and more significant invasion, by the Normans in 1169.

Nevertheless, Brian Boru left behind an ideal of national unity, expressed in a 12th-century saga, *The War of the Irish with the Foreigners*, to be recalled whenever the cause of nationalism sought its historical roots.

6

France: Powerful Dukes, an Embattled King

From the ruins of Charlemagne's empire emerged a family who would counter anarchy and lay the foundations of a unified France.

As the millennium approached, the western remnants of Charlemagne's 9th-century Frankish Empire had collapsed into a patchwork of robber baronies that gave no hint of future nationhood. The Roman popes, local bishops, rival claimants – all were at loggerheads. Brittany was a Celtic stronghold, Normandy was under the firm hand of former Vikings. The warlords of Flanders paid only nominal allegiance to Charlemagne's heirs, whose last king, Louis V, died in 987. In the south, the people of Provence and Aquitaine, speaking the *langue d'oc* (saying *oc* instead of *oui*), were almost as foreign to Parisians as were the Celts and the Norse.

To the northern parts of this semi-tribal scattering, one man brought a new sense of unity: Hugh, known as Capet (from the 'cape' he wore when he was an abbot). It was not a unity imposed from above. It grew from below, from the seed of a well-run estate. Hugh, the greatest of the French nobles, inherited huge areas of land around Paris, the region called both Francia and the Île-de-France, an 'island' then as now only in that was defined by rivers, principally the Seine and Oise.

Hugh had no direct claim to the throne. Like any leader, he needed God on his side. Luckily, he had as counsellors one of Europe's greatest churchmen, Adalbero, Archbishop of Reims, and his protégé, Europe's greatest scholar, Gerbert, both of whom had opposed the Carolingians. Reims was to be the key to Hugh's success. Standing at the crossroads of ancient trade routes across Gaul, its archbishop had traditionally crowned Frankish kings for the previous 500 years. It was probably Gerbert who suggested a way forward: that nobles should elect their new

king rather than accept a hereditary ruler. This had long been practised in Germanic tribes in cases of disputed succession – once even for a Carolingian (Pepin III in 751) – and it would later become an integral part of the administration of the Holy Roman Empire. It worked. Hugh was proclaimed king in 987.

Hugh began the slow task of imposing his will, working from the centre outwards. With ingenious diplomacy, he held off Otto, the German emperor, and Charles, the Carolingian claimant based in Lorraine. Six months after his own coronation, he had his son, Robert, crowned heir-apparent to ensure an orderly succession. After Adalbero's death in January 989, Hugh ensured that Gerbert emerged from a flurry of infighting as archbishop of Reims.

The same year saw the first manifestation of a movement that was both a threat and a promise: a threat to rulers, a promise of better times to ordinary people.

It came from the anarchic south, a land whose barons hardly recognized their own ruling house, let alone Hugh, and it came not from any leader but from the people and the Church. It arose from the abuse of a system by which small estates and church property were handed over – 'commended' – to a local lord for administration and protection. Frequently, nobles simply took over the lands and expelled the owners. Their hunger grew as it was fed. In the words of one commentator, 'Evil-doers had sprung up like weeds, and wicked men ravaged the vineyard of the Lord.' Across the land, prime Church land was at risk.

Appalled, churchmen began a movement to impose peace. Its focus was a monastery in Charroux, 50 km (30 miles) south of Poitiers. Here, on 1 June 989, crowds gathered, summoned by the bishops of Bordeaux, Poitiers, Périgueux, Limoges and Angoulême. 'The bodies of many saints were brought along to reinforce the pious by their presence and dull the threats of the wicked. The divine will … illuminated that council by frequent miracles.' Resolutions were passed to excommunicate anyone who infringed the sanctuary of a church, or seized church property, or assaulted an unarmed clerk.

This was the beginning of what came to be called the Peace of God. It spread rapidly. In Narbonne (990) and Anse (994), church councils promised to wield 'the sharp blade of anathema'. Noblemen complied. The aims became more

Literally and symbolically a pinnacle of Christianity, the 11th-century St Michel d'Aiguilhe stands on one of the volcanic obelisks of Le Puy, southern France.

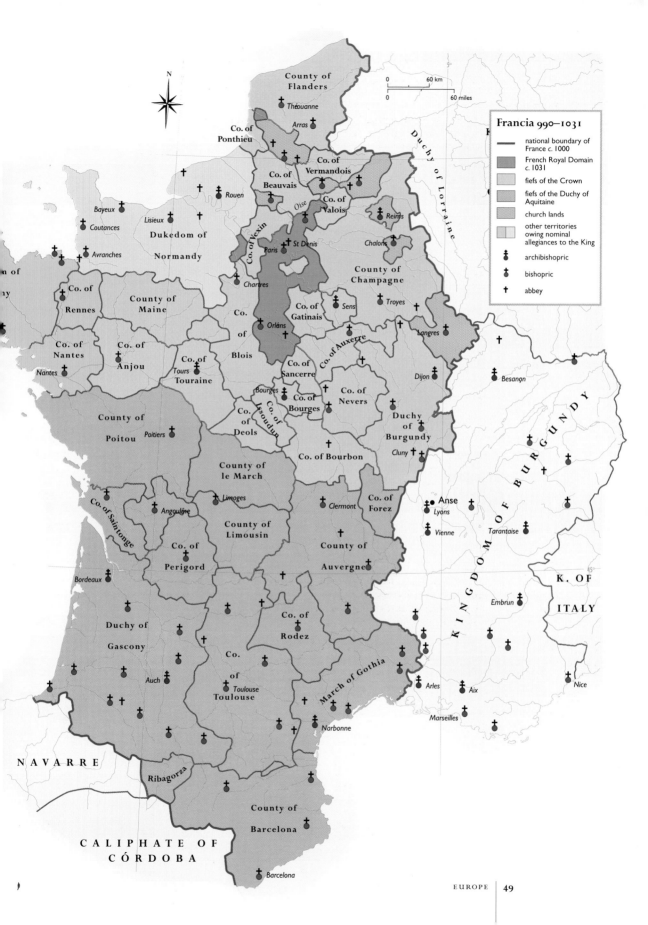

Francia 990–1031

Legend

- national boundary of France c. 1000
- French Royal Domain c. 1031
- fiefs of the Crown
- fiefs of the Duchy of Aquitaine
- church lands
- other territories owing nominal allegiances to the King
- ♟ archibishopric
- ♟ bishopric
- ✝ abbey

County of Flanders

Thérouanne

Co. of Ponthieu

Arras

Co. of Vermandois

Co. of Beauvais

Co. of Valois

Rouen

Reims

Bayeux

Lisieux

Co. of Vexin

Chalons

Coutances

Paris St Denis

County of Champagne

Avranches

Dukedom of Normandy

Chartres

Troyes

Co. of Rennes

County of Maine

Co. of Blois

Co. of Gatinais

Sens

Orléns

Langres

Co. of Nantes

Co. of Anjou

Co. of Touraine

Co. of Auxerre

Besançon

Nantes

Tours

Co. of Sancerre

Dijon

Bourges

Co. of Bourges

Co. of Nevers

Co. of Isoudun

Co. of Deols

Duchy of Burgundy

County of Poitou

Poitiers

Cluny

County of le March

Co. of Bourbon

Anse

Lyons

Limoges

Clermont

Co. of Forez

Angoulême

Vienne

Co. of Saintonge

County of Limousin

Tarantaise

Bordeaux

Co. of Perigord

County of Auvergne

K. OF ITALY

Embrun

Duchy of Gascony

Co. of Rodez

Auch

Co. of Toulouse

Arles

Aix

Nice

Toulouse

March of Gothia

Marseilles

Narbonne

NAVARRE

Ribagorza

County of Barcelona

CALIPHATE OF CÓRDOBA

Barcelona

Duchy of Lorraine

KINGDOM OF BURGUNDY

0   60 km
0   60 miles

N

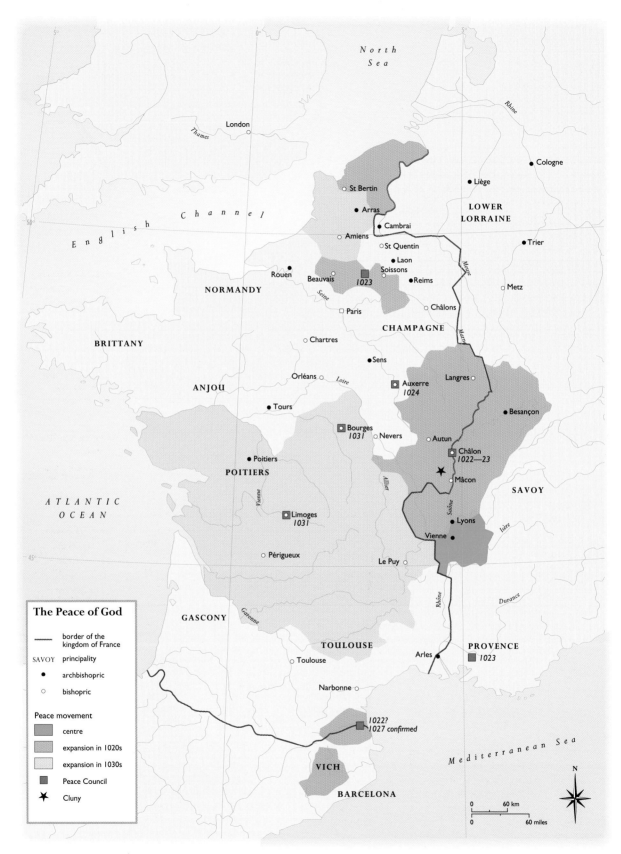

The Peace of God

border of the
kingdom of France

SAVOY   principality

●   archbishopric

○   bishopric

Peace movement

centre

expansion in 1020s

expansion in 1030s

Peace Council

★   Cluny

From Viking to Norman

British history has been largely defined by the Norman invasion of 1066. It was an event with unlikely origins. As the name implies, the Normans were 'Norse-men' – from Denmark, not Norway. Initially, in the late 9th century, they were Viking raiders. When the first arrivals went off to find easier pickings in England, those left behind were granted land around Rouen. From there, the Normans spread westwards, to Bayeux (924) and the Cotentin Peninsula (933). They made little impression farther west, where the Bretons had thrown out their would-be Viking conquerors.

By 1000, Normandy was in effect independent. In theory, its dukes owed allegiance to the Francian king. In practice, they controlled everything that mattered – military service, the building of castles, the money supply, the law, taxation, Church appointments.

Quite quickly, the Normans had begun to forget their northern heritage. Trade with the north dried up. By 1000, only the old had Danish as their first language. The last Scandinavian poet visited Rouen in 1025. Villages ending in -bec, or starting with the name of some forgotten Danish settler, recalled Norse origins (as they still do), but by 1000 their inhabitants were Norsemen no more. They were culturally Francian – their scholars and legal system and social organiza-

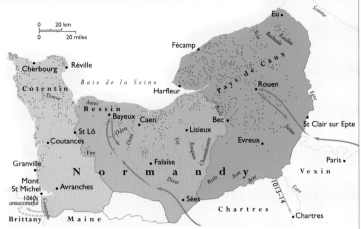

tion imbued with Latinized Christian feudalism. It was this, rather than their coarse Scandinavian heritage, that gave them their later historical impact.

As with Europe's other dynasties, family was all, a fact that would have peculiar significance for England. In 1000, the Duke

was Robert – Robert the Magnificent to some, Robert the Devil to others. His sister, Emma, married England's King Ethelred in 1002. This gave the Norman dukes a tenuous claim to the English throne. Ethelred's son, Edward, was educated in Rouen, where he promised to help his

Norman family make good that claim, should the need arise. When, as King Edward the Confessor, he died without an heir in 1066, Robert's son, William of Normandy, took up the offer made by his late cousin, with a consequence that changed the course of English history.

---

general – individuals were expected to take personal control of their behaviour. The Peace became a focus for moral revival. Over the next 40 years the revolution rolled on, across Burgundy and northwards, wherever relics could focus feelings and inspire miracles. In Glaber's words, 'Bent legs and arms were straightened … skin was broken, flesh was torn and blood ran freely … and all cried out with one voice to God, hands stretched out, "Pax, Pax!"'

All this was too much for the established Church and the nobles of the north. Peace was surely the prerogative of the King, not the Church and people. Where would it end, asked the Bishop of Laon – with bishops pulling ploughs, and knights as priests, and every peasant a king?

When Hugh died in 996, Robert took over. Born in about 970, Robert the Pious, as he was known, had had the good fortune to be educated in Reims with Gerbert as his tutor. The friendship shattered when Gerbert refused to sanction Robert's marriage to his cousin Bertha. Intelligence, education and experience acquired under his father allowed Robert to preserve his shaky inheritance. He did so by supporting, and in effect subverting, the Peace of God. His purpose was political, not moral – to limit peasant

unrest and suppress feuding knightly families.

In places like Anjou and Champagne, great abbey-estates, owing allegiance only to the King and God, chose to impose their own peace, more by applying the rule of law than by force. From 1027, noblemen began to hijack the principles of the Peace, declaring certain times, places, people and routes free of violence. This, the so-called Truce of God, slowly allowed the laity to reassert its authority over what had so nearly become a popular revolution.

From this, over the next century or so, would grow the new stability of feudalism: a ruling hierarchy of king, counts, barons, knights and serfs, all bound by mutual obligation. (And new ideals: the Christian knight would become the hero of medieval French epics.) Legal systems, once a local mix of Roman law and Frankish custom, became regional.

Robert inherited more than estates and a crown: good genes, good luck. When the Duke of Burgundy died in 1002, Robert staked a claim and took over the province. He produced sons, and secured the succession. On his death in 1031, the Capetian estates were a foundation on which, over the next 350 years, Francia would be turned into France, with Paris as northern Europe's greatest city.

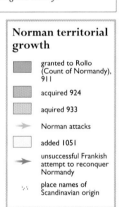

Norman territorial growth

- granted to Rollo (Count of Normandy), 911
- acquired 924
- aquired 933
- → Norman attacks
- added 1051
- → unsuccessful Frankish attempt to reconquer Normandy
- ·:· place names of Scandinavian origin

7

Viking + Greek = Russian Orthodox

How a vicious, womanizing pagan adopted Orthodoxy, and became a saint.

In origin, St Vladimir, King of Kievan Rus, was anything but a saint. Part Viking, part Slav, Volodimir (as he is in another spelling) was an enthusiast for ancient Slavonic gods. In a civil war before his succession, he gathered a Viking army from Scandinavia with which he seized the old Viking base of Novgorod and then the capital, Kiev. He came to the throne by killing his brother. He had four wives and (it was said) 800 concubines, a fair figure, perhaps, given that he reputedly gave vent to a ferocious sexual drive in every town and village he visited.

On his succession in 980, he put up statues to his pagan gods in Kiev, and celebrated by sacrificing 1,000 victims in public. One of them was the son of a Christian aristocrat, who refused to give up the boy, defending him with brave words. 'Yours is not a god,' he told the crowd, 'but a piece of wood.' Father and child were slaughtered by the outraged mob.

Vladimir was in a position to see that such acts would do him little good. Kiev was the centre of a great 'water road' of rivers, principally the Dnieper, linking Scandinavia and Byzantium. Men of many religions gathered there: Christians, Muslims, even some Jews. Eastwards lay pagan warrior nomads, the Pechenegs, who were a constant threat. South and west were rich Christian kings. To an ambitious leader, it must have been clear that monotheistic religion spelled civilization, stability and wealth, while paganism, reviled by literate and rich foreign traders, would lead to war, with the attendant risk of defeat and poverty.

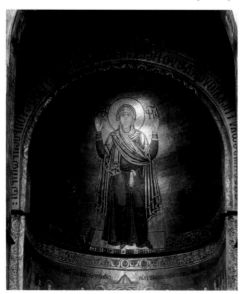

In Kiev's cathedral, St Sophia still recalls Orthodoxy's Byzantine origins.

The Russian Primary Chronicle, edited by a Kievan monk, Nestor, in about 1100, tells a famous story. In 987, Vladimir decided he needed a new religion. But which? He sent out a team of researchers. When they returned, he went through the options. The Jews were scattered, and powerless, so Judaism was out. Islam was discarded when Vladimir learned that they were against alcohol; for Russians, he said, happiness was quite impossible without strong drink. The Catholics looked to the Pope, and one thing Vladimir did not need was the challenge of another strong leader. The Bulgarians were defined by 'sorrow and a dreadful stench'. In Germany 'we saw no beauty'.

But in Constantinople lay perfection. His delegates reported that in the great church of St Sophia a ceremony was put on for them. Its awe-inspiring theatricality – gorgeous costumes, imposing priests, incense-laden air, music to seize the soul – staggered them. Their words to Vladimir have often been quoted: 'We knew not whether we were in heaven or on earth, for on earth there is no such vision or beauty, and we do not know how to describe it; we know only that there God dwells among men.'

It is a good tale, which conceals as much as it tells. Vladimir's grandmother, Olga, had been baptized in Constantinople in about 957. As regent of Kievan Rus, Olga, the first Russian saint, was one of the most formidable ladies of her age. In the words of Nestor's chronicle, she 'was radiant among the infidels like a pearl in the mire'. With her as an example, Vladimir must have had a fair idea of the benefits of Orthodoxy, without inquiring too deeply into alternatives.

There were other complexities. Vladimir did not simply convert, inviting in a foreign culture that might threaten his independence. It was a decision taken as part of a portfolio of military, political and cultural considerations. His father Svyatoslav, once held captive by the Byzantine emperor John Tzimesces, had gained his freedom only by promising to send help if needed. Vladimir's window of opportunity came when Basil II, John's heir, found himself in trouble (p. 64) and sought Vladimir's help. He sent it, in exchange for a promise of Basil's sister Anna in marriage. When Vladimir's 6,000 Russians arrived in Constantinople a year later, Basil used them to save his empire. But where was the promised bride? Vladimir, suspecting treachery, invaded Cherson (or Korsun, present-day Sebastapol) in the Crimea, then a city of Greek and Orthodox culture. Basil had no choice: Anna was sent off weeping. Vladimir married her, handed back the Crimea as his traditional bridegroom's gift to his wife's family, and allowed himself to be baptized by a local bishop.

Back home in Kiev, where Vladimir was escorted by clergy from Cherson, the Orthodox priests set about the job of converting the Slavs of Rus to the new religion. Since Vladimir's aim was as much political and economic as spiritual, conversion during the 990s was not left for the individual to decide. The people of Kiev were simply baptized, by edict, en masse. It took force to prevail in Novgorod, Vladimir's original base, the most Scandinavian, the most conservative of his towns. In Rostov, Russian and Finnish inhabitants martyred several missionary monks. But mostly, along the great 'water-roads', bishops from Constantinople made willing converts. Perun, the old god of gods, with his silver head and golden moustaches, was toppled from his hilltop shrine above Kiev and rolled into the Dnieper. In the 1050s, Hilarion, the first Russian Metropolitan, recalled those days: 'Angel's trumpet and God's thunder sounded through all the towns. The air was sanctified by the incense that ascended towards God. Monasteries stood on the mountains.'

Anna's fate was not as bad as she had feared. Vladimir turned from womanizing to converting, acting as godfather to hundreds, opening schools, setting up courts, and building innumerable churches and monasteries, including Kiev's great Cathedral of the Tithes. He died in 1015, and in due course was made a saint.

The consequences of Vladimir's action

transformed Russian culture. Russian churches, with their central and subsidiary domes, were Byzantine. Kiev, with its own St Sophia, became 'the glory of Greece'. Byzantine law became the basis of Russian law. Missionaries spread the script adapted from Greek by St Cyril to bring Christianity to the Slavs in the 9th century; and Cyrillic remained the Russian script (and that of other Orthodox Slav cultures – Belorussian, Serbian, Bulgarian, Macedonian, Ukrainian). When Constantinople fell to the Turks in 1453, it was the Russian church that became the champion of Orthodoxy. 'There exists only one true church on earth,' wrote the Metropolitan, 'the Church of Russia.'

Kievan Rus

- Rus 972
- Rus 1054
- → Vladimir's invasion of the Crimea 990
- — main trade route

Otto III's Teenage Dreams of Imperial Grandeur

An ambitious teenager almost turned his dreams of a new and grander Rome into reality.

By the turn of the millennium, the region now known as Germany was supreme in western Europe. The empire of Charlemagne, defunct for 100 years, had been reborn, and the Pope was an appointee of the Saxon emperor.

These were surprising developments, given that only a couple of generations before 'Germany' had been a kaleidoscope of rival princes, all claiming their share of the eastern section of Charlemagne's empire.

The groundwork had been laid by Henry I, who at first was little more than the local ruler of Saxony. From there he beat off both the Danes and the Magyars. To do this, Henry secured the help of other German princes. After victory, their provinces fell to him. A judiciously arranged marriage gave him sway over land west of the Rhine.

His son and successor, Otto I (936–73), built brilliantly on these foundations. From the start he had pretentions to re-establish the empire of Charlemagne over all of present-day France, Germany and northern Italy. Francia, the heart-land of France, would remain out of reach, but campaigns against the Slavs won him present-day east Germany. More marriages and campaigns secured Swabia, Bohemia, Bavaria and the Italian throne. Several invasions put the Pope in his pocket. When rebels threatened, luck intervened. The Magyars went on the warpath again. Rebels and king united, and crushed the Magyars in one of history's most decisive battles, Lechfeld, in 955. Thereafter, Germany's eight dukedoms were secure, a nation waiting to be born.

In pursuit of his imperial dream, Otto had himself crowned by the Pope and called himself 'Augustus', deliberately claiming political descent from ancient Rome and from Charlemagne. This was the foundation of what would later become known as the Holy Roman Empire, the original 1,000-year Reich. As befitted such power, he funded an artistic renaissance, encouraging an international literary circle of scholars from Ireland, England, France, Italy and Greece. He also married off his son, another Otto, to a Byzantine princess, Theophano, a niece of one of the greatest of Byzantine emperors, John Tzimesces, a deal that secured an uneasy peace between the two growing empires.

But it was security that had to be bought from nobles, by establishing bishoprics loyal to the monarchy, and by rewarding allies with new lands – in the Slav borderlands to the east, in southern Italy. This was not easy. When he

succeeded his father, Otto II failed to beat the Arabs in southern Italy, a defeat that inspired a Slav revolt.

His death in Rome in 983, aged 28, left the problem of how and where to expand. His son, Otto III, was only 3. A solution would have to wait until he was old enough. Meanwhile, he was in the hands of a tough and able woman, his mother, the Byzantine princess Theophano. She had been sent as a teenager into a land of which she knew nothing. But she was intelligent and ambitious. She determined that her son would have not only the brilliance of her own culture – which she could give him personally – but also the power of her father-in-law, Otto the Great.

Young Otto grew up with a dream, which he set about fulfilling when he was declared of age at the age of 14. He was born doubly 'to the purple', the heir – perhaps – to two empires: his father's, Rome; and his mother's, Byzantium. His dream was nothing less than to reunite the two. He would marry a Byzantine princess, and be another Constantine.

Naturally, Otto fell in love with Rome, the fount of his pretensions. Rome, he said, was 'head of the world' and 'mother of all churches', but she had been betrayed by negligence, ignorance and squabbling. He would restore and increase its glory. He built himself a grand palace, and encouraged missionaries to seek converts in Poland, Hungary and the Balkans. He probed Vladimir of Russia about the possibility of adopting Catholicism. He appointed his 23-year-old cousin, Bruno, as the first German Pope. As Pope Gregory V, Bruno anointed Otto Emperor of the West on Ascension Day, 21 May 996, in St Peter's (the old one, built by Constantine in the 4th century).

Bruno didn't last long: when Otto left for Germany, an Italian noble, Crescentius, announced Bruno's removal and appointed John Philagathos, Archbishop of Piacenza, in his place. John, Greek by birth, was Otto's godfather and former tutor, and a friend of Theophano's. He was already a man of some power. He had just returned from Constantinople, where he had opened negotiations for a Byzantine wife for Otto. The visit, as his fellow-envoy Leo recorded, infected him with a severe attack of ambition. He, a Greek, would surely be a better man to link Rome and Constantinople. Besides, Gregory V – a young German – was unpopular in Rome. But to allow himself to become Crescentius's puppet was a big mistake. Technically, Bruno was still Pope, with John as an 'anti-pope'.

John's punishment for betrayal was dire. Otto returned and captured John. What happened next was described by his colleague, Leo, in a letter:

KINGDOM OF DENMARK

Baltic Sea

North Sea

Oldenburg

Lübeck

County of Holstein

Mecklenburg

Slavinia

Duchy of Pomerania

Hamburg

Ratzeburg

1181 imperial fief

Prussia

Lüneburg

Bremen

Verden

March of Havelberg

Brandenburg

Brandenburg

Gniezno

Friesland

Duchy of Saxony

Minden

Brunswick

Osnabrück

Hildesheim

Magdeburg

Halberstadt

Duchy of Lausitz

1158 joined to Empire

Duchy of Silesia

1163 imperial fief

KINGDOM OF POLAND

Utrecht

Nijmegen

Detmold

Paderborn

Goslar

Mühlhausen

Merseburg

Naumburg

Meissen

Neisse

Opol and Ratibor

Brabant

Duisburg

Dortmund

Landgrayate of Thuringia

Altenburg

March of Meissen

1163 imperial fief

Bruges

Antwerp

Duchy of Lower Lorraine

Cologne

Aachen

Remagen

KINGDOM OF GERMANY

Oberwesel

Eger

Prague

Olomouc

KINGDOM OF BOHEMIA

March of Moravia

Flanders

Hainault

Liège

Cambrai

Trier

Mainz

Frankfurt

Gelnhausen

Bamberg

Würzburg

Reims

Verdun

Kaiserslautern

Trifels

Worms

Franconia

Nuremberg

Regensburg

Passau

Duchy of Austria

Linz

Vienna

Bratislava

Esztergom

Metz

Speyer

Heilbronn

Eichstatt

Freising

Duchy of Bavaria

Toul

Weissenburg

Esslingen

Hohenstaufen

Ulm

Augsburg

Munich

Salzburg

Chiemsee

1156 imperial fief

Budapest

Troyes

Strasbourg

Duchy of Swabia

KINGDOM OF FRANCE

Duchy of Upper Lorraine

KINGDOM OF HUNGARY

Basle

Besançon

Constance

Zurich

Innsbruck

Seckau

Gurk

Graz

Solothurn

Bern

Fribourg

Chur

Duchy of Carinthia

Lavant

Duchy of Styria

County of Burgundy

Lausanne

Disentis

Brixen

Geneva

Sitten

Trent

Duchy of Carniola

Patriarchate of Aquileia

March of Carniola

Lyons

Savoy

Aosta

Como

Bergamo

Vicenza

Treviso

Aquileia

Vienne

Tarentaise

Ivrea

Milan

Brescia

Verona

Padua

Grado

Novara

Lodi

March of Verona

Venice

KINGDOM OF BURGUNDY

1033 joined to Empire

Turin

Vercelli

Cremona

Mantua

Valence

Asti

Piacenza

Die

Embrun

Tortona

Parma

Modena

Ferrara

Comacchio

Viviers

Saluzzo

Alessandria

Bologna

Ravenna

Adriatic Sea

Avignon

Digne

KINGDOM OF ITALY

Emilia

Romagna

Rimini

Fano

Arles

Provence

Nice

Genoa

Luna

Pisa

Ancona

Aix

Fréjus

Florence

March of Ancona

Marseilles

Siena

Duchy of Spoleto

Camerino

Toulon

Tuscany

Perugia

Spoleto

Mediterranean Sea

Corsica

Sutri

Patrimony of St Peter

Rome

Tivoli

Anagni

KINGDOM OF SICILY

1194 conquered by Henry VI

N

Sardinia

0   100 km

0   100 miles

The Empire in the 10th and 11th centuries

Empire border, 1152

kingdom of Germany

kingdom of Italy

kingdom of Burgundy

imperial land in Italy

ecclesiastical land

● archdiocese

○ diocese

Gerbert, the Wonder of the World

In a century when scholarship was still dim, Gerbert was a star. Born in the early 940s, he was educated in the Benedictine abbey of St Geraud, in Aurillac, then studied in Catalonia, on the edge of the Muslim world, where he learned Arabian science and mathematics. Taken by patrons to Rome, he met Otto I and his son in 970, and impressed them both. When he came to the throne Otto II made Gerbert head of the monastery at Bobbio. His brief stay (982–4) implanted in him a passion for the Ottonians and their imperial zeal, which he nurtured on his return to Reims as head of its cathedral school.

At Reims, he confirmed a growing reputation for brilliance. He was a master of all seven subjects of medieval education, the trivium (grammar, rhetoric and logic), which ordered knowledge, and the quadrivium (mathematics, astronomy, geometry and music), which applied it. His library was one of Europe's finest. He constantly badgered friends, agents, and colleagues to acquire manuscripts for him.

For a towering intellect, he had a rare technical talent. To teach astronomy, he made elaborate globes showing the movements of the heavenly bodies, which he swapped for rare manuscripts. For mathematics he constructed a 1,000-counter abacus. He was said to have masterminded an ingenious timepiece. His practicality even extended to music – he was reputed to be a builder of organs.

Among his pupils was Robert, son of Hugh Capet, would-be unifier of France. This would prove another good contact. When Gerbert's mentor, Archbishop Adalbero, died, his replacement tried to play kingmaker by undermining Hugh. When Hugh captured Reims and its archbishop, Gerbert emerged in 991 as Archbishop of Reims.

But when his friendship with young Robert turned sour, he fled to the court of his greatest supporter, Otto III, who made him archbishop of Ravenna, then in 999 Pope as Silvester II. As Pope, Gerbert buttressed Otto's dreams of a restored and expanded empire. But he also had his own agenda for Christendom that was outside imperial control. In 1000, he established an archbishopric in Gniezno, Poland, and supported Stephen of Hungary's Christianizing influence.

When he died in 1003, his reputation stood so high that he soon became part of European folklore. The credulous said he was a black magician, and mentioned him in the same breath as supposed wizards like Merlin and Simon Magus. To others he was simply stupor mundi, 'the wonder of the world'.

'Well, first the Church of the West dealt him anathema; then his eyes were gouged out; third his nose, and fourth, his lips, and fifth that tongue of his which prattled so many and such unspeakable words, one by one, were all cut from his face. Item six: he rode like a conqueror in procession, grave and solemn on a miserable little donkey, hanging on to its tail; a piece of old hide from some animal covered his head … Item seven: he was brought to trial and condemned. Then they put on him the priestly vestments, back to front, the wrong way round; and then they stripped them off again. After this he was pulled along the church, right through it and out of the front portico to the court of the fountain. Finally, for his refreshment, they threw him into prison.' Otto finally allowed his erstwhile ambassador to retire to a German monastery where he lived on, in a fashion, for another 15 years. Crescentius had it easier: he was publicly beheaded, and his wife taken by Otto as a concubine.

Meanwhile, the great scholar Gerbert of Aurillac had fled to Otto's court. He flattered and encouraged his dreams. 'Ours, ours is the Roman Empire! You are our Caesar, our Augustus. You spring from the noblest of Greek blood. You surpass the Greeks in empire, you rule the Romans by hereditary right, and you surpass them both in wisdom and eloquence.' In 999, Otto rewarded Gerbert by appointing him the first French Pope, who took the title of Silvester II. The name was symbolic – Silvester I had crowned Constantine.

Another Silvester – another Constantine; and

another Caesar, another Charlemagne. Besides terming himself 'Augustus' as his father and grandfather had done, Otto devised a seal that read on one side 'Renovatio Imperii Romanorum' – 'Renewal of the Empire of the Romans'. On the other side was the imperial head – Charlemagne's head. This, then, was Otto's dream: a 'Frankish' – i.e. German-dominated – Latin-speaking, Christian empire of all Europe. German officials ruled in Rome. Roman rituals governed daily life in Otto's palace. For a brief moment, Roman church and German state, German emperor and Italian nobility, were united. One contemporary painting in a book of Gospels commissioned by him shows him receiving tributes from Rome, Gaul, Germany and 'Sclavinia'.

In 1000, Otto went with great pomp to Charlemagne's tomb in Aachen and opened it. According to one macabre story, he found Charlemagne's body seated on a throne 'as though he lived', crowned and sceptred, except that his nose had decayed. The corpse was wearing gloves, 'through which the nails had grown and pierced'. Otto re-dressed his hero's corpse in white, gave it a new golden nose, cut the nails, and 'made all good'.

There remained a longer-term agenda. One day, Byzantium too would be his. Some of his officials had Greek titles, and wrote their names in Greek characters, surely a habit that increased the antipathy of the Romans towards their foreign ruler. In February 1001, the threat of violence forced Otto out of Rome. Looking beyond this temporary embarrassment, he sent a second embassy to Basil II, one of whose nieces, Zoe, was despatched to be his bride.

Fate intervened. In a castle near Civita Castellana, 50 km (30 miles) north of Rome, Otto died of a sudden fever, perhaps smallpox, on 24 January 1002, still aged only 21. Zoe, who had just landed in Bari, the capital of Byzantium's colony in southern Italy, went home again. No link with Byzantium was made.

Otto's empire, with its rival princedoms and its peculiar Franco-German-Roman-Christian ethos, would never be as united or dominant as the three Ottos had envisioned. The Holy Roman Empire would always be at most a patchwork Germanic Reich, with a German-speaking heart that would wait another 860 years for nationhood. Yet the dream lived on. Otto was buried beside his hero, Charlemagne, in Aachen. The Empire's 'Roman' element ensured that for centuries it would remain an ideal, an empire of the spirit, if never a political reality.

On Europe's Slavic Fringes, a Nation Grows

Though the Slavs produced few records since their arrival in eastern Europe in the 6th century, archaeologists have established that they developed an advanced culture. The southern Slavs, divided from their northern neighbours by the influx of Hungarian nomads, remained impoverished. But in the richer lands of today's Poland, the Czech Republic and Slovakia, villages that formed the hearts of present-day Poznan, Gniezno, Gdansk and Prague were strongholds protecting workers of metal, leather and fur. On this foundation arose a version of feudalism, drawing raiders from the former Frankish empire eager for 'slaves'.

To these incipient nations of Bohemians and 'Polanies' came missionaries from both branches of Christianity: Roman (Catholic) and Greek (Orthodox). Bohemia was already in the Roman orbit by the early 10th century. A few decades later, the northern Slavs were also being drawn into the Christian world. Mieszko, prince of the Polanie, faced not a religious but a political choice: between accepting the Catholic faith directly from Germany or from its dependent, Bohemia. In 965, he opted to hold Germany at arm's length, and married a Bohemian princess, Dubrava. She brought with her Christian priests and books, and converted her new husband. Mieszko built himself a new residence in Gniezno (Gnesen), with a chapel dedicated to St George, and in due course a bishop. The faith spread – a mission station in Poznan, two Benedictine monasteries – and so did Mieszko's political reach.

But Germany, needing stability on its eastern frontier, was not easily excluded. In 996, Otto III appointed a missionary bishop, Adalbert, to shepherd the Poles, now under Mieszko's son Boleslaw, into Germany's fold. Adalbert of Prague had been born Vojtech, but changed his name to that of his mentor Adalbert of Magdeburg. After a somewhat erratic career, having been forced out of Prague for criticizing polygamy and quarrelling with the king, he served Otto rather better than he might have wished. This ambitious and impulsive prelate, hardly pausing in Gniezno, moved directly on into the pagan lands which would one day be known as Prussia. There, in April 997, the locals slew him. When his two companions arrived back in Gniezno with his body, a papal decree instantly made him a hero: St Adalbert the Martyr.

To his shrine, in March 1000, came Otto III himself. In a magnificent ceremony, he embraced Boleslaw as friend and ally. With such a backing – the Pope made Gniezno an archbishopric – Boleslaw emerged as the region's most powerful and ambitious leader. He imposed his rule westward, to Otto's borderlands, south into Prague (in 1003 he blinded the Bohemian king and seized the throne) and east to Kiev, where he placed his son-in-law on the Russian throne.

Recognition became complete when Boleslaw – 'the Brave', as his biographer called him – was acknowledged by the Pope as king of an enlarged and united Poland. He was crowned in 1025, a few months before his death, leaving a new nation that would remain a bastion of eastern Catholicism.

The Coming of the Ashkenazim

Though small in numbers, the Jews of medieval Europe ensured vital contacts with other cultures, as well as nurturing their own.

Ever since the defeat of the Jews' last anti-Roman revolt in 135, Jewish history had been the story of the diaspora (dispersion). Though the homeland of Israel vanished as a political entity, Jewish communities survived. From Palestine and from Babylonia, the land of the ancestral Jews, they spread. Over eight centuries, their traditions became woven into the fabrics of the Middle East, North Africa, Spain, western Europe and Byzantium. For all that time, the sages of Palestine and Babylonia preserved and developed legal, social and religious teaching. By 1000, educated Jews from Mesopotamia to northern France were studying their own copies of the Talmud, the vast compendium of law, commentary, folklore, science and theology that had been recorded in Palestine and Babylonia.

In Europe, after the destruction of their nation, they were at first recognized under Roman law. That had allowed them to move freely and settle, mainly in Italy and Spain. Then, with the coming of Christianity, had come restriction, and sometimes oppression. When Rome fell in the 5th century, barbarian rulers let them be. But under Charlemagne, whose reunited Europe inspired an artistic and economic revival, European Jews began to flourish. Hundreds

migrated north, to France and Germany.

These were very different people from their land-based co-religionists in the Middle East. Among Europe's land-owning aristocracies and ancient peasantry, with its estates and its network of feudalism, there was little room for land-working migrants. Nor could they win advancement by force of arms; there were no Jewish knights.

But the new arrivals had something of their own to offer. They had contacts in both the former Roman Empire – Italy, Byzantium – and in what had become the Muslim world. Their cultural network gave them access to luxury goods brought along the medieval trade routes from India and China. Though outside the feudal network, they found support from kings and nobles. For Charlemagne and his heirs, they became sources of textiles, spices and perfumes. They came to dominate the trade in humanity centred on Prague and Verdun, where Slav captives became slaves destined for Christian and Islamic courts.

Ashkenazim

⟶ migration 500–1000

✡ town with significant Jewish settlement, c. 1000

Jewish cultural areas

▢ Spanish or Sephardi

▢ South Italian

▢ Ashkenazim, c. 1000

Where dealers came, families and communities followed. By 1000, the Jewish population of Europe north of the Alps numbered some 4,000 families – perhaps 20,000 people – living in 50 towns across eastern France and central Germany. Though few and scattered, they were close-knit. They took on and modified the language of their hosts, creating their own Judisch-Deutsch – Judeo-German – mixture, soon to be known as Yiddish. They would, in years to come, refer to themselves as those who lived among the descendants of Ashkenaz, the son of Noah's third son Gomer (Genesis 10:3), whose language was traditionally equated with German. The Ashkenazim, a term which came to embrace all the Jews of northern Europe, nurtured their emerging talent for enterprise, jealously controlling their family-based trading empires, keeping in touch with rivals and colleagues to preserve traditional rights and iron out disputes.

From the start, their position in European society was unique. Franks and Germans had no easy way to place them. On the one hand, they could be respected as the people of the Old Testament, the Greek version of which was a foundation of European literature and its Christian religion. And they had economic power. But their loyalties were as much to themselves and a non-existent foreign homeland as to the land and people around them. They were neither citizens nor alien, yet something of both. These paradoxes would always aid and oppress them. In different times and different places, Europeans would come to admire them for their scholarship, history, financial skills and social commitment, and despise them as 'Christ killers', slave-dealers, usurers and potential traitors. Here they would live in wealth, security and honour; there, in a ghetto (like the Chanel des Juifs in Paris). Europeans never resolved the conflict within themselves. In bad times, tolerance would flip into hatred and murder, as when in 1012 some 2,000 Jews were expelled from Mainz. Later, in the 12th century, oppression would force many to flee eastwards.

As always, Jews took care to nourish their historical identity. If this was a cause of the intolerance they endured, it was also their solace, their security and the root of their self-confidence.

The communities had a focus: the Rhine Valley, around Mainz and Worms. In Mainz, which had risen to prominence in Charlemagne's time, there was an academy for the training of rabbis headed by a renowned scholar, Gershom ben Judah (c. 960–1028). Titled 'Rabbenu' ('our master'), and known as the 'Light of the Diaspora', Gershom was the first to bring copies of the Talmud to western Europe from Palestine and Babylonia. He wrote his own commentary and passed on his learning, ensuring that European Jews had a basis

for literacy and learning to match that of Christianity. The Rhineland became the focus of European Jewry as students and community leaders sought him out.

To a people working out a new way of life, he provided numerous *takkanot* ('directives') to help Jews adapt to European laws and practices. Though little of his actual writing survives, he is said to have prohibited polygamy – a practice that survived among Jews in the Muslim world – and limited a husband's right to divorce without his wife's consent. Among other *takkanot*, he ruled on matters of law, taxation and finance. He forbade the defrauding of Christians, and advocated tolerance to create stability. Jews who underwent forced conversion to Christianity were not to be harassed, while plaintiffs were allowed to speak out, even if it meant interrupting prayers.

So powerful was his influence that all across Europe Jewish communities took to excommunicating those who broke his rulings. With this unique status, he became the foundation on which later Ashkenaz scholars built, in particular Rashi (an acronym of his title and name, Rabbi Shlomo ben Isaac) of Troyes (c. 1040–1105), one of the greatest of biblical and talmudic commentators.

These responsa, from the Jewish head (gaon) of one of Baghdād's two religious academies, were replies to queries about Jewish practices from Rabbi Meshullam ben Kalonymos, the head of an eminent Italo-German family of merchants and scholars. He was buried around 1020 in Mainz.

The Emergence of Hungary

Of all Europe's nations, none has its roots so firmly in the millennium as Hungary. Within a few years, Magyar nomads devoted to war and pillage reformed themselves and settled. There they have remained ever since, their language remaining as living proof of their origins on the steppes of Central Asia.

Under pressure from other tribes, the Magyars had swept over the Carpathians in about 900, bringing the name of their federation with them: On-Ogur ('Ten Arrows'). Soon, everyone knew them by a corrupted version of that name – Hungarians – and their ruling dynasty as the Arpads, after the leader who brought them to their new home. For a century, the Magyars, originally from beyond the Volga, had controlled the central European grasslands, raiding at will into western Europe – Bulgaria, France, Italy, and in particular Germany – until Otto I defeated them outside Augsburg, on the banks of the river Lech in 955.

Thereafter, their chiefs were forced to consider the fact that there was nowhere left to migrate to, and no one weaker to raid. They would have to settle down and behave if they wished to live well. They might have looked south, to Constantinople and Orthodoxy. Instead, in the 970s, the current leader, Geza, sent an embassy to the German emperor, Otto II, and had himself baptized. The deal was this: Otto and the Pope would recognize him as a fellow-ruler if he promised that no Christians would be kept as slaves. To seal the bond, Geza married off his son Vaik – renamed Stephen (or Istvan) – to Gisela, daughter of the King of Bavaria, one of Otto's subsidiary provinces. But the clause about not owning Christian slaves did not endear him to his countrymen, and Hungary was still seething when Geza died in 997.

It was Stephen, aged a mere 22, who finally asserted royal authority, crushing the rebels with Bavarian troops at Veszprem, just north of Lake Balaton. When the time came for his coronation in 1001, legend has it that the Pope, Silvester II – Otto III's placeman, the brilliant scholar Gerbert – sent a crown for him. In any event, Stephen's power was assured. It was this tough, smart, tolerant monarch who dragged his unruly subjects into the new millennium and into the European community with a new social and political structure.

Old tribes vanished. On the model of Charlemagne's empire, Stephen divided the country into counties, appointed sheriffs to rule them,

handed out estates to his former chiefs, and took over what remained for himself. Slaves – conquered Slavs and other former captives – were upgraded to serfs and included in what was in effect instant feudalism. For the Church, Stephen – Saint Stephen as he became in 1083 – established ten dioceses under two archbishops, had churches built, and acted as patron for a number of monasteries. Since at the time there was no formal split between Rome and Byzantium, Stephen answered to the Pope but favoured Greek monks (Greek monasticism in Hungary lasted until the 13th century).

In 38 years of rule, Stephen masterminded the creation of a new world for his subjects. A high-ranking Hungarian who started out in his youth as a marauding, pagan nomad chieftain could well have ended his life as a landed Christian nobleman, his children able to converse in Latin with scholars across western Europe.

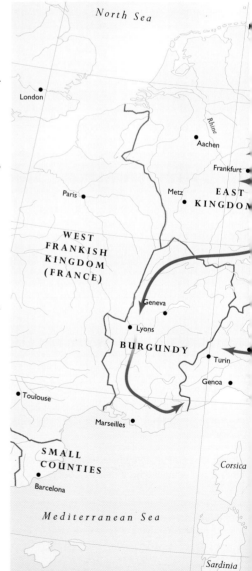

Hungary's Crowning Glory

In 1986, Budapest celebrated a great anniversary: the millennium of their country's foundation. Its focal point was the crown, which was said to have been sent to Stephen for his coronation in 1001 by the Pope, Sylvester II. Tradition claims that it was worn by all Hungarian kings from Stephen to the last

Habsburg Emperor, Franz-Josef. Experts doubt its authenticity, but no one doubts its significance, emphasized by its present position in the Hungarian National Museum. It consists of two crowns, a Greek and a Roman one. With its great golden band and its raised plaque of Christ, its imperial portraits, saints and archangels, and its gemstones and enamel, the crown symbolizes Hungary's two great traits: its position in the heartland of Christian Europe and its durability.

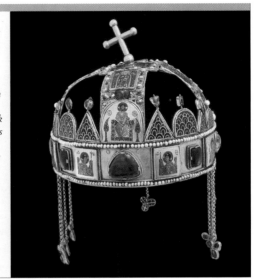

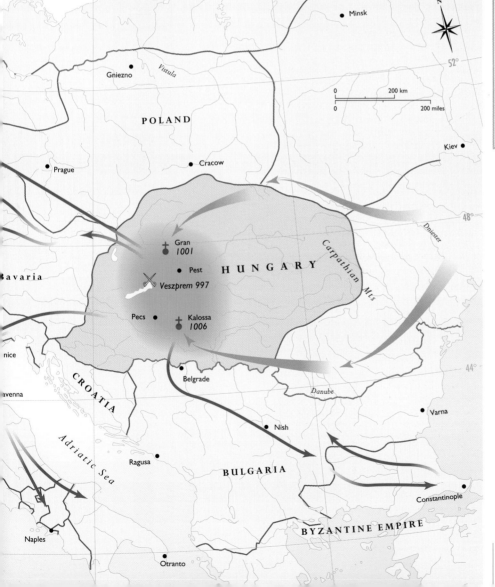

The emergence of Hungary

→ Magyar migration into central Europe, c. 895

▨ area of settlement by 900

→ major Magyar raid, 900–955

▨ Hungary by 1000

☫ archibishopric, with date of foundation

Minsk

Gniezno

Vistula

POLAND

Prague

Cracow

Kiev

☫ Gran
1001

Pest

✗ Veszprem 997

Pecs

☫ Kalossa
1006

HUNGARY

Carpathian Mts

Dniester

Bavaria

nice

CROATIA

avenna

Belgrade

Danube

Varna

Adriatic Sea

Ragusa

Nish

BULGARIA

Constantinople

Naples

BYZANTINE EMPIRE

Otranto

0   200 km
0   200 miles

II

Byzantium: Fighting to Preserve the Glory

Constantinople saw itself as the centre of the post-Roman world. But even as western Christendom arose, its eastern counterpart was starting its slow-motion fall.

Imagine hovering above the river of time, with the year 1000 below. Ahead, for the those living in the eastern Mediterranean, and its capital, Constantinople, we can see rapids. We know their world will end when it is seized by the Turks in 1453. But the inhabitants could not have guessed at such a disaster. Their world wore the mantles of Greece and Rome. Their capital was Rome's natural successor, with a Christian heritage that conferred a moral superiority – this was the city of Constantine, after all, the man who brought Christianity to Europe. With the blessing of Constantinople's Patriarch, the Byzantine

emperor knew himself to be the true conduit for Christian truth, God's agent on earth, his grandeur stated by glorious works of art and surrounded by ritual designed to hide him in mystery and induce awe. Constantinople's civilization, Byzantium, looked back 1,500 years. There was no reason to think it would ever end .

It was, by 1000, a very different world from that of the Latinized west of which it had once been a part. The coronation of Charlemagne, the Frankish king, as an alternative western emperor in 800 had introduced a permanent threat to the claims of the eastern empire to universal authority. Doctrinal differences – mainly the Filioque clause (p. 35) – were intensified by linguistic and social ones. Greek, not Latin, had been its main official language for 300 years.

True, this was an empire which was always

Venice: New Power, New Wealth

As a city-state straddling a few low offshore islands at the head of the Adriatic, Venice in the late 10th century did not look well placed for expansion. Arrogant rulers had alienated both Rome and Constantinople – her nominal overlord – and inspired dissension at home.

But she had advantages. Her citizens, deliberately turning from mainland possessions, had committed themselves to sea trade. They had acquired a firm sense of their own identity, focused by the (supposed) body of St Mark retrieved from Alexandria in the 9th century. In 991, they elected a new leader (or doge, a local name deriving from the Latin dux, from which duce and 'duke' also derive). He was the brilliant, 30-year-old Pietro Orseolo. It was his ambition and diplomatic skill that underlay Venice's future rise to commercial and maritime supremacy.

Pietro first reapproached the Byzantine Emperor Basil II and negotiated

beneficial trading terms, promising in return to help ship Byzantine troops wherever and whenever necessary. He also won the admiring support of the young emperor of the west, Otto III, who granted Venetians tax-exempt rights to trade inland. He even acted as godfather to Orseolo's third son, named Otto in his honour, and would later (in February 1001) make a secret visit to Venice to seal the bonds of friendship. Venetian goods flowed northwards into mainland Europe, south to Byzantium, and even to the Islamic world scorned by other Christian powers.

One major obstacle stood in Orseolo's way: the Slav pirates who dominated the Dalmation coast. For decades, Venice had actually been paying off these seafaring gangsters with protection money. Orseolo put a stop to that, and sent ships to seize a pirate stronghold, the island of Vis. The pirates, in their fury, turned on the Latin inhabitants along the coasts of present-day Croatia and Bosnia. Though Basil was their overlord, he could offer no protection. Orseolo took on the task.

In May 1000, Orseolo led a great seaborne expedition southwards along the coast, being greeted with joy and promises of tribute. In Split, local pirates came to talk, and backed down. Other bands, based on the offshore islands of Korcula and Lastovo, gave up after brief resistance. Venetian merchants flocked south. Soon, Venice had warehouses and trading posts, secure food supplies and fine sources of timber for their ships. Orseolo, with Basil's blessing, named himself the Duke of Dalmatia.

After Otto III's death, Orseolo kept his shrewd diplomatic balance between east and west. Otto's successor, Henry of Bavaria, became godfather to Orseolo's youngest son. He married his eldest, Giovanni, to one of Basil's nieces. The wedding capped a remarkable resurgence of Venetian power and influence. In 1005, plague took Giovanni and his young wife. The shock destroyed Orseolo, who died in 1008, aged only 47, but he left behind a republic that was a rich and increasingly independent power in its own right.

fighting off religious and territorial challenges. Heresies and sects nibbled at the flanks of Orthodoxy. One concerned Christ's nature while he was on earth. Was he man and god, or all god? Traditional Orthodoxy stated the former, several heresies the latter. Some of these heretics, the so-called Monophysites, had broken away to form their own churches in Ethiopia, Syria and Armenia. Persians, Avars, Arabs, Bulgarians, Slavs, even other Christians harried imperial border-lands. The Bulgarians, having accepted the faith, then had the temerity to establish their own patri-arch and build their own empire. Several times, the Rus – the Norsemen of what was becoming Russia – attacked Constantinople itself. In the west, the empire was left with mere toeholds in southern Italy and Sicily. It took every form of state action to stave off challenges: war, oppres-sion, diplomatic alliances, bribery, intermarriage.

Nevertheless, as the millennium approached, the empire seemed more secure than it had been. This was an unlikely position, given the empire's record of intrigue (it would get worse: later, 'Byzantine' became a synonym for scheming and murder). The throne, technically held by two boys aged 6 and 3, had twice been seized from under them, once by a brutal assassination, opening the way for two other rebels to stake claims. Still, the assassin, John Tzimesces (John I, 969 – 76), had seen off the rebels and dealt with another major threat, imposing his rule as far as the Danube, seizing eastern Bulgaria from the clutches of the Russian leader Svyatoslav. Bulgaria's ruler, Boris, was brought back to Constantinople and made to abdicate in St Sophia. The Bulgarian Patriarchate was abolished. Eastern Bulgaria became part of

Byzantine victory

- Byzantine empire, c. 950
- gained by Byzantium, 971
- lost by Byzantium to Bulgaria, 986
- Samuel of Bulgaria attacks Larissa, 986
- Basil's unsuccessful attack on Sofia, 987
- Samuel attacks Basil's retreating army, 987
- Basil attacks Bulgarian army, 987
- Byzantine empire, 1025
- under Venetian influence

The Blinding of the Bulgarians

In 1000, though eastern Bulgaria had become part of the Byzantine Empire, a new and ambitious young ruler, Samuel, had taken advantage of Basil's troubles at home to build up a new empire to the west, centred on Macedonia, but reaching east to present-day Sofia and Plovdiv.

Samuel, Basil's greatest threat over 30 years, proclaimed himself tsar and appointed his own patriarch, reviving the empire destroyed by John Tzimesces. In 986, he besieged Larissa in Greece, took it, and carried off its holiest relic, the bones of a sainted bishop, to his capital, Prespa.

This was a challenge Emperor Basil II took up instantly, in a campaign that ended in disaster. After an unsuccessful siege of Sofia, he retreated across the plains southwards towards the Maritsa river, into a mountain pass known as Trajan's Gate. There, on 17 August, Samuel ambushed the Byzantine army and seized its treasure. After years of work securing his power-base at home, Basil's first great foreign campaign had ended in humiliation. When he returned to Constantinople with the tattered remains of his army, he swore revenge on the Bulgarians. It would take almost 30 years for him to make good his oath.

In 991, now secure at home, Basil set up a forward base in Thessalonika, from where he intended to grind Samuel slowly into submission. Samuel wisely held back, trusting that some crisis would draw Basil's attention.

He was in luck. In 995, the Egyptian caliph threatened to take Aleppo (today's Halab in Syria). Basil took a force south and east, saved Aleppo, then returned to Bulgaria. In his absence Samuel had struck westwards, into present-day Albania, Bosnia and Montenegro, only to be blocked by the Venetians under Pietro Orseolo II.

Basil could now return to his original strategy of attrition, spread over years interrupted by other foreign and domestic matters (one was an approach for a bride from Otto III, p. 54). Of this campaign between the two ageing adversaries, few details are known. But after 10 years Basil's superior power and wealth told. Bribery eroded Samuel's support, and all eastern Bulgaria once again fell into Byzantine control.

That the empire would win in the end was virtually inevitable. But there was nothing inevitable about the horrific way it happened. The showdown came in 1014, when Basil was 57, Samuel 60. The setting was a narrow gorge leading west from the River Struma, just north of the town of Serres (today's Serrai, in northern Greece). The gorge itself, known as both Cimbalongus and Clidion, was a regular route for Basil's armies. Samuel had occupied a fort overlooking it, Belasitza, and blocked the valley with a palisade. One of Basil's generals proposed a raid along a forested crest to take Samuel from behind, while Basil attacked head-on. It worked. On 29 July, Samuel's force was overwhelmed.

There followed an atrocity that seared itself into Bulgaria's soul. Basil took some 15,000 prisoners. Samuel himself escaped, eventually reaching Prespa. Back on the Struma, Basil took a terrible vengeance on the people who had troubled him so long. He had almost all of them blinded, leaving just one in a hundred with one eye. These were sent off leading 100 blind men each back to their king in Prespa. Weeks later, the ruined army straggled in. Samuel fainted at the ghastly sight, and died two days later.

Four years later, all Bulgaria submitted, and Samuel's cracked empire was at an end.

Blessed by angels, adored by his people, Basil II is portrayed in full military regalia in a Byzantine psalter. He laboured for 50 years to stem the slow decay of his ancient empire.

the empire. In the south, John took back part of Palestine from the Muslims, and secured peace with the west by marrying off his niece Theophano to the youthful Emperor Otto II.

When John died in 976, the empire came at last to the two boys Constantine and Basil, now teenagers. The two ruled as co-emperors, though Basil was the senior. Constantine was reserved to the point of invisibility; Basil II was short and rotund, but charismatic, with brilliant blue eyes, and noted for his austerity – he wore the most ordinary unimperial clothes. He was also a terrific horseman. It was he who took on all the burden of government from his unassuming brother.

At home, Basil did not have an easy run. The first 13 years of his rule were overshadowed, first by his great-uncle and chamberlain, also named Basil, and then challenges from the two rebel commanders, brothers named Bardas. Astutely, Basil risked giving power to one, Bardas Phocas, by setting him against the other, John's brother-in-law Bardas Sclerus. Sclerus was a huge man and notorious fighter – in the words of the 11th-century scholar, Michael Psellus, 'whole armies trembled even when he shouted from afar'. When the two armies met, Sclerus challenged his opponent to single combat. Phocas could not refuse. When they charged each other, both were wounded – but it was Sclerus who fell. He fled to safety with the caliph in Baghdād.

In 985, the young emperor discovered evidence of collusion between Phocas and his chamberlain. He arrested and exiled the old man – just in time to confront a new challenge from beyond the frontier, in Bulgaria, again. That campaign ended in personal and national humiliation (see Box), which gave both Phocas and Sclerus second chances. Each raised their own army. But Phocas, who had more support from disaffected officers and from the aristocracy, managed to have Sclerus arrested, and prepared to invade across the Bosphorus.

What was Basil to do? He turned for help to the Russians, of all people. The Russian ruler Svyatoslav had escaped from John Tzimesces only by promising help. Basil now asked Svyatoslav's son, Vladimir, to honour that promise. Vladimir, seeing a chance for a great alliance, demanded Basil's sister Anna in marriage. A deal was done: the sister in exchange for a 6,000-strong guard of Varangians (one of several names for the Rus that came into general use in Byzantium).

It took a year for the reinforcements to arrive, during which time Basil's navy kept Phocas's ships at bay. Early in 989, after a ferocious winter that froze the sea off Constantinople, the Russians came. A night-time crossing of the straits and a dawn assault led to the massacre of Phocas's army. Phocas, though, was elsewhere, with reserves.

These he turned on the city of Abydos, at the Gallipoli end of the Dardanelles. Basil and his Varangians followed. There followed a hard battle, which left Phocas facing defeat.

The revolt ended in a strange incident. According to Psellus, Phocas remembered the man-to-man combat that had served him in good stead with Sclerus. He charged Basil, approaching 'like a cloud driven by a hurricane'. Then, un-accountably, to the astonishment of Basil and his officers, Phocas reined up, stopped, and toppled slowly from his horse. Basil and his followers rode up, puzzled, wondering if Phocas had been felled by a stray arrow. No: he had had a stroke or heart attack, brought on (we must suppose) by intense strain.

For two years, Sclerus had been a captive, and might now have re-emerged as a danger. But in that time he had developed cataracts, and was going blind. There would be no further challenge from him. Basil offered him and his entourage generous terms – freedom, wealth and titles – in exchange for loyalty. When the two finally met, Basil gasped at the sight: 'Can this old dotard truly be he whom I have feared for so long? See, he can hardly walk by himself!'

Now came the reckoning. Vladimir had sent the promised troops, and they had saved Basil's empire. Now he wanted Anna, and invaded Cherson in the Crimea to get her (p. 52). Vladimir married her, converted to Orthodoxy, and handed Basil back the Crimea.

Both sides got the best deal they could, and both had good reason to stick to the terms. This was close to a medieval equivalent of a Cold War stand-off through 'mutually assured destruction'. Both sides had, in effect, provided hostages as insurance of good behaviour. Vladimir had Anna, in case Basil should be tempted to send his armies north. Basil secured the service of 6,000 hefty Varangians, and the freedom to re-exert his authority in his Bulgarian borderlands.

He did so with a terrible ferocity (see Box) that won him the title of 'Bulgaroctonus' ('Slayer of the Bulgars'). All of present-day Bulgaria, Macedonia, Serbia and Bosnia were his. He ruled from the Adriatic to the Azerbaijan. He failed only in one thing: he did not marry, and thus failed to produce a successor. When he died in 1025, the empire he had spent a lifetime securing resumed its slow decline.

Byzantine Empire

Byzantine empire, c. 970

Bulgaria, c. 1000

EMONA
Aquileia
Siscia
Mursa
CROATIA
Pannonia
Viminacium
Singidunum
Drobeta
Ancona
Ras
Nish
Oescus
Novae
Durostorum
Duklja
Sofia
Marcianopolis
Scodra
Scupi
Philippopolis
BULGARIA
Dyrrhachium
Stobi
1014
Bari
Adrianople
Naples
Avalona
Thessalonica
Constantinople
Tarentum
Philippi
Chalcedon
Codenra
Larisa
Alexandria
Bithynia
Messina
Nicopolis
BYZANTINE EMPIRE
Palermo
Patras
Rhegium
Sardes
Sicily
Athens
Ephesus
Iconium
Syracusae
Miletus
Sparta
Attalia

THE WORLD
OF ISLAM

*A Political Patchwork,
a Cultural Unity*

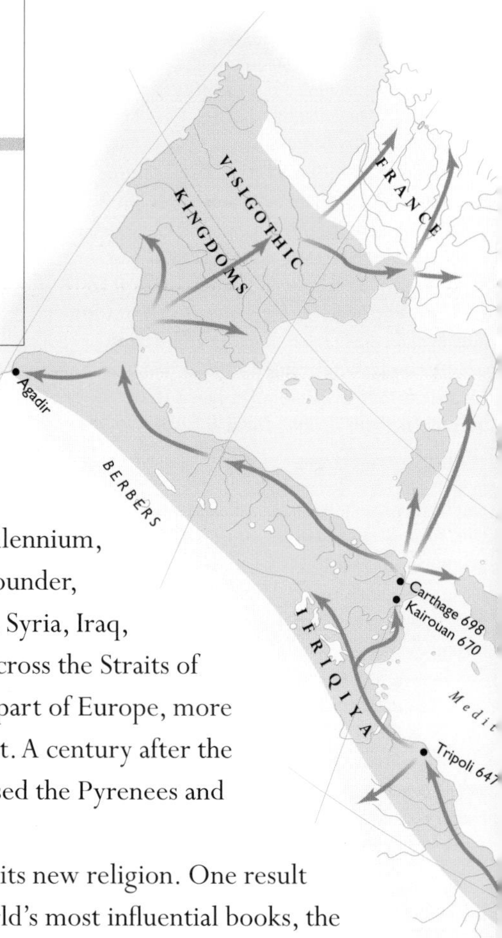

VISIGOTHIC KINGDOMS

FRANCE

Agadir

BERBERS

Carthage 698
Kairouan 670

IFRIQIYA

Medit

Tripoli 647

*In 1000, the Arabs
no longer ruled
all Islam. But
the empire they
had founded lived
on as an empire
of themind and
spirit.*

Over 300 years before the turn of the millennium,
Arabs, drawing inspiration from Islam's founder,
Muhammad, swept outwards over Persia, Syria, Iraq,
Egypt, North Africa, Central Asia, even across the Straits of
Gibraltar – making southern Spain less a part of Europe, more
a part of North Africa and the Middle East. A century after the
Prophet's death, Arab armies briefly crossed the Pyrenees and
reached Kashgar in western China.

For a while, this empire was unified by its new religion. One result
of Muhammad's work was one of the world's most influential books, the
Koran, which, as the Authorized English translation of the Bible did, distilled
and stimulated a language at a crucial moment in its evolution. Muslims point to
its beauty as a proof of Allah's existence. On this foundation arose another doctrinal
source, the Sunnah, the deeds and sayings of both the Prophet and his successors.
Together, these two streams of doctrine gave Arabic culture a lasting vigour, infusing
every aspect of life – government, law, knowledge, behaviour, creativity. In Islam
there is no clear distinction between Church and state, sacred and profane: all should
be sacred. The new faith also provided a political focus for a loyalty to something
above the merely tribal. Islam, more intensely than its paler rival Christianity, was to
be a 'brotherhood of believers'.

But ruling an empire seized by force was very different from ruling a desert kingdom inspired by religion. A great dynasty, the Umayyads, seized power, shifting the
empire's centre north to Damascus. The religious heartland, Arabia, became an economic and political backwater, known more for its pilgrim-site, its singers and its
thoroughbreds. Ruling with their supporters, the Sunnis, the Umayyad Empire was
as much Greek and Persian as Arab.

The cultural and political shift inspired hostility. One fount of opposition came from the Shi'ite sect (from 'Shi'at Ali', Party of Ali), who claimed that Islamic authority should derive not from any dynasty but only from Muhammad's descendants, through his son-in-law Ali, from whose ranks a divinely appointed imam would emerge as Mahdi, or messiah. Another faction, basing itself on the claims of Muhammad's uncle, Abbas, arose on the empire's fringes, notably in Iraq, where local non-Arab administrators resented their pure Arab rulers. In 750, rebellion here brought in a new dynasty, the Abbasids. The empire's centre of gravity jumped again, eastwards this time, to Baghdād.

Such a vast entity could not hold. Southern Spain broke away as 'al-Andalus' under its own rulers. In 973, the Shi'ite Fatimids established their own dynasty

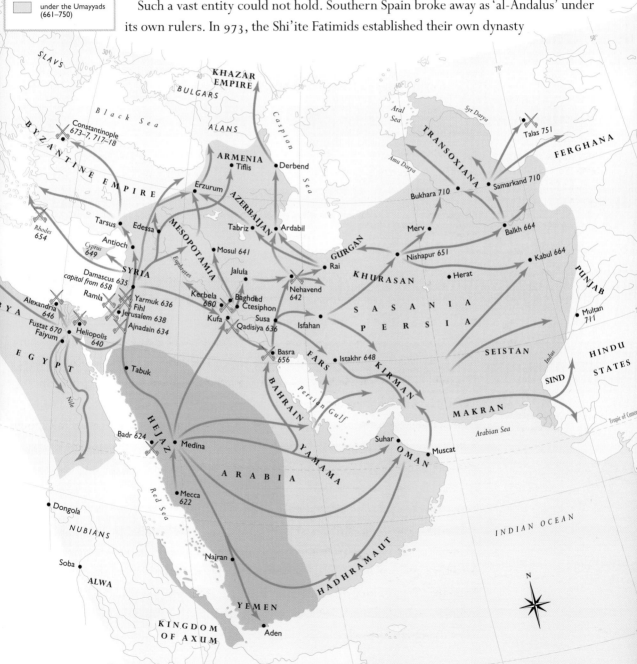

Expansion of Islam

→ Arab advance

✕ battle (with date)

▨ under Muhammad's control

▨ under the Umayyads (661–750)

across North Africa. In the east, today's Afghanistan became the seedbed of an empire that briefly reached from Persia to northern India. The great Silk Road entrepôts of Samarkand and Bukhara were virtually independent from the early 9th century. North Africa became a focus for those seeking to control the trans-Sahara trade in gold and black slaves. At the imperial heart, local rulers turned the Abbasid Empire into a shifting kaleidoscope of petty dynasts. By 1000, the Islamic world, created as one imperial river by the Arabs, had divided into a delta of five major streams and dozens of minor ones.

But unity of a sort endured. Muslim scholars of the year 1000, from the Hindu Kush to southern Spain, all worshipped the same god, honoured the same prophet, spoke and wrote the same language, and inherited the same astonishingly rich intellectual mantle. All Islam shared in its economic strength, with trade linking North Africa, Europe, Russia, the Middle East, India and China. Since Islam accepted the enslavement of non-Muslims, all benefited from a lucrative trade in slaves, whether African, Turkish, Indian or Slav. Arab coins found their way north as far as Finland, and Muslim merchants wrote cheques honoured by banks in major cities. One trader had a warehouse on the Volga, another near Bukhara and a third in Gujarat, India.

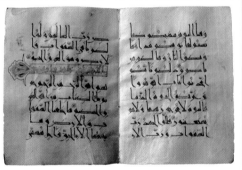

This 11th-century Qur'an (Koran) from the great medieval Islamic centre of Kairouan, in today's Tunisia, would have been familiar the length and breadth of Islam. The Kufic script includes the warning to unbelievers in sura (chapter) 45: 'The evil of their deeds will manifest itself to them, and the scourge at which they scoffed will encompass them.'

Fuelled by staggering wealth, medieval Islam hungered for learning, and inspired brilliant scholarship. The Arabic literature of the time was so vast that much still remains to be researched. Paper displaced papyrus, bookshops thrived, libraries graced the homes of the rich. Mosul's library supplied students with paper free, Basra's offered scholarships. Since Arabic was the language of divine revelation, the written word was venerated and calligraphy became an art-form valued above painting.

But this was not a world of inward-looking fundamentalism, for medieval Islam, assured of its superiority, was innovative, curious, and surprisingly tolerant of other cultures and faiths. The Arabs, looking back to the Greeks for the foundations of science and philosophy, translated Greek classics en masse. Many other languages and creeds – Persian, Sanskrit and Syriac, Christianity, Judaism and Zoroastrianism – also formed part of this rich amalgam.

The arts flourished. Urbanized literati found patrons for the ornate and elegant creations of poets, who were much given to romanticizing Arabian desert life that few ever experienced. Historians recorded and honoured Islamic achievements. From the 10th century dates the first draft of the *Thousand and One Nights*, which would be vastly amplified in later centuries. Though Islam discouraged (and later banned) human likenesses in art, there was nothing to inhibit design and architec-

An Empire of Gold and Silver

From the late 7th century, Islam's economic dominance was underpinned by gold – seized in conquest, taken from the tombs of the pharaohs, and extracted from mines in the Caucasus, Armenia, Nubia, and East and sub-Saharan Africa. The gold was minted into dinars, the coin that became standard from Spain to India (the name derives from the Latin denarius, which in English was shortened to

'd.' to stand for the old penny).

A dinar, with a purity of about 90%, weighed 4.25 grams (about 0.15 oz). For centuries, the coins poured in their millions from dozens of mints. Giving equivalent values in current terms is hard. Today, its gold content would make a dinar worth about £25 ($40), but its antique value gives it a worth of about £160 ($250).

Almost as vital in Islamic commerce was the silver-based dirhem (from the Greek, drachma), which was worth one-twentieth of a dinar.

ture. Wonderful domed mosques arose. Potters tried to match Chinese porcelain (they failed, but they created lustrous, wonderfully decorated glazes). Stuccoed and frescoed palaces displayed an ornate style emulated throughout Islam.

Science too blossomed. 'Arabic' numerals, derived from Indian ones, provided a far more powerful mathematical tool than any previous system. Though Arab scientists remained convinced that gold could be produced by the transformation of metals, their rigorous search for the 'philosopher's stone' that would cause this to happen created the bridge between alchemy (*al-kīmiyā*, 'transmutation') and modern chemistry. The need to determine the direction of Mecca demanded a good knowledge of geography. Muslim travellers wrote reports of China, Europe and much of Africa. European languages, enriched by translations from Arabic into Latin, still contain many other tributes to Arab scientific predominance: zero (from *sifr*, 'empty'), algebra (*al-jabr*, 'reunion'), star-names such as Betelgeuse (from *bayt al-jawza*, 'the house of the Orion') and Altair (*al-tā'ir*, 'the flyer'), zenith, nadir, azimuth.

At the turn of the millennium, this great empire of the mind was not only the patrimony of Muslims from the deserts of Central Asia to the heartland of Spain. It was the cultural foundation that would fuel Europe's medieval revival in learning, and the basis for even further expansion in the future, into Africa, south-east Asia, and western China.

Baghdād: The Heart of Islam

One of the world's greatest glories became the capital of a rump empire, and its caliph a mere puppet in the hands of outsiders.

Most of Islam's web of scholarship and trade was spun during the 200-year cultural and scientific golden age of the Abbasids. As much Persian as Arab in tradition, Arabic in language and religion, the Abbasids had made their capital, Baghdād, into one of the greatest cities of the world.

Its position was ideal. Straddling the Tigris, one of Mesopotamia's two major rivers, it was also on a canal that linked with the other, the Euphrates. Since the Euphrates degenerated into swamps downriver, Baghdād dominated Mesopotamia's major water routes, and its trade. On this ancient site, the 8th-century Abbasid ruler al-Mansur had 100,000 workers create a wonder. Planned as a perfect circle, with four gateways piercing its walls and a palace and mosque at its centre, Baghdād was surrounded by a vast triple rampart of earth guarded by 360 towers and a moat. The Round City, as it was known, soon became a magnet for traders, scholars and artists from as far afield as Spain and northern India, and spilled over its walls, spreading south to a trading suburb, al-Kharkh, and east, across the river, which was crossed by a pontoon bridge. In the 9th century it was abandoned when the caliph al-Mutasim fled to Samarra, 60 miles (96 kms) up the Tigris, after violent confrontations between the restless populace and the city's Turkish garrison. His successor's return 55 years later led to yet more building on the east bank, reached by two other pontoon bridges.

In the 10th century, Baghdād grew to become one of the largest cities in the world, equalling Constantinople – about the same size as Paris at the end of the 19th century – with wealth to match. One caliph greeted a Byzantine ruler with a pageant of 160,000 cavalrymen and 100 lions, conducting the awed visitors to a palace decorated with 38,000 curtains and 22,000 rugs. The city's wharfs harboured vessels bringing porcelain from China, silk, musk and ivory from east Africa, spices and pearls from Malaya, Russian slaves, wax and furs. To supply a scarce resource, timber from Armenia was floated down the Tigris.

The study of medicine conferred on the Abbasid state a remarkably modern, even benign aspect. In the early 10th century, Baghdād had 860 certified physicians, who were allowed to administer drugs. Some were licensed to make daily visits to prisons. Major cities had state-run hospitals, with their own libraries and dispensaries. One of the greatest physicians, al-Razi, who wrote some 140 books on medicine and alchemy, is said to have chosen the site for one of

Baghdād's hospitals by hanging up raw meat around the city to identify the place least subject to contamination.

But in 1000 Baghdād was the caliph's in name only. For 50 years either side of the millennium (945–1055), Baghdād was in the hands of ruthless kingmakers, the Buwayhid (or Buyid) family. In 945, the three sons of the dynasty's eponymous founder, Abu Shuja Buwayh, led their own army, raised in the mountains to the south of the Caspian Sea, into Baghdād. The Buwayhids were Shi'ite, Baghdād was Sunni.

This spiral minaret, recalling an ancient Babylonian ziggurat ('high place'), rose beside the great mosque of Samarra, the temporary Abbasid capital in the 9th century. In Baghdad itself, no buildings survived later wars.

The Turkish guards fled, and the caliph, al-Mustakfi, was forced to acknowledge the leader of these upstart conquerors, Ahmad ibn-Buwayh, as *amir al-umara* ('emir of emirs') with the grand title of Muizz al-Dowlah – 'he who renders the state mighty'. It didn't save al-Mustakfi. The next year, the brothers blinded him (a common mutilation, for Islam forbade the disabled from rule), and replaced him with their own puppet.

Briefly uniting Persia and Iraq, a second-generation Buwayhid amir, Adud al-Dowlah ('Supporting Arm of the State') aimed to found a lasting empire. He married the caliph's daughter – and forced his own daughter on the caliph, in the hope of producing an heir to the caliphate. He adopted the ancient Iranian title of 'Shahanshah', King of Kings, and set about creating the foundations for lasting greatness, with mosques, hospitals, public buildings, roads, bridges and libraries. Poets sang his praises, writers dedicated their works to him. His greatest achievement was

Baghdād's Bimaristan (hospital), completed in 978–9 with a faculty of 24 doctors.

Adud's son, Baha al-Dowlah ('Honour of the State', 989–1012) fought off rivals with wealth secured by deposing the caliph al-Tai and seizing his fortune. Rebels still tore at the state's flanks, but Baha at least put cash at the disposal of his vizier Sabur ibn-Ardashir, who was responsible for building a library in Baghdād containing 10,000 books.

This was the high point for the Buwayhids, and the beginning of Baghdād's decline. The Buwayhids had always squabbled, and as Shi'ites they would never win acceptance in Sunni Baghdād. In 1055, the Turks (pp. 78–9) arrived from the east. The military commander, al-Basasiri, fled with his troops – who were themselves Turkish – and the caliph al-Qaim welcomed the incoming tribal chief, Tughril, as a deliverer. When al-Basasiri attempted a comeback, he was executed.

For two more centuries, the puppet Abbasid caliphs danced to new masters, in a capital that never again matched its previous glory.

Baghdād map

to Mosul
al-Holig
to Mosul
Nahrawan
to Khurasan
upper port
ar-Rusafa (al-Mahdi)
the Tahirids
round town of Dar al-Khilafa
the Barmekids
al-Mu'tasim's
al-Khuld (al-Amin)
al-Mu'tadid's 'Pleiades'
to the Euphrates (Anbar)
Syria gate
Firdaws
al-Hasani Taj
al-Amin's
Kufa gate
Basra gate
al-Mansur
lower port
al-Karkh (market)
Zubayda's
Tigris
Kalwadha
to Wasit
to Basra
to Kufa

Baghdād
— wall
— town expansion
— canal
— palace

Islamic states, c.1000

- Abbasid caliphate at its greatest extent
- Abbasid caliphate, c. 900
- major battle
- Abbasid palace
- Abbasid mosque

Regional map

BYZANTINE
Black Sea
KHAZARS
Caspian Sea
TURKS
Aral Sea
Syr Darya
Constantinople
EMPIRE
Tiflis
Derbend
Amu Darya
Bukhara
Samarkand
Erzurum
SAMANIDS
Tarsus
Tabriz
Ardabil
Merv
Balkh
Antioch
Edessa
Tigris
Mosul
Nishapur
Kabul
Damascus
BUWAYHID EMIRATES
Rai
Herat
Ghazni
Euphrates
Jalula
Jerusalem 977
Kerbela
Nehavend
MAHMUD OF GHAZNI
Multan
Alexandria
Heliopolis
Baghdad
Isfahan
Susa
Cairo 969
Faiyum 971
Istakhr
Tabuk
Basra
Karmatians
Indus
Medina
Persian Gulf
Arabian Sea
Tropic of Cancer
Badr
Suhar
MAKKURA
Muscat
Dongola
Nile
Mecca
Red Sea
N
0   300 km
0   300 miles
Soba
Najran
INDIAN OCEAN

2 The Slaves of Islam

Slavery was part of Islam's heritage from the past, as natural to them as it had been to the Greeks, Romans and many other civilizations.

Yemeni slave-traders haggle over their African captives. This illustration is from an edition of the maqamat *of al-Hariri (1054 – 1122), anecdotes revered for their stylistic excellence.*

Slaves were the labourers of the Islamic world, an underclass used everywhere, in vast numbers. One 8th-century campaign in North Africa netted 300,000 captives, all destined for slavery. Umayyad princes in Spain commonly had 1,000 or more slaves. When the wave of conquest, with its backwash of captives, ceased its forward roll, trade continued the supply.

Slaves were in demand for all forms of labour, working in gangs on plantations and in mines, alongside freemen as builders in towns, in domestic service and as soldiers – particularly as soldiers, for Muslims argued that once cut from their traditional roots slaves would be more loyal to their masters than free warriors. Female slaves formed harems for sovereigns, guarded by other slaves who had been castrated – a brutal operation done without anything to deaden the pain – on their way from initial captivity to slave-market. Some harems were as large as small armies: Abd al-Rahman's harem in Córdoba in the mid 10th century numbered 6,300 women, and the Fatimid palace in Cairo had 12,000. Special schools in Baghdad, Medina and Córdoba trained musicians and dancers.

Islamic slavery had three main categories of slaves – the Slavs of eastern Europe, the Turks of Central Asia and the blacks of sub-Saharan Africa – with lesser streams of Indians and Anglo-Saxons. It was a trade in which any group with the power to do so sought the benefit of partnership, from the Christians of western Europe and Byzantium, the Jews of Europe and the Islamic world, Vikings, frontier tribes of eastern Europe, central Asia and the African interior.

Slavs captured by Christian Europe were taken south as trade goods, through France via Verdun and Lyons to Córdoba and Cairo. Another route carried Slav captives to the castration centre of Prague, then on to Regensburg and Venice, the hub of the Mediterranean slave trade. The Rus of Kiev also seized captives from neighbouring tribes, trading them in Constantinople. Armenia was a noted castration centre for those Slavs who were delivered through Khazar lands to Itil at the mouth of the Volga.

Turkish slaves from Central Asia flowed into Islam through the slave markets of Bukhara, Samarkand, and Urgench, which dealt with both Slavs and Turks. All three were castration centres for those slaves destined for domestic service. Turks had been favoured as soldiers by Persian rulers, and the fashion spread westwards, with the result that slave armies became

significant political forces in many major cities.

Sub-Saharan Africa was a region so vast that it made up many sources and many exit routes for the thousands captured and sold by rulers and middlemen. Western Sudanese captives – Sarakole from Takrur in today's Senegal, Soninke from ancient Ghana (p. 114), Songhai from Gao and Sao from Kanem – were taken across the Sahara for sale in Morocco and Spain, or eastwards to Egypt, and beyond. Nubians of the Upper Nile were imported via Aswan, another castration centre. Ethiopians were taken down the Blue Nile or to the Red Sea ports. Somalis were exported to Aden. And east Africans – known as Zanj, whether they were Bantu or Nilotic – were taken to the island of Socotra or Aden, for shipping onwards up the Red Sea to Egypt or up the Persian Gulf to Mesopotamia.

Given that slavery is now seen as an offence against humanity, it takes an effort of imagination to see it through the eyes of the past, before attitudes were coloured by the peculiar brutalities of the Atlantic slave trade. Muslims, like Christians, saw nothing wrong with it, with one proviso: that the slaves were not of their religion.

By hindsight, this implies a tacit recognition that there was something inhuman about the practice. Yet no one saw this, for many reasons. In medieval times, slavery was accepted uncritically as necessary to economic well-being. Since slaves were outsiders, not part of the 'civilized' world, they could be treated differently. The beneficiaries, Muslim and Christian alike, simply disregarded the cruelty involved in acquiring slaves. It was, after all, no more cruel than war, than plague, than the usual tribulations of life itself.

Besides, slavery embraced a wide range of practices. Slaves may have been merely oppressed labourers or abused concubines; but they also climbed social and political ladders, starting as

al-Andalus

Córdoba

Agadir

Fez

UMAYYAD EMIRATE

Maghreb

FATIMID

from West Africa

house-servants perhaps, and then becoming wives, husbands, adopted children, scholars, bureaucrats, ministers. If taken into military service, a man did not even have to overcome the stigma of servitude. A slave soldier could rise to become an officer, a general, an army commander, a provincial governor, even a sultan.

The steps away from outright bondage were part of Islamic law. The liberation of slaves was regarded as a 'good work' that would be rewarded in the next world. If a concubine produced a child, for instance, she became a 'mother of children' who could not be sold and who became free on her master's death. Many Abbasid caliphs were the sons of slave women, who then assumed influential roles. Once free, power was within reach. The Mamluks (*mamluk*, 'owned') – the slave army that in the 9th cen-

tury consisted of 24,000 Turks and 40,000 blacks – played a pivotal role in Egyptian history for 600 years. Abu-al-Misk Kafur, briefly ruler of Egypt (966–8) before the Fatimids came to power, was a black eunuch who had been bought by his master and predecessor from an oil merchant.

For centuries, slavery was a door through which uncounted hundreds of thousands entered the Islamic world, and influenced it profoundly. As Slavs turned Christian and Turks became Muslim, supplies dried up, undermining Islam's economy, writing new rules. The old trade routes now became warpaths for Turks, Almoravids, Normans and Crusaders. Still no one saw slavery as anything but a necessity. For slavery to be seen as an unmitigated evil, a slave trade of a different sort – the transatlantic trade from West Africa to the Americas – would have to strip away every positive and neutral element. That was a change that would take the best part of another millennium.

Slave origins and trade routes

▨	major Muslim states
→	slaves from Europe
→	slaves from Africa
→	slaves from Asia
○	collection centre
●	castration centre

The Fatimids: Ambition, Power and Madness

In its early days, Cairo was a prey to, and beneficiary of, one of the world's most eccentric rulers.

As Islam disintegrated, as its disparate parts fell away from Abbasid rule and reinvented themselves, an ambitious new dynasty, the Fatimids, rose to power in North Africa.

Their origins were curious, for their claims to authority derived from separate strands of Islam. As their name suggests, they claimed to descend from the prophet's daughter Fatima and her husband Ali, and therefore to be the true rulers of all Islam. In addition, their beliefs made them a sect within a sect: the Ismaili branch of Shi'ite Islam. Ismailis, taking their name from their 8th-century figurehead, saw hidden, mystical meanings in the Koran and predicted the return of Ismail's son Muhammad as the Mahdi, or messiah. From the 9th century on, they constituted an anti-Abbasid underground. Naturally, Ismaili religious claims and Fatimid political ones were both bitterly opposed by the Abbasids, forcing the Fatimid/Ismaili leadership to flee their first base in Syria in 909. They seized Ifriqiya – modern Tunisia and eastern Algeria – took over the trans-Saharan gold-

and-slave trade, built two great capitals – first Kairouan, then nearby Mahdiyya – and set up an autonomous state far from the reach of Baghdād. But, as is usual with dynasties, this one was riven by power struggles; and as usual, it took one supreme leader to unite the squabblers and build an empire.

That man was Jawhar al-Rumi, known as al-Siqilli, 'the Sicilian'. On behalf of his caliph, al-Muizz, this former Christian slave completed the Muslim conquest of Sicily, conquered Egypt in 969, and began to lay out a new town alongside the old capital of Fustat. The new quarter he named al-Kahira – 'the victorious'. It was to this new town, the heart of today's Cairo, that al-Muizz moved his administration. At the heart of the Nile's dense-packed ribbon of humanity, Cairo grew fast, booming on gold which flowed from Nubia, Ethiopia and the newly opened tombs of the pharaohs.

Egypt was to be a mere stepping stone to all Islam. Ismaili missionaries began to spread the word across the Muslim world. Armies followed, bringing Fatimid rule to Palestine and Syria.

The year 1000 saw this ambitious empire ruled by al-Hakim (born 985, ruled 996–1021), who has a rare claim to fame: he ranks high in a list of those few rulers who were both psychopaths and megalomaniacs.

Al-Hakim, who was only 11 when he succeeded, was murderously unstable even as a teenager. Once, finding his studies irksome, he took his tutor for a walk and led him into the arms of an assassin. He soon displayed the unpredictability of a Caligula. He grew his hair long and took to wearing a coarse woollen garment. His moods swung between depression and exhilaration, generosity and insane extortion, and he responded to each mood on the instant, without a qualm. In the words of a contemporary, 'his actions were without reason, his dreams without interpretation'. The history of the period is largely a history of the 'Mad Caliph's' lunatic acts.

He could punish a man by cutting off his hands, then load him with gold. He supported and then persecuted those who observed the times of fasting during Ramadan. He killed off officials by the dozen. In 1004, he ordered all Cairo's prisoners that year to be executed. Once, out walking with his entourage, he seized a butcher's axe and felled a courtier with one blow, then ignored the bloody corpse and walked on unconcerned, with his entourage following in stricken silence. According to one story, a general accidentally came across him cutting up a child. Knowing himself to be doomed, the general hurried home and set his affairs in order before Hakim's executioner arrived.

Ancient Cairo

- ▬ wall
- ▪ 7th century
- ▪ 8th century
- ▪ 9th century
- ▫ 10–11th century

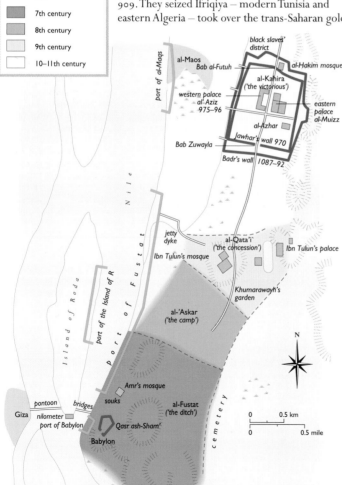

Some edicts, made and often rescinded with equal randomness, might have been merely eccentric, except that infraction might be punished by death. He forced both Christians and Jews to identify themselves by wearing black belts and turbans. He briefly banned chess, wine and certain vegetables. He forbade women to weep at funerals, and also ordered women to stay indoors after sunset, enforcing the order by banning the manufacture of women's shoes. Other orders were openly destructive, tearing at the fabric of society. He unleashed a week of rioting in old Cairo, asked plaintively, 'Who gave orders for this?' and then took a ringside seat to watch the flames from Cairo's hills. In one thing he remained steady: he was equally capricious, equally appalling to all those not of his narrow and ever more fervent and self-centred faith. The great Jewish synagogue in old Cairo (Fustat) was ransacked. Among the Christian churches he destroyed was the Holy Sepulchre in Jerusalem, an act that was later used by Christian crusaders as a reason for invasion.

Yet Cairo continued to prosper, despite, and sometimes because of, al-Hakim's volatility. The al-Azhar mosque, started by Jawhar in 972, developed into the first Islamic university. The royal library, the Dar al-Hikma (House of Wisdom), contained some 200,000 books. Al-Hakim, a dedicated astrologer, had an observatory built on the desert hills of al-Moqattam, now part of eastern Cairo, where he would retire to record the position of stars with a giant copper astrolabe. This passion, combined with the presence of the university and the library, made the city a home for the great astronomer Ali ibn-Yunus, who compiled an updated list of observations known as the Hakemite Tables after his patron. The physicist Ali al-Hasan ibn al-Haytham wrote a book of optics here that made his Latinized name, Alhazen, famous in medieval Europe. He also dreamed up a scheme to regulate the flow of the Nile; when he failed, he feigned madness in order to avoid al-Hakim's own madness, recovering his wits on al-Hakim's death.

Al-Hakim's lunacy had a lasting influence on Islam. In 1017, under the leadership of a Persian

felt-maker, Hamza ibn Ali, there arose a messianic group who developed a mystical faith in the physical presence of God. By an astonishing coincidence, declared ibn Ali, this godhead was none other than al-Hakim himself, who in his divine capacity had created five cosmic leaders, of whom the principal one was (of course) Hamza. The notion appealed to both al-Hakim (naturally) and a Turkish teacher from Bukhara, al-Darazi, whose name became a label for his group: the Druze. A year later, al-Darazi died, probably at the hands of an assassin.

This odd offshoot of Ismailism – a sect of a sect of a sect – might have died with its figurehead al-Hakim, when on the night of 13 February 1021, he went for a walk on the al-Moqattam hills, and simply vanished. Possibly, he was assassinated on the orders of his sister, with whom he had had a row. But the obscure circumstances of his death left a mystery upon which the Druze extemporized. In a reflection of the Shi'ite belief in the imam's return as Mahdi, the Druze claimed that al-Hakim did not die at all, but simply 'withdrew' pending his return in glory to initiate a golden age (along with Hamza, who 'withdrew' soon after al-Hakim). That remains one of the tenets of the austere, secretive and intractable Druze, who today number between 200,000 and 400,000, mainly based in Syria and Lebanon.

Later schisms undermined the Fatimids. The Yemen, Sicily, western parts of North Africa all fell away, and their rule ended in 1171.

In an ivory plaque done under Fatimid rule, a field-worker harvests grapes while his master enjoys a cup of wine. The Koranic ban on alcohol was seen to apply only to some brews, not all.

Fatimid North Africa

- Fatimid caliphate at its maximum extent, c. 1000
- breakaway principality, with date
- movement of Arab peoples (Banu Hilal and Banu Sulaim), c. 1000
- Fatimid caliphate, c. 1055
- Sulaim and Hilal attacks, late 10th–early 11th centuries

4 Islamic Spain: Glory and Egomania

Spanish Islam surged outwards for the last time thanks to the ambitions and ferocity of one man, al-Mansur. But his revolution tore the fabric of his state beyond repair.

In the mid-990s, Europe seemed safe from the expansionist forces of Islam. In southern Spain the Arabs had been blocked when they tried to cross the Pyrenees, and were now held back by Christian buffer states: León, Castile, Catalonia. Pilgrims from the north had begun to beat a safe path to the great shrine of Santiago de Compostela.

But that security was about to be threatened again by the growing might of Córdoba, the centre from which Arab rulers had slowly welded their diverse peoples – long-established Arabs, Berber newcomers from North Africa and indigenous Spaniards – into a strong, independent state. No need now to fear 'Firanja' – the still disorganized kingdom of Francia (p. 48).

For almost two centuries the rulers had been amirs who were in effect independent of Damascus and Baghdad. When the Abbasids seized power from the Umayyads, an Umayyad prince, Abd al Rahman, brought his army to Spain, and took over. His descendant, Abd al Rahman III (912–61), upgraded himself to Caliph. Passionately interested in both science and religion, and ambitious to establish the pre-eminence of his kingdom, he set Andalusia (al-Andalus) on its own rise to intellectual and political greatness. Under his successor, al-Hakam (961–76), Andalusia became a power to equal other Islamic

regions. And with firm roots in rice-rich, well-irrigated land, it soon outshone Christian states to the north.

Córdoba, the capital, rose to match Baghdad, Damascus and Bukhara. After Constantinople, it was Europe's second-largest city. As the millennium approached, it had a population of over 100,000 (perhaps twice the size of Paris), 700 mosques, 300 public baths and 70 libraries. A 400-room palace, the Madinat al-Zahra, built by 10,000 workmen over 12 years, arose on the foothills of the Sierra Morena. Here the caliph lived in style, protected by a private army of 'Slavs', some 13,000 prisoners of war brought from northern and eastern Europe, which became a political force in its own right. In Córdoba itself, people could stroll at night beneath Europe's first street lights. Once, they had aped Baghdad. 'If a fly starts buzzing in the depths of Syria,' wrote a 9th-century playwright scathingly, 'they fall flat on their faces as if before an idol.' But now the people of Córdoba were renowned on their own account, for their leatherwork and for their fashions – the palace weavers produced a superb dark cloth for winter-wear, an innovation for Arabs.

And renowned too for their learning. Its scholars included some of Islam's greatest geographers, astronomers, mathematicians and physicians. A visiting intellectual could hope to talk with the mathematician Maslamah al-Majriti, who re-defined the positions of the stars and coordinated Islamic and Persian chronologies; or al-Zarqali, known in Europe as Arzachel, who compiled tables to relate Coptic, Roman and Persian calendars to the phases of the moon; or one of the few great Arabic surgeons, Abu al-Qasim al-Zahrawi (Abulcasis in Latin), who wrote a summary of medical knowledge which, when translated into Latin, became one of Europe's leading medical textbooks.

In the last two decades of the 10th century, Córdoba was more than a jewel of intellectual and artistic ability. It was the centre for an expansion that once again threatened the borders of Christian Europe. The author of this challenge was the vizier, al-Mansur, 'the Victorious'. Ibn abi Amir, as he was originally known, was of humble origin. During al-Hakam's reign he had been administrator for the caliph's wife, a beautiful Basque ex-slave and singer named Subh. According to rumour, he quickly graduated from administrator to lover. Ambitious and well-connected, he was made political boss of Umayyad-held areas of Morocco.

When al-Hakam died in 976, the struggle over the recognition of the teenage crown prince, Subh's son Hisham, revealed Amir's ruthlessness and talent for intrigue. He had Hisham's uncle, a

Islamic Spain, c. 1030

(shaded)	Christian states
(white)	Caliphate of Córdoba to 1031
Murcia	Islamic kingdoms after 1031
☩	archdiocese
✡	important Jewish community

Population
(vertical lines)	Christian
(diagonal lines)	mostly Berber and converts
(cross-hatch)	mostly Arabic

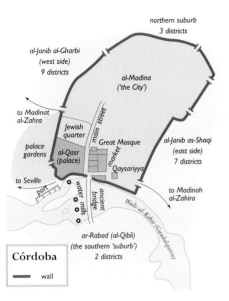

Córdoba

— wall

northern suburb
3 districts

al-Janib al-Gharbi
(west side)
9 districts

al-Madina
('the City')

to Madinat
al-Zahra

Jewish
quarter

main street

Great Mosque

al-Janib as-Shaqi
(east side)
7 districts

palace
gardens

al-Qasr
(palace)

market

Qaysariyya

to Seville

port

water
mills

ancient
bridge

to Madinah
al-Zahira

Wadi-al-Kebir (Guadalquivir)

ar-Rabad (al-Qibli)
(the southern 'suburb')
2 districts

bi-Allah, Victorious by the Grace of God, which in its north European form of Almanzor made him feared throughout Christendom.

Then, as has often been the way of dictators, he ensured unity at home by foreign adventures, justified by religious ideology. He carried with him a Koran copied in his own hand and a linen winding-sheet made of flax woven by his daughters. He purged al-Hakam's great library of less-than-orthodox books, and crucified a scholar accused of heresy. Everywhere he went, he collected dust to be mixed with the perfumes that would sanctify his body after death.

Declaring a jihad, a holy war, he turned north, against the infidels, the Christians, in raid after raid, over 50 of them. Navarre, Castile, Zamora, Barcelona, Léon – all fell to him. In 997, his armies demolished the glorious church of Santiago de Compostela, which, as the supposed burial-place of St Iago (St James the Apostle), was on its way to becoming one of Christian Europe's greatest shrines. Though the tomb itself was left intact, the bells and doors of the church were carried back by Christian prisoners to Córdoba.

Here, the chained captives were forced to build them into the Great Mosque, which al-Mansur vastly extended. With its 850 pillars, it became the largest sacred building in Europe until the building of St Peter's in Rome, and the largest in the Islamic world after the Great Mosque in Mecca (later, under Christian rule, it became today's cathedral).

Al-Mansur died in August 1002, at Medinaceli, about 100 km (60 miles) north-east of Madrid, on the borderlands of Islam and Christendom. Good riddance, implied one Christian chronicler in a terse comment: 'Almanzor died, and was entombed in hell.' The dust he had collected on his campaigns was buried with him.

And so were his achievements. His power was all military show, which destroyed its own foundations. His Berber troops owed everything to him, nothing to the state. Al-Mansur had made his office hereditary, but his chosen successor was poisoned by a brother, who foolishly proclaimed himself heir to the caliph. For the people, this was one claim too many. In the revolt that followed, he was executed. Hisham was dragged out of seclusion, to no avail. Andalusia fell into near anarchy. Finally, the people of Córdoba took matters into their own hands. They shut poor Hisham into a room beside the mosque, where he died in 1027. In 1031, they abolished the caliphate altogether.

The state collapsed into a score of rival regions. In the north, Christians looked to their defences, and to vengeance. It would take another 400 years, but the decay caused by al-Mansur's excesses would allow all Spain at last to be brought into the mainstream of European Christian culture.

The forest of two-tiered arches in Córdoba's mosque (now its cathedral) exemplify the ambition of southern Spain's Islamic rulers to make their realm – al-Andalus – a rival to Baghdād.

claimant to the throne, strangled in front of his family, and therafter rose rapidly to absolute power. After two years he was chamberlain (*hajib*) and vizier, which allowed him to dismiss the caliph's 'Slav' bodyguard and replace it with his own trusted Berbers from Morocco.

This gave him his power base. Subh, realizing her lover would never let her son rule, tried to seize the palace treasury to finance his removal. He moved faster, and put the young caliph under house arrest in his palace, announcing that the boy had decided to devote himself to religion, in isolation. Subh was sidelined – she died a broken woman in 999 – and Amir set about creating a cult of personality to rival any modern dictator.

Scorning the vast royal suburb of Madinat al-Zahra, Amir ordered a monumental palace of his own, giving it a confusingly similar name – al-Madinah al-Zahirah (The Town in Bloom), which later came to designate the city's eastern suburbs. He had his name included in official prayers, imprinted on coins, woven onto his golden-thread robes. He became an absolute monarch, except in name: he kept on young Hisham as a front for his authority.

Next, he extended his reach by reforming the army to prevent any unified resistance, introducing Berber, Christian and Slav regiments, and crushing rival commanders. He paid them by imposing new taxes on the peasantry, a policy that would in the long run undermine his economic base and popular support. But it served his immediate aims. With his new army, he began two decades of military adventures. In 981 he invaded North Africa, seizing control of a major source of gold in Sijilmasa (today's Tafilalt), south of the Atlas mountains. After this conquest, he awarded himself the title by which he is known: al-Mansur

5

Central Asia: The Coming of the Turks

For years, the Turkish barbarians had been at the gates of Islam. The turn of the millennium saw them seize power – the first step in a long expansion into new homelands.

The mausoleum of Ismail Samani, who made Bukhara into one of Islam's most glorious cities, was one of the few buildings to survive the Turkish invasion. Its clay bricks, bound with egg yolk and camel's milk, are arranged in 18 different basket-weave patterns.

For over a century, the ancient oasis cities of Samarkand, Bukhara and Merv, the eastern out-posts of Islam, were ruled by a family that looked back to their 8th-century Persian ancestor, Saman Khudat. The Samanids, originally viceroys, had thrown out their Arab overlords and built their own civilization – Islamic, but Persian – spreading east into Afghanistan, holding off the Arabs to the west and a new challenge from the north: Turkish nomads, eager for the wealth of Islamic society.

The three cities were all on rivers running from the Pamirs into the wastes of the Kyzyl-Kum, all sustained by intricate canal systems and underground channels (qanat), all walled against enemies and the encroaching sand. They had long been the rich bulwarks of the provinces of Khurasan and Transoxiana (the land beyond the river Oxus, today's Amu Darya). All three were trade emporia linking east and west. In a list of products recorded by the late-10th-century geographer al-Muqaddasi, the region's exports included soap, sulphur, silks, sable, leatherware and ornamental arms. Water melons packed in snow were couriered along the the great highway that led westwards to Baghdad. Paper from Samarkand was in demand all over the Muslim world. Caravans the size of small armies – one numbered 5,000 men and 3,000 horses and camels – ranged back and forth to eastern Europe, trading silks, copper bowls and jewelry for furs, amber and sheepskins. From China came pottery and spices, in exchange for horses and glass.

Bukhara, the capital, with a population of 300,000, was a match for Baghdad and Córdoba. Its scholars and poets, writing in both Arabic and Persian, made it the 'dome of Islam in the east', in a common epithet. In the words of an 11th-century anthologist, al-Tha'alabi, it was the 'focus of splendour, the shrine of empire, the meeting-place of the most unique intellects of the age'. Its royal library, with 45,000 volumes, had a suite of rooms, each devoted to a different discipline. This tolerant environment, with its mix of Arabic and Persian language and culture, and its equally rich mix of religions and sects, did much to ensure Islam's appeal to other cultures.

All of this was under threat towards the turn of the millennium. Its secondary source was dissension: the Buwayhids challenged from the west, while local dynasties made southern Samanid lands independent fiefdoms. This coincided with

economic and social decline. The Samanids lost control of their silver mines on the Zarafshan river. Land values dropped, the coinage was debased, trade shrank. Peasants crowded into the cities. Writers complained of Bukhara's crowds, of alleys made impassable by garbage, of stench and pestilence. The 11th-century minister and historian Nizam al-Mulk described how rival factions squabbled for power, 'the smallest person demanded the biggest title', authority crumbled.

But the primary and decisive threat came from the north, from the Turks. As part of a west-ward drift of Turkish tribes that had been going on for centuries, one particular group, the Ghuzz or Oghuz, had colonized the steppe and desert regions of today's Uzbekistan and Turkmenistan. These people, with no records of their own, were named for their leaders, or 'khans'. But the names given to them were various, and confusing. Later, non-Turks called them either 'Ilek Khans' (a combination of two separate chiefly titles) or 'Kara (black) Khans' (Qarakhans). As they settled, they converted to Sunni Islam, and also acquired Muslim names and titles, adding to the confusion over terminology.

The shadowy Muslim/Turkish borderland had seen a constant interplay of war and collaboration for two centuries. Non-Muslim Turks were commonly captured or bought as slaves – a good Turkish boy or girl could fetch as much as 3,000 dinars. And Turks made good soldiers, lacking local loyalties yet retaining a strong sense of their own identity. So it was with the Turks employed by the Samanids, with dramatic and lasting effects. Over time the Turkish troops acquired their own officers, who were used as local governors and inherited the possessions of the slain,

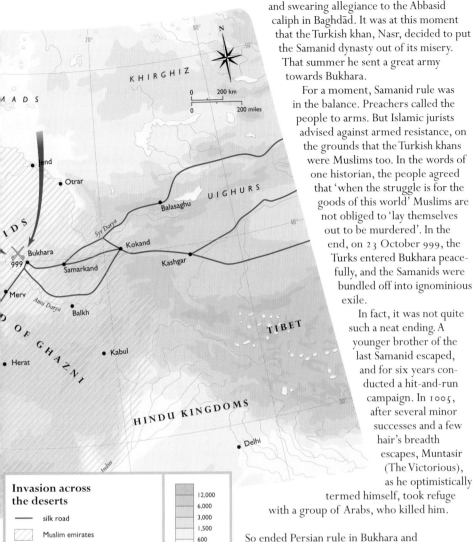

and swearing allegiance to the Abbasid caliph in Baghdād. It was at this moment that the Turkish khan, Nasr, decided to put the Samanid dynasty out of its misery. That summer he sent a great army towards Bukhara.

For a moment, Samanid rule was in the balance. Preachers called the people to arms. But Islamic jurists advised against armed resistance, on the grounds that the Turkish khans were Muslims too. In the words of one historian, the people agreed that 'when the struggle is for the goods of this world' Muslims are not obliged to 'lay themselves out to be murdered'. In the end, on 23 October 999, the Turks entered Bukhara peacefully, and the Samanids were bundled off into ignominious exile.

In fact, it was not quite such a neat ending. A younger brother of the last Samanid escaped, and for six years conducted a hit-and-run campaign. In 1005, after several minor successes and a few hair's breadth escapes, Muntasir (The Victorious), as he optimistically termed himself, took refuge with a group of Arabs, who killed him.

So ended Persian rule in Bukhara and Samarkand. It was an odd outcome. For generations, the Turks had been infidels to be slain, enslaved, and converted. But when they became Muslims, attitudes changed. They became acceptable, useful, and then powerful enough in their own right to turn from slaves into masters.

The Samanid dynasty was not the only one to suffer the consequences. Turkish military prowess plus Islam was a winning combination. The same process would continue for another 450 years, until the Turks worked their way through all Islam to Constantinople, and beyond. Bukhara's fall in 999 thus created a cascade of consequences, one of which was to intensify intractable ethnic and religious problems in the Balkans a thousand years later.

Invasion across the deserts

— silk road

▨ Muslim emirates

→ Turkish advances

▨	12,000
	6,000
	3,000
	1,500
	600
	0 ft

thus creating a power base that would act as a springboard when the time was right.

Throughout the 990s, the time was almost right on several occasions. In 992, perhaps in collaboration with rebels, the Turkish khan Bughra chased the amir, Nuh, from Bukhara. Luckily for Nuh, Bughra fell ill and died, allowing Nuh to return. Five years later, a flurry of alliances, betrayals and battles between half a dozen protagonists — one of them Mahmud of Ghazni (p. 80) — was interrupted by the coincidental deaths of four leaders, including Nuh. Backed by a Samanid rebel, a Turkish general, Begtuzun, entered Bukhara in February 999, blinded the amir, expelled him and replaced him with their own puppet. Mahmud outflanked his Turkish rivals by turning from his nominal overlords, the Samanids,

6

Mahmud, Scourge of Northern India

How the son of a slave became a career iconoclast, built a short-lived empire and brought Islam to north-west India.

By 1000, eastern Islam – today's Iran and Afghanistan – had acquired a dictator who was extending Islam's boundaries while serving his own hunger for empire.

Turkish in origin, he emerged from the peculiar and ever-shifting mix of Arab, Persian and Turkish cultures that disputed the desert-and-oasis lands of southern Central Asia (p. 79). In the late 10th century, when the Samanid rulers of Bukhara routinely used Turkish officers as local governors (p. 78), one of them, Alp-tigin ('tigin' being a Turkish title), conquered most of present-day Afghanistan and became its governor, administering his domains from Ghazni, which stood on the crest of a great plateau 150 km (100 miles)

south of Kabul, dominating the route into India.

After Alp-tigin's death, several of his Turkish officers inherited command in sequence, until one, Sebuk-tigin, proved a lasting success. By 997 he was in effect the undeclared ruler, on behalf of his nominal overlord Nuh, in Bukhara, of a province reaching from the Oxus (Amu-Darya) across today's eastern Iran and Afghanistan. In that same year, both Sebuk-tigin and Nuh died.

Sebuk-tigin's son, Mahmud, then aged 26, was presented with an opportunity that comes to few: an army, a province, and suddenly no overlord. His only problem was that his father had named a younger brother, Ismail, as successor. Mahmud, experienced in both fighting and politics, did not let his father's wishes stand in his way. He turned on his brother, imprisoned him, and then sent him into exile.

That put him in a good position to take advantage of revolution in the Samanid Empire. In 999, when the Turks chased the Samanids from their home bases of Bukhara and Samarkand (p. 79), Mahmud quickly declared allegiance to the caliph in Baghdād, who acknowledged Mahmud as the lesser of two evils, terming him his 'right hand of government'. So he proved to be, in his own interests more than the caliph's, seizing Samanid lands and those of half a dozen lesser dynasties, and fighting off his own Turkish rivals three times. In the next 30 years he pushed his frontiers west almost to the Persian Gulf, south to the Arabian Sea and eastwards through Afghanistan, creating the greatest empire since the Abbasids at their height.

It was in northern India, in the Punjab and today's Rajasthan, that his conquests had the most lasting effect. From 1000 onwards, when he made his first tentative foray, he was drawn by one thing: loot, which he needed to finance his campaigns in Persia. In the autumn of 1001 he took 15,000 horsemen towards Peshawar, where the local ruler, Jaipal, opposed him with 12,000 cavalry, 30,000 footsoldiers and 300 war-elephants. On 27 November, Mahmud's cavalry scattered Jaipal's forces, leaving 5,000 of them dead. The victory gave Mahmud the beginnings of a vast fortune. Jaipal, captured together with 15 sons and grandsons, paid 250,000 dinars and 50 elephants for his freedom, leaving a son and grandson as hostages. The humiliation was too much for Jaipal: he burned himself to death the following year.

That was the first of some 16 campaigns in India, in which Mahmud showed himself a general of genius, as fearless in battle as he was ruthless. One source records that he was wounded 72 times in the course of his campaigning life. In 1008, a campaign against an alliance of local rulers in present-day Lahore ended in Mahmud's capture of a fort, Nagarkot, which contained a

The Poet and the Iconoclast

For all his destructiveness, Mahmud financed a court of a sophistication surprising in one whose father had been a pagan nomad. He set up a university, and employed 400 poets, rewarding them with 'elephant-loads' of gold and silver. Among them was one of Islam's greatest scientists and scholars, al-Biruni, brought as a prisoner from his native Khwarazm, and who then among his many works wrote a history of Mahmud's Indian campaigns.

Another was Abul Qasim Firdawsi, Persia's most famous medieval poet. His stay in Ghazni, though, was brief and ended in bitterness. Firdawsi spent a good deal of his long life (c.935–c.1020) in his Persian homeland, Khurasan, writing the Shah-Nama, a history of the kings of Persia in nearly 60,000 sonorous couplets – over twice the length of

the Iliad – which is still revered by Iranians as their national epic. By the time he had finished it in about 1010, Khurasan was part of Mahmud's empire. Firdawsi was ageing and impoverished. Many people copied his great work, he said, 'but I received in return only praise.' So he turned to Mahmud – no Persian, certainly, but now the greatest Muslim ruler of his time.

According to an anecdote by the 12th-century writer Nizami-yi Arudi, the king offered 60,000 dirhams, one for each couplet. Then came second thoughts. Firdawsi was a Persian Shi'ite, Mahmud a Turkish Sunni, and other court-poets were jealous. Mahmud backtracked, and handed over 20,000 dirhams. Perhaps most galling of all was Mahmud's indifference – 'such a monarch,' Firdawsi wrote later, 'so generous, so shining among the sovereigns, did not glance at my poem.'

Insulted beyond measure, the poet stormed off with his fee to have a bath, 'and on coming out bought a drink of sherbet (a sort

of beer) and divided the money between the bathman and the sherbet-seller.' Then, fearing Mahmud's anger, he fled to the court of a local ruler in Tus, in northern Persia.

Years later, when Mahmud was bearing yet more treasure back from an Indian campaign, a local chief quoted some beautiful verses to him. Mahmud asked whose verse it was. 'Poor Abul Qasim Firdawsi composed it,' came the reply. 'He who laboured for five and twenty years to complete such a work, and reaped from it no advantage.' Mahmud was shamed. 'I deeply regret that this noble man was disappointed by me,' he said, and ordered him to be sent 60,000 dinars-worth of indigo – a stupendous sum.

By the time the huge gift was arranged, it was too late. As the camel train arrived in Tus, Firdawsi's coffin was being carried out. His daughter haughtily refused the gift, which was sold off on Mahmud's orders, the proceeds being used to restore a local rest-house.

temple of legendary wealth. He netted another fortune in coins, gold and silver ingots, a collapsible house of silver measuring 27 by 14 metres (90 by 45 feet), and a vast linen tent with poles of gold and silver. It was more than enough to beautify Ghazni and finance future raids.

Year followed year, raid followed raid, each one aiming at some rich temple, each one starting at harvest-time and ending with a rapid retreat beyond the Punjabi rivers before they were swollen by monsoon rains. One by one, local sultans were swept away (one of them, Daud of Multan, was an Ismaili Muslim – Mahmud slew co-religionists as well as Hindus). In 1018 Mahmud advanced again, to Mathura, Krishna's mythological birthplace; then on down the Ganges to Kannauj, northern India's greatest city; and so to Kalinjar, an immense star-shaped fortress, with seven gates, one for each of the known planets. This proved too strong even for Mahmud. He made peace with the sultan, Ganda, defining the far eastern limits of his authority, returning with more booty in 1023 to embellish Ghazni.

Finally, in his most famous exploit, Mahmud undertook a 1,000-km (650-mile) march across the Thar Desert of north-west India to the coastal town of Somnath. Here on the shore stood a statue, which Hindus worshipped as the linga or phallus of Mahadeva, and which they claimed was 30,000 years old. Its fame was legendary. Since it was washed by the tide, Hindus proclaimed that even the moon and ocean were perpetually occupied in worshipping it. Pilgrims came in their tens of thousands, numbers that had increased as Mahmud's rampage destroyed lesser shrines. Its wealth, flowing from the 10,000 surrounding villages and the crowds of pilgrims, matched the veneration in which it was held: 1,000 Brahmins presided over its rituals, 300 musicians and dancers performed at the temple gates, and every day relays of runners brought water 800 km (500 miles) from the Ganges to bathe it. The linga was housed in a stone temple, beneath a pyramidal roof supported by 56 teak columns and topped by 14 golden orbs. Surrounding it were gold and silver idols and jewelled chandeliers, while nearby hung a 180-kg (400-pound) bell on a golden chain. How could Mahmud resist such treasure?

It took his 30,000 cavalrymen, with two camels each as water-carriers, six weeks to get there from Multan. In the two-day assault in January 1026, some 50,000 Hindus are said to have died, either in the temple or in the shallows as they tried to escape. Mahmud did not linger. He seized the treasure – according to one estimate, 20 million dinars-worth, some 85 tonnes in gold – and burned the temple. (Though today's temple is a later reconstruction, with little hint of past glories, its museum preserves a few statues and friezes that survived Mahmud's attack.)

His return was not so easy – it took three months – but he had accomplished one of the greatest feats of military adventure in the history of Islam, or, if you prefer, one the greatest acts of desecration in Hindu history. To Muslims, he became an epitome of courage, skill and crusading energy; to Hindus, he was a thieving iconoclast, his army a juggernaut of destruction.

His empire as a whole did not long outlast his death in 1030 (though Ghaznavid rule in Ghazni itself endured another 150 years). Ten years after his death, his son was defeated by the Turks, who began their long expansion westwards. But the effects of his most destructive conquests endured. The Punjab, its economy ruined, fell to later Muslim invaders, and became the heart of Islam in India. It is in part thanks to Mahmud that the subcontinent is divided in religion, that Pakistan and Bangladesh exist, that Kashmir remains a disputed borderland.

Ghaznavid Empire

under Mahmud's direct rule

under Mahmud's suzerainty

campaign, 1025–6

Beneath its later accretions, the temple at Somnath preserves something of the aura of wealth that attracted Mahmud's attention.

Judaism: A Faith Toughened by Trials

In the shadow of Islam, the Jews preserved the old, adapted to the new, and ensured a foundation for their survival.

Across and beyond the Islamic world, the Jews formed a diffuse network of communities linked by religion, culture and trade.

Once an agricultural people, the Jews under Muslim rule came to dominate long-distance commerce. Known as 'Rhadanites' (probably deriving from the name of the Jewish quarter in Baghdād), Jewish merchants created trade routes that ran from North Africa to the Middle East and India, then north of the Caucasus through the lands of the Khazars (a Turkish people whose trade-loving elite had actually converted to Judaism) to Russia, Germany, France and thus full circle to Spain. Islam, Orthodoxy, Catholicism, paganism – all were linked by Judaism.

The Muslim takeover made the preservation of a centralized Jewish authority even more essential. That authority was underwritten by common beliefs, practices and languages (in the Muslim world, Jews used Judaeo-Arabic, Arabic written in Hebrew characters). But it was threatened by four main channels of dispute: between the academies of the two great regional centres of Judaism, Babylon and Palestine, in present-day Iraq and Israel (both of which had produced versions of the Talmud, the book of law, ethics and information that governs every aspect of Jewish life); between sects; between the academies and the supreme political authority, the Exilarch, a highly esteemed member of Baghdād's establishment; and finally between central authorities and the distant Jewish communities in North Africa and southern Spain.

Steadily the academies acquired secular as well as religious power, with Jerusalem shepherding local communities and Baghdād guiding more distant communities in North Africa, southern Europe and Persia. Since many North African Jews were emigrants from the Baghdād area – 'Babylon' – the Jewish community centred on Baghdād gained dominance.

By 1000, the geonim (*gaon*, 'head') of the two Babylonian academies, Sura and Pumbedita, had become the greatest authorities over Judaism in Muslim lands. They were not, however, supreme – in 1006, the revered Hai ben Sherira of Baghdād's Pumbedita Academy failed to have his rule accepted by Spanish rabbis. When Hai died in 1038, aged 91, the great age of the geonim died with him.

Division, in what some call outright heresy, also came from those who questioned the rabbinical tradition and its rich oral heritage. This group, the Karaites (from the Hebrew meaning 'to study the Scriptures'), arose in the 8th century to proclaim the absolute authority of the Bible. In their view, God, not Man, made the Law, which had no need of rabbis and their oral traditions as recorded in the Talmud to interpret it. Their puritanical fundamentalism set them apart from mainstream Judaism. But the faith nevertheless inspired both brilliant scholars and determined missionaries, eager to

The influence of the academies

— Rhadanite trade route

● major commercial centre

Jerusalem, and its influence

Baghdād, and its influence

✡✡ major Jewish communities

area under Muslim control

area under Christian control

other religions

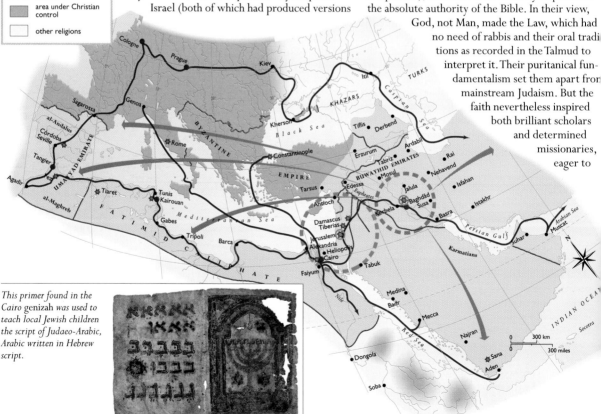

This primer found in the Cairo genizah was used to teach local Jewish children the script of Judaeo-Arabic, Arabic written in Hebrew script.

shepherd their scattered flock back to the Promised Land. Through the 10th century, it spread from its Middle Eastern heartland through the Diaspora, westward through North Africa, north into the Byzantine Empire, and east towards Bukhara and Samarkand. In the heart of Zion, Jerusalem, the 'roses' – as they termed themselves, as opposed to the Rabbinical 'thorns' – formed a majority of Jews around the turn of the millennium. Some 27,000 remain in Israel today, with several thousand more in the USA.

A further source of disunity was the growing independence of the Jews of North Africa and Spain. A popular legend of the 990s captures a historical truth: in the Legend of the Four Captives, four sages are captured by pirates and ransomed by four different communities, each of which is then established as an independent centre. The centres, which vary in their identity, may be seen as Egypt, Tunisia, Spain and Europe.

Certainly, the Tunisian town of Kairouan (Kayrawan or Qairwan in other spellings), the religious centre from which the Arabs had launched their conquest of all the Maghreb, emerged as a Jewish base of importance, with an eminent talmudic school. Soon after the dawn of the millennium, two Kairouan rabbis, Hananel ben Hushiel and Nissim ben Jacob ibn Shahin, wrote the earliest commentaries on the Babylonian Talmud. Nissim, the head of the Kairouan academy, was also renowned as the author of the first stories in medieval Hebrew.

In Islamic Spain, Jews had welcomed the Islamic conquest as a release from Catholic oppression, and made important contributions to science, poetry, philosophy and Biblical studies. On Islam's borderland, Toledo had two synagogues, where Jewish scholars adept in Hebrew, Latin, Greek and Arabic formed important intellectual links between the ancient world and the three contemporary cultures.

Córdoba, which had a school of Talmudic studies, was fertile soil for Jews before and after al-Mansur's extremism. In the mid 10th century, Caliph Abd al-Rahman's vizier had been the Jewish physician and scholar Hisdai ibn Shaprut, famous for an attempt to forge a link with the Jewish ruler of the Khazars, Joseph. After the Córdoban state fell, the vizier of one of its successors, Granada, was Samuel ha-Nagid (993–1055/6), author of treatises on Jewish law and poems that mark the beginning of a great age of Jewish poetry in Spain. As the leader of Spanish Jewry – hence his nickname *nagid*, meaning 'governor' – he worked hard to strengthen Jewish links across the Muslim world. He married his son to the daughter of Kairouan's leader, Nissim, and among many charitable works he supplied all Jerusalem's synagogues with olive oil.

The Cairo Genizah: A Hidden Treasure of Jewish Archives

In about 1003, when al-Hakim (p. 74) turned against the Jews and other non-Ismaili sects, Cairo's wealthy Jewish leaders decided to save Jewish records in a special sanctuary, a genizah, built into their greatest religious centre, the building now known as the Ben Ezra Synagogue in Fustat (Old Cairo). Many synagogues had a genizah for old bibles, prayer books and ritual objects, but this one was unique. The elders stored away anything written in Jewish script, whatever its origins or language (Hebrew, Arabic, Persian, Spanish, Greek, even Yiddish). For over 200 years the collection built up. Then, perhaps in the face of some unrecorded outbreak of violence, the room was sealed, and forgotten for 700 years.

In 1896, two learned, intrepid and wealthy Scotswomen, widowed twins named Agnes Lewis and Margaret Gibson, were on a trip to Cairo, where they bought a bundle of ancient Hebrew manuscripts from a dealer. Back home in Cambridge, they showed them to the eminent Romanian-Jewish scholar, Solomon Schechter, the university's Reader in Talmudic. He was astonished to discover that one of the fragments was intellectual dynamite. It was a leaf of a 10th-century copy of the book written by Joshua ben Sira in the 2nd century, but relegated from the Bible to the Apocrypha. Until then, it had been known only in Greek.

If there was one such fragment, there should be more. But where? The word 'Fustat' appeared on several fragments. Backed by the Master of St John's College, Charles Taylor, Schechter headed for Cairo. There the Chief Rabbi showed him several possible sources. One, of course, was the newly opened Genizah itself, from which many documents had already been sold elsewhere. Instantly, Schechter recognized it as a treasure trove that demanded proper preservation and research. With the Chief Rabbi's agreement, Schechter filled sacks with documents and shipped them to Cambridge.

In a fury of excitement, Schechter, Taylor and several others set about recording and storing the 140,000 items – approaching half a million individual pages. Such an immense and significant task attracted eminent scholars, but not the necessary official commitment. Disillusioned, Schechter left England in 1902 to head the Jewish Theological Seminary in New York, where he remained until his death in 1915.

In Cambridge, it took half a century to assess the first 30,000 fragments. Only then did the archive receive the backing it

Cambridge, 1898: Solomon Schechter pores over some of the genizah's time-damaged documents.

deserved, with the founding of the Taylor–Schechter Genizah Research Unit in 1974. Since then, the unit has completed the task of conserving the remaining 110,000 items – 32 crates – but assessment of the finds will absorb scholars for decades to come.

In a century of work, scholars have come to see this as one of the world's greatest stores of medieval manuscripts, and of unique significance for Jews. The items throw light on every aspect of medieval Jewish culture: prayer, education, poetry, music, science, philosophy, history, commerce, court records, private letters, a 10th-century children's reader, references to medieval massage techniques. The trove unveils relations between Karaites and Rabbanites, and between Jews, Muslims and Christians. It preserves a text by the heretical Zadokites who wrote the Dead Sea Scrolls, found in 1947. It gives insights into the evolution of the Midrash, the Talmud, synagogue practices, Hebrew and Judaeo-Arabic. It is a bridge between the Biblical past and modern Judaism, and a symbol of Jewish tenacity in the face of persecution and dispersal.

ASIA

Two Suns and Their Planets

Of the two suns of Asian civilization, India radiated the more brightly, casting a glow of scholarship and religious fervour that reached to Japan. Its ancient traditions arose from more ancient roots in the rich plains of the Indus, dating back to before 2000 BC. Though largely protected from invasion by mountain bulwarks, India's culture was largely defined by Aryan invaders. From their presence sprang the complex and enduring system of castes that still divides and governs Indians, and the rich pantheon of Hindu gods and goddesses.

Another of India's greatest legacies arose in the 6th century BC, when the Buddha, Gautama Siddhārtha, taught that truth and spiritual freedom were to be sought through self-denial. This offered an escape not only from the round of human suffering, but also from the rigidity of the caste system. In the end, the caste system and Hinduism predominated in India itself. By 1000, Buddhism had become one of India's most influential exports, spreading down the south-east Asian peninsula to the Indonesian archipelago.

By then, India's patchwork of kingdoms was being reformed, in the north by the first major incursion of Islam in the destructive form of Mahmud of Ghazni (p. 80), and in the south by the rise of Tamil culture and its driving political force, the Chola Empire. Here, geography underlay politics. The highlands lay to the west, lowlands to the east. In both, kingdoms sought to control the eastbound rivers. From the confusion of half a dozen southern kingdoms the Cholas emerged supreme, reaching out to seize Ceylon (Sri Lanka), and jousting for dominance with the two great empires of south-east Asia, Kambuja (as Cambodia then was) and Śrīvijaya in Sumatra.

These were not the only states in south-east Asia. On the lowlands of the south-east Asian peninsula, Kambuja had three rivals. One to the north-west, on the upper Irrawaddy, was growing at the expense of the older Mon state lower down the river. This was the core of what would become Burma, centred on its capital Pagan, soon to become one of the world's greatest Buddhist sites. To the east, controlling the coast of what is now central Vietnam, lay Champa, supplying exotic forest products like camphor, rhinoceros horn and kingfisher feathers to China. In the north-east was the Viet state of Dai Co Viet, which had prised itself from Chinese control in the mid 9th century, and in 1000 was already beginning to rival Champa for the east coast.

By comparison with India, China was culturally the less radiant, but her size and economic power ensured her influence. In 1000, China had the world's most ancient surviving civilization, with written records dating from 500 BC, references back to 750 BC and archaeological evidence from 1,000 years before that. Its heart was the 'Chinese Mesopotamia' of the two great rivers of the north and centre, the Yangtze and the Yellow River (Huang He). Together, they nourished another sort of river, a stream of culture, language and administration. From this spun artistic and technical innovations: great cities and roads, luxury goods and trade routes – one of which ran west across the western deserts and mountains to the Middle East and Europe. All Asia breathed China's air, and most adapted, by choice or constraint.

This vast cultural unity lacked historical continuity. In fast-forward, a sequence of Chinese historical atlases would look like a film-loop of a growing cell, constantly buffeted by the surrounding 'barbarian' cells, constantly dividing and re-uniting, nuclei jumping this way and that, until a return to a new beginning back on the rich loess of the northern plains.

Under the T'ang Dynasty (618–907), Chinese civilization had seen something of a golden age. The T'ang Empire covered the heartland of modern China, with a tongue of territory reaching west to the Himalayas. The cosmopolitan capital, Ch'ang-an (today's Xian), attracted merchants and scholars from India and Iran, while its armies imposed unity and guarded the western borders against the threat of Islam. Central Asia, Tibet, Korea, Japan, south-east Asia – all felt T'ang influence.

Unity and continuity were underpinned in part by China's remarkable civil service, a force at once deeply conservative and surprisingly open. Its members, tens of thousands strong, had been imbued with the morality and language of the philosopher Kung Fu-tzu (551–479 BC) – 'Master' Kung, Latinized by 17th-century missionaries as Confucius – for over 1,000 years. This social and political bedrock was open to anyone who could pass its demanding exams. Learning, not breeding, was the key to success.

But Confucian conservatism and T'ang power were subject to long-term changes. One of these was the slow shift of population (roughly 50 million nationwide in the middle of the 8th century) from the northern grasslands to the richer soils of the Yangtze valley, where the farming of rice in paddy fields allowed numbers to grow. Between about 600 and 750, the population of North China fell from about 37 million to 26 million, while that of the lower Yangtze tripled to 10 million. The growth of towns brought increasing complexity. The first paper money dates from 650. Woodblock printing extended literacy after about 700.

Internal and external pressures multiplied. Peasants, who all too easily had their lives ruined by war, disease, famine, flood or taxation, tended to revolt, emerging from obscurity to make sudden marks on China's history. Imperial rule could no longer depend on its conscript armies. Empires arising on the western and northern borders posed new threats, forcing China to focus more on the coast. The old and glorious cosmopolitanism of the T'ang degenerated. Buddhism, though long established in Chinese society, was reduced by a xenophobic purge in the mid 9th century. Local warlords staged uprisings in remote areas. In the 880s, the T'ang capital, Chang'an – a place of perhaps two million inhabitants – was reduced to burnt ruins by 600,000 insurgents.

Eventually, in the early 10th century, the T'ang collapsed into a succession of five dynasties, all failing to impose their will on their own patch, let alone the 10 or so independent states to the south. In 960, the 'mandate of heaven' was handed to another dynasty, the Sung, with remarkable consequences.

As it happened, the Sung dynasty came to power just as two other central Asian peoples, the Tanguts and the Khitans, were also emerging from the flux of competing pastoral nomadic tribes. As the two new empires – Hsi-hsia and Liao – jockeyed for power with the Sung, western Chinese states in the late 10th century were caught in a chaotic dance of diplomacy, treaties, broken promises and wars. Farmers and pastoral nomads worked together no better then than they ever had, or ever would. It was this endemic instability that would, two centuries later, allow the Mongols their hour upon the world's stage.

Offshore lay Japan, close enough to feel China's breath, close enough to have ambitions of its own to rule on the mainland, but far enough for this rich and mild land to develop a unique culture. China offered a model of civilization, with firm central government, a rigorous bureaucracy and literary traditions. The Japanese copied, in their legal system, the style of their official histories, their religion (all the great Buddhist sects were inspired by Chinese originals), city-planning (the capital Heian, today's Kyōto, was modelled on Chang-an). Japan even used Chinese copper coins as its own currency.

Japan copied – and then modified. Its writing models the process: Chinese script remained in use but the Japanese also adapted it to create two entirely Japanese syllabaries (*hiragana* and *katagana*), with a consequent flowering of calligraphy and literature. Socially, too, the Japanese created something of their own that was the very reverse of their model: central authority eroded, localized clans ruling supreme.

This was a system that evolved unplanned in response to local conditions. In the 7th century, Japan's clans acknowledged an emperor. His court at Heian was a

Having spread through Asia for 1,000 years, Buddhism was established in its most easterly outpost, Japan, in the 6th century. This 11th-century painting on silk shows Fugen, a boddhisattva ('enlightenment-being' in Buddhist mythology), riding on an elephant.

powerful social and artistic lure, and observance of Shinto and Buddhist rites gave the island a strong cultural unity. But political unity was not easily imposed. Mountains cut the island into regions that worked better under local rule, even if that leader spent his time at court, occupied with rituals, social niceties and versifying.

Compared with civilizations elsewhere, Japan had much to recommend it. Since Japan had no enemies and no ambition for foreign conquest, there was no need for an army. The only national defence force, the coastguards of the west, fished and slept until they were disbanded. In Heian, the City of Peace, the only soldiers were the imperial bodyguard, whose lives were no more dangerous than those of beefeaters at the Tower of London. With no need for a vast flow of taxes (other than to fund imperial fancies), the system that emerged was marked by strong families made stronger by the grant of tax-free lands, a weak emperor, a hereditary bureaucracy and a court dominated by intrigue and empty ritual – all exact inversions of the traits that mark China's history. Even in its astonishingly rich artistic and intellectual life, which evolved with a steady awareness of Chinese precedents, Japan went its own way.

One family, the Fujiwara, proved supreme at manipulating Japan's unique social and political elements. Venerating the emperor, dominating court bureacracy, expert in intrigue, they married their daughters into the imperial family, and acted as regents, often persuading adult emperors to retire in favour of a compliant child-heir. High-minded officials complained about corruption, luxury, moral laxity and educational decline. But Fujiwara self-interest served the national interest surprisingly well, and for a surprisingly long time. For over 300 years, from 858 to 1185 (most of the so-called Heian Period), the Fujiwara were the country's puppet-masters. They prepared the way for the local military dictators, the shoguns, with their warrior culture, which dominated Japan until the arrival of Europeans in the 16th century.

China: The Success of the Sung

To western eyes, the millennium coincides neatly with a paradox: foreign threats to the stability of the nation, combined with an economic and cultural upsurge which has been called a Chinese Renaissance.

The Chinese, of course, did not know and would not have cared about a Christian millennial milestone. To them, it was the third year of the Emperor Cheng-tsung, a time when it was possible, after half a century of collapse, to nourish a cautious optimism.

Underlying the domestic changes was a new wealth growing from the paddy fields of the Yangtze. The bounty, which had been increasing for some 400 years, soared again after 1012 when a new variety of early-ripening rice appeared, producing two harvests every year. China's astonishingly detailed records show that the annual harvest of rice and cereals in the 11th century amounted to some 2.6 million tonnes.

From this surplus sprang population growth. Though numbers rose slowly by today's terms, they rose steadily, doubling in 500 years from about 53 million to over 100 million. Increases in food and population combined to stimulate a multiplicity of changes: political, economic, social, scientific, artistic.

In the mid 10th century, China was a patchwork of some ten major and dozens of minor independent states, with no central rule. In 960, a general, Chao K'uang-yin, seized the capital,

K'ai-feng, in a military coup and established a new dynasty, which he named Sung. Later events decreed that his dynasty be divided; they ruled as the Northern Sung for 175 years, after which defeat sent the remnants to Hangchow, where their rule continued as the Southern Sung until 1279.

The Sung effected a remarkable turnaround. Building on reforms initiated by the last in a line of five brief dynasties, the first and second Sung emperors took just 20 years to reconquer six independent kingdoms, imposing imperial rule across an area twice the size of western Europe. Expansion was halted only when the new mercenary armies ran up against the strong, ambitious empires emerging on China's borderlands: the Khitan Empire of Liao (p. 94), which had eaten into the north-east, the Tanguts of Hsi (Western)-hsia in the north-west, Yunnan in the south-west, and Vietnam.

The need for unity, efficiency and financial controls inspired reforms that provided public welfare by attacking privilege. The civil service became more independent, the emperor more presidential than dictatorial. Under the second emperor, T'ai-tsung (976–7), a council of state, responding to summaries of official reports, funnelled decisions past the emperor to three departments: economic and financial; military; and legal and personnel, which managed the civil service, with its demanding examinations. The civil service, which had formerly subjected limited numbers of hopefuls to many tests, was thrown open to a wider range of candidates in one examination. Brilliance had to be matched by character: candidates were backed by recommendations, but to limit favouritism the authors had to bear responsibility for their protégés. Later reforms tackled economic and social problems, setting up orphanages, hospitals, schools and grain reserves.

All of this revolutionized Chinese society. Self-supporting, patriarchal aristocratic estates continued to decline in importance. Ordinary people started tilling land for themselves, especially in the rich Yangtze valley. Taxes, once based on the number of people of working age, were now related to agricultural production. A new class of tenant-farmers emerged. These landowners, relying on a steward to manage the peasant workers, often lived as absentees in a town.

The changes released social and economic forces that have a remarkably modern ring. Peasants fled the countryside for the cities, seeking work in new industries – mining, metallurgy, ceramics, paper, printing, salt-works. It was as if the whole country was on the move. Carts and boats could be hired everywhere, carrying traders, merchants, artisans, and ordinary people in search of a better life.

Ch'ang-an

- ● Taoist monastery
- ● Buddhist monastery
- ● Manichean, Nestorian and Mazdaist church

N

0   1 km
0   1 mile

Imperial Park

Ch'ung-hs an Gate

Da-ming Palace

Imperial Park

Imperial Park

Chin-huang Gate

Imperial City

Ch'eng-tien Gate

Administrative centre

Hsing-ch'ing Palace

Ch'un-ming Gate

Western Market

Eastern Market

Yen-p'ing Gate

Yen-hsing Gate

Hibiscus gardens

Ming-te Gate

Ch'ü-chiang Lake

Sung China

K'ai-feng, inherited as the capital by the Sung, grew explosively, like many other cities. It had already burst over its inner circuit of walls, acquiring a second ring in 954. With the boom in commercial activity, markets soon sprang up outside these as well. This was a new type of city – lower-class, bustling with a life that ignored the old rules by which crafts and businesses had been limited to their own areas. Merchants and craftsmen banded together in guilds to protect their own interests. The streets thronged with shop assistants, inn-workers, street hawkers, and the domestic staff of merchants' houses, the crowds providing oppor-tunities for pickpockets, muggers and prostitutes of both sexes. The *wa-tzu* (entertainment quar-ters), with their story-tellers, actors, mime-artists, musicians, animal trainers and puppeteers, stayed open throughout the night.

Economically, the changes reinforced each other, creating a system of production and commerce that provided a new base for state finances. Reunification paved the way for a single economic unit based on Sung copper coins, which were issued in 'strings' of 1,000. In the year 1000 itself, the state issued 1.3 million such strings – 1.3 billion coins – in just one year. But coins are cumbersome. For over a century, provincial gov-ernments had been issuing certific-ates of deposit to rich merchants, who used them as cheques, so-called 'flying money'. In 1024 the state printed the first banknotes, which would become the main means of exchange for the next four centuries. Soon, merchants and financial officials were writing cheques that could be cashed in exchange offices across the empire.

Since more people were now freed from the need to grow food, more could work in other areas. The increase in manpower was matched by technical advances.

In porcelain, China led the world, with styles and glazes, particularly those from the royal kilns in K'ai-feng, which are still ranked among the greatest. Iron, copper, lead and tin all saw big increases in production. Explosives were used to blast out coal more quickly, hydraulic machinery kept mines free of water. In 1078, cast iron pro-duction exceeded 114,000 tonnes, while one iron foundry in Kiangsu province employed 3,600 workers – a respectable figure for a British foundry at the beginning of the Industrial Revolution 800 years later.

The products of all this enterprise were traded across the empire and beyond, a good proportion being carried along the 50,000-km (30,000-mile) network of waterways created by the Yangtze, its tributaries and the canals that linked Hangchow to

A late 10th-century hemp banner portrays a 3rd-century hero, Kuan-yü. Renowned for his loyalty to his leader, he became a favourite with Sung story tellers and artists keen to reassert their cultural heritage.

Chen-chiang and Yangchow to K'ai-feng. Luxury items like incense, ivory, ebony and sandalwood flowed in from abroad, paid for either in copper coins, which became common in every Asian country, or with tea, silk and silver.

China, once a predominantly agrarian economy, was rapidly becoming a state based on production, commerce and trade, with great benefits for state finances. In the early 11th century, income from taxes and monopolies began to rival revenues from agrarian taxes. The sums involved were staggering. Official receipts for one year (1077) included about 2 tonnes of silver, 5.5 billion copper coins, 100,000 tonnes of rice and cereal, and 2.6 million rolls of silk.

One major problem for the Sung was defence, especially along their northern and western frontiers. Conscription had not worked: conscripts failed to save K'ai-feng when it was ransacked by the Khitan in 947. The Sung policy of recruiting mercenaries did not work either. Under the threats from the Liao Empire of the Khitan (p. 94) and the Tangut Empire of Hsi-hsia (p. 96), numbers increased – from 378,000 in 975 to an astonishing 1.25 million under arms in 1045 – but standards dropped. Nomads refused to sign up. Recruiting officers became the scourge of the countryside; recruits were from the landless dregs of society; and discharged soldiers became bandits. Later reforms replaced the mercenaries by peasant militias, making regions responsible for their own defences, but meanwhile the Sung were never able to command the compliance of their ambitious neighbours. They discouraged attack with defences designed to frustrate nomadic cavalry: three million saplings planted, canals dug, 200,000 men placed in border garrisons. But the best defence proved a diplomatic one – the treaty of 1005, which removed Liao from the equation.

One consequence of the new threats from beyond the border and the poor state of the army was a new interest in weapons. A military treatise of 1044 mentions a flame-thrower with an ingenious double-acting piston which blew out a continuous jet of flaming paraffin. The most significant advance, however, was the development of gunpowder. For over a century, Chinese alchemists had known of a sort of gunpowder made from coal, saltpetre and sulphur. In 904–6, projectiles somehow filled or impregnated with this mixture had been used in warfare. By the early 11th century, Chinese generals had the use of catapult-launched grenades that would carry smoke and fire. Armourers also knew how to enclose the mixture in a container which exploded under the pressure of the fire within. This was in effect the first use of an explosive shell. The 11th century also saw the development of bamboo tubes filled with gunpowder – prototypes of rockets and mortars. Later, in the 13th century, these weapons were made of metal. They became known in the Islamic world and Europe after the Mongols adapted them and used them in their western campaigns.

Political and economic changes were matched by intellectual and artistic ones. This Renaissance, underpinned by new money, dismayed traditionalists, but also encouraged open-mindedness, curiosity, practicality. Fashions changed. Physical activity – hunting, soldiering – was out; Buddhist mysticism was out; the arts and sciences were in. The rich of the Sung Dynasty created an enduring image of the Chinese intellectual as the lover of garden design, calligraphy, book-collecting and art.

During the 10th century, printed texts became part of life for ordinary well-to-do families. With paper, which had been in use for centuries, and woodblock printing, used since about 800, printers produced the first printed texts. The first popular works – Buddhist texts, lexicons, manuals – appeared later in the same century. By 1000, printed texts were common, and many have survived. Some of the text collections were massive. One year, 983, saw the completion of two such works: the basic Buddhist texts – 260,000 pages engraved on two-page blocks – and an encylopedia of 1,000 chapters. Sung institutions built up vast libraries – the imperial palace library in K'ai-feng, founded in 978, had 80,000 volumes.

Not long after this, around the mid 11th century, came the first use of movable type, establishing a tradition of typography long predating printing in Europe. Though the techniques were different – Chinese woodblock printing did not need a press, and therefore could not mass-produce so effectively – woodblock printing was cheap and easy to revise, whether for text or illustration, and gave literate Chinese a range of high-quality illustrated texts far beyond anything available in Muslim lands and Europe for another 500 years. This combination of technical advance and curiosity soon inspired a mass of works on a huge range of subjects, from the broad-ranging – astronomy, architecture, geography, mathematics – to the minutely specialized, like a *Manual of Crabs*, written by a certain Fu Kung in 1059, and a catalogue of ancient inscriptions compiled in 1063.

This was just a foundation for what was to follow: a flowering of art, philosophy, history and science, that would make the three centuries that ended with the Mongol invasions one of the great ages of intellectual achievement, and social ferment. It was an age in which the Chinese sought to revitalize an ancient faith that state and society, administration and education, could be united, and take civilization forward to a new level.

A Genius for Seafaring

At the beginning of the Sung Dynasty, two economic factors – the boom in trade and the closure of Central Asia by rival empires – drove forward the evolution of one of China's greatest icons: the high-seas junk.

The design that emerged from centuries of trial-and-error evolution was probably refined in the lower Yangtze, where the great river merges with the ocean. These were superb vessels. A typical large junk, capable of holding 1,000 people, had four decks, watertight holds, six masts and twelve mainsails, of either canvas or matting. With a drop-keel, it could sail in shallow waters. With its canvas sails, it could sail close to the wind, while those of rigid matting provided an extra turn of speed with following winds. The vertical rudder gave easy control under sail, and oars allowed for manoeuvring close inshore and in a dead calm.

Junks carried Chinese goods to every Asian culture, from Korea and Japan, southwards to south-east Asia, and on round the coasts to India, even the Persian Gulf and the rich markets of the Islamic world. Every captain would have been expert in inland navigation, using an intimate knowledge of currents and depth; and Sung maps were the best in the world at the time.

Quite possibly he would also have had the use of a compass. Lodestones had long been used by geomancers to establish the most auspicious alignment of buildings, and the first maritime compasses were recorded in 1090, probably several decades after they were actually in use on board, and two centuries before they came into wide use in Europe.

'Going up the River at the Spring Festival' – an ink-on-silk drawing from a Sung scroll records a busy scene on the Yangtze.

One of the many unforseeable consequences of this Renaissance was its impact beyond China's frontiers. Almost all its great advances – paper, compass, stern-post rudder, gunpowder, printing – became seeds which, when planted in Europe, became part of another Renaissance, which would eventually allow European technology to match, then outdo, the society from which these novelties had sprung.

2 | Tibet's Dark Age

Tibet, once a great empire, had collapsed into anarchy. But this time of confusion and terror inspired the beginning of a religious revival that would underlay the nation's later cultural strength.

Emerging from prehistory in the 7th century, Tibet had acquired an empire that spanned the high heartland and northern deserts from the Chinese capital of Ch'ang-an, over halfway across present-day China, to the Oxus (Syr Darya). But tensions increased when a 9th-century king became a fanatical advocate of Buddhism, which, despite being made the state religion in 779, had made little headway against the Tibetans' original shamanistic faith, Bon. Or so Buddhist sources portray this and later events, obscuring personal, social and political complexities with a partisan agenda which has Buddhism emerging victorious after a time of persecution. But this may have been a straightforward power struggle, as Buddhist monks, deriving wealth and power from their newly founded monasteries, challenged traditional rulers. In any event, Bon nobles revolted. In 838 they killed the king by twisting his head off his body, and installed his younger brother, who was himself assassinated five years later. Buddhists were persecuted, monasteries destroyed and Indian monks expelled, and the work

of translating texts stopped. The empire collapsed into a patchwork of minor kings and feudal lords.

One final attempt to restore the empire ended in a defeat by the Uighur army in 966. Politically, Tibet fell into a historical black hole until the arrival of the Mongols in the mid 13th century. Prince fought prince, family displaced family. Without central rule, with the monasteries in ruins, there were few records.

From this wreckage, Buddhism re-emerged. It took many forms, predominantly Mahayana, with its complex, mystical belief in the multiple manifestations of Buddha and transcendent beings, or *bodhisattvas*. This and other forms were embraced with a particular emphasis on Tantric Buddhism, with its emphasis on spells, mystic syllables and diagrams, as the highest and best type of practice. In Tibet, though, all Buddhist beliefs and practices took on peculiarly Tibetan forms by adapting Bon chants, rituals and deities.

The seed of revival in the east grew from the action of three Buddhist monks, later known as the Three Men of Khams, who escaped the persecutions and fled with their books of monastic discipline to Amdo, present-day Qinghai, on the headwaters of the Yellow River. There they lived in a cave, devoting themselves to re-establishing monastic life. The new order carried Buddhism west to the Tibetan heartland.

From about 950 onwards, a monk from Amdo

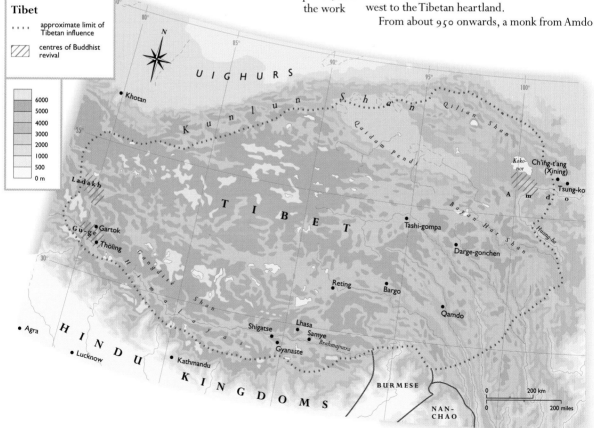

Tibet

. . . . approximate limit of Tibetan influence

centres of Buddhist revival

| 6000 |
| 5000 |
| 4000 |
| 3000 |
| 2000 |
| 1000 |
| 500 |
| 0 m |

named Klumes (or kLu-mes in one of several possible transliterations) drove forward the Buddhist renaissance. In what is known as the 'second introduction of Buddhism', old monasteries were repaired, new ones founded. Klumes himself restored Tibet's first monastery at Samye, on the Brahmaputra, south-east of Lhasa.

A similar but better-documented revival occurred in the far west, where a member of the royal family had fled when the empire collapsed. He and his descendants created three tiny kingdoms: Mar-yul (roughly present-day Ladakh), Purang (sPu-hrangs) and Gu-ge, on the upper Sutlej river, near the borders of present-day India.

Gu-ge in particular became a centre for the Buddhist revival in the western Himalayas, then populated by Tibetans. The Gu-ge king became the 'royal monk', Ye-shes-'od (or Yeshe-Ö). He arranged for 21 young Tibetans to study in India; 19 died there. One of the survivors returned after 17 years, and went on to become one of Tibet's most famous medieval scholars, Rinchen Zangpo, the 'Great Translator' (958 – 1055). He founded a monastic complex at Thöling which remained in use until parts of it were reduced to ruins in the Cultural Revolution.

This period was marked by intensive programmes of building and restoring monasteries, and translating texts. One of the works translated into Tibetan was the *Kalacakratantra*, which set out Tibet's 60-year calendar, with its cycle of 12 animals and 5 elements. The greatest expert on this system was an Indian teacher and master, Atisha. Ye-shes-'od issued an invitation to Atisha, to be backed by an offer of gold which he set about collecting himself, with tragic and significant results.

On one of his gold-collecting expeditions, Ye-shes-'od was captured by Karluks, a tribe of eastern Turkestan. They put a price on his life: either he had to convert to Islam or pay his own weight in gold. He chose to pay. But when a princely nephew arrived with the gold, he didn't have quite enough: he lacked the weight of the royal monk's head. The Karluks refused to release him. The nephew promised to return with the outstanding gold, but Ye-shes-'od declined, saying that he was old, and it was better to spend the cash on Atisha. Sorrowfully, the prince obeyed, leaving his uncle to be executed.

Atisha duly arrived in Gu-ge at the age of 60 in 1042 – a vital date, because it acts as the baseline for Tibet's lunar calendar with its 60-year cycles. Atisha stayed in Thöling monastery for three years, then travelled in Tibet until his death in 1054. In that time he laid the foundations for Buddhism's fully fledged revival. Reting monastery, founded in 1056, was associated with

A Tibetan Outpost on China's Fringes

The high, windswept grassland around Lake Kokonor, now the eastern end of China's Qinghai province, was in 1000 a remnant of the old Tibetan Empire that still dominated the trade route westwards. Known as Tsung-ko (Tsongkha in Tibetan), this remote region was for almost two centuries the pivot of three cultures: Tibetan to the south-west, Tangut to the north, Sung to the east.

In 1001, a warlord, P'an-lo-chih, came to power, perhaps with the backing of the Sung as a counterweight to rising Tangut power. It was he who arranged the ambush of the Tangut leader Li Chi-ch'ien in 1003 (p. 96), an act for which he was himself assassinated by Tanguts shortly afterwards.

After a brief interregnum, a boy-king was found and in 1008, at the age of 12, he was enthroned as Ku-sso-lu – the start of a reign that would last for 57 years. In 1015, Tsung-ko sent an embassy to the Sung, offering their 60–70,000 troops to head off Tangut advances. No lasting alliance followed. In 1032, after the Liao pushed further south, Ku-ssu-lo set up his headquarters in Ch'ing-t'ang (today's Xining), which remained an independent base controlling east–west trade until the Sung finally took it over early in the 12th century.

Thöling monastery, once the heart of the ancient kingdom of Gu-ge, played a crucial role in the revival of Buddhism in Tibet in the late 10th century. It was in use for another 1,000 years, until 1966, when it was ransacked during the Cultural Revolution.

him through his favourite disciple, Bromston.

In 1076, a great council in Gu-ge, linking eastern and western Buddhists, put a stamp on the revival. The translation of Buddhist literature into Tibetan accelerated. This was to prove vital work for a religion that was to decline in India under the pressure of Islam. Tibet, with its massive collection of translations, was to become the chief inheritor of Indian Buddhism.

Atisha's pupil, Dromtönpa, founded the Kadampa order, and Atisha's teachings were absorbed by the 15th-century Gelugpa school, the inspiration for the subsequent revival of monastic discipline. But the struggle between Bon and Buddhism was not yet over. After lasting almost 1,000 years, it finally ended in the 17th century, when Gelugpas, with Mongol help, killed the last political claimant to the throne. The way was open for the rule of the joint spiritual and political kings, the Dalai Lamas.

The Liao: A Challenge from the North

On China's Central Asian borders an empire emerged, created by a people virtually unknown to the outside world, yet whose name would for Europeans become synonymous with China itself.

To the north-east of China, in the grasslands east of present-day Mongolia, pastoral nomads known as Khitan had formed a confederation of tribes in the 9th century. Since they left few records, they remain a shadowy people to historians. But their impact was immense. They, like the Huns, Juan-juan, Turks, Tartars and Uighurs before them, were another of those nomadic groups that wrote the agenda for much of China's foreign policy, and defined its northern and western borders.

The Khitan (or Ch'itan) claimed to have orginated from a tribe of pastoral nomads living in the valley of the river now known by its Mongol name, Khar Moron (also transliterated as Shira Muren, or Siramuren). To the Chinese it was the Hsi Liao, the western branch of the River Liao. By the 8th century, the Khitan were a hierarchy of tribes ruled by a chieftain. Like other pastoral nomadic groups, they could not build up the kind of wealth that Chinese city-dwellers and farmers could amass, and relied on trade and war to supply luxury goods. For two centuries, they remained relatively impotent and impoverished. But in about 907 the tribes were welded into a nation by a chief named A-pao-chi, later sanctified as the emperor T'ai-tsu (Liao rulers, like their

Chinese counterparts, had half a dozen personal and honorific names; T'ai-tsu was his post-mortem 'temple title').

Under T'ai-tsu, the Khitan expanded fast, absorbing the little neighbouring Chinese-style kingdom of Po-hai, north of Korea, and driving west and north into the rolling heart of present-day Mongolia, creating an empire that would in its mid-11th-century heyday be over 2,000 km across, twice the size of Germany and France. In his homeland, T'ai-tsu adopted the Chinese custom of using forced labour to build a Supreme Capital (Shang-ching) with 15 km (10 miles) of walls, palaces, ministries, and Confucian, Buddhist and Taoist temples.

After T'ai-tsu's death, during a time when China collapsed into separate provinces, the Khitans seized their chance, driving west to K'ai-feng itself and sweeping on to Peking. The assault on K'ai-feng over-extended the army, and it retreated in disorder after five months. But they held Peking and renamed it Nanjing – their 'southern capital'. The emperor named his newly established empire 'Liao', after the Chinese name for the river of his homeland. The two empires, Sung and Liao, now faced each other along a frontier that stretched from the Yellow Sea to the Yellow River, with both sides eyeing border territories held by the other. Further war was virtually inevitable.

In 983, an 11-year-old, Lung-hsü, inherited the throne. Under his imperial name of Sheng-tsung, he would reign for the next 48 years. But until he came of age, power was in the

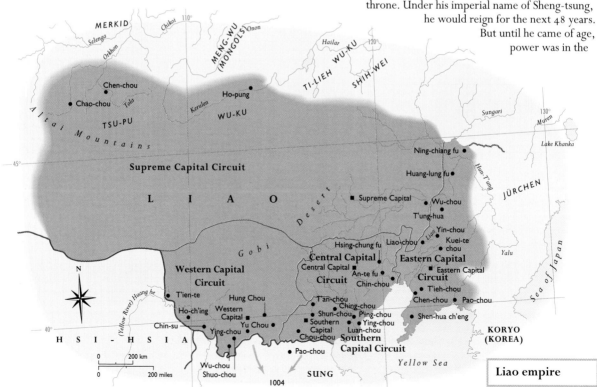

A silver-and-gilt Liao crown displays imperial symbols.

hands of the regent, his mother, the Empress Dowager Ch'eng-t'ien. She was one of a line of women who exercised authority thanks to an anthropological quirk. The Khitan royal family took their wives from one particular 'consort' clan, which also provided companions to princesses and had traditional rights to several high offices. Ch'eng-t'ien was no stranger to power when, at the age of 30, she suddenly found herself ruling an empire. She continued to do so even after her son came of age, for this extraordinary woman, virtually unknown except to specialists, was one of history's most talented leaders: politician, administrator, military commander – she controlled her own regiment of cavalry, a so-called 'ten-thousand'.

It was mainly under her direction that the Liao adopted an official patina of Chinese culture: institutions, titles, bureaucratic examination system, and two Chinese-like scripts which have been only partially deciphered. On top of its pastoral-nomad roots, the Liao acquired a class of farmers and merchants, iron-founders and weavers with the trappings of Sinified modernity.

It was the Sung who, in 986, opened the next round of war, only to be forced back after heavy losses. For the Liao, this campaign marked the start of a series of wars which lasted for over 40 years, ending only when the empire had found a balance with its neighbours that would last for a century. After forcing both Korea and the Tanguts into surly alliances, the Liao turned on China. Two opening campaigns, in 998–1000 and 1002–3, ended with no lasting gains. In the autumn of 1004, a third invasion, under the direction of both the emperor and the empress-dowager, drove south. In two months the army covered 300 km (200 miles), to confront the Sung army drawn up in a strong position at Shan-yan, just north of the Yellow River.

At this point, the Liao paused. They had taken the territory they claimed, and were within 100 km (60 miles) of the Sung capital. The Sung had stopped them advancing further, and stood ready to cut off their enemy's retreat. Neither side wanted to break the stalemate, and risk defeat.

A senior adviser to the Liao, a Sung who had been taken prisoner and then offered his services to them, suggested making peace. Good sense prevailed. The bottom line was this: the Liao wanted their gains formalized; the Sung refused, but offered to pay. The negotiations involved an intricate diplomatic dance to save face, with clauses specifying that the two emperors should call each other brothers, and that the empress-dowager should become the Sung emperor's 'aunt'.

The heart of the Treaty of Shan-yan, confirmed in 1005, was the Sung's compensation, an annual tribute of 2.8 tonnes of silver and 200,000 rolls of silk – though the clauses diplomatically avoided the word tribute, referring to it as a 'contribution to military expenses'. The 'contribution' was to be handed over at the border, not at the Liao court, in the face-saving pretence that it was not really tribute at all.

This agreement laid a foundation for a century of peace. Both sides benefited. The Sung paid up, but saved far more on military expenditure. The flow of wealth went to extend the Liao Empire and beautify it. At one point, its shifting frontiers stretched across the Gobi to the Altai mountains, including almost all of present-day Mongolia. 'Oh! What prosperity!' crowed the 14th-century history, the *Liao Shih*. Liao ships sailed to Japan, and their overland traders – following the Silk Routes westward – reached Baghdād, where the caliph asked for a Khitan princess in marriage.

Wealth was too much, yet not enough. Luxury undermined the old Khitan military spirit. Constant war, or the threat of war – if not against the Sung then against the Tanguts or envious nomadic tribes to the north – made too many demands on ordinary people. In 1125, two centuries after its foundation, the Liao Empire, softened by security and urbanization, gave way to new conquerors, the Jürchen of eastern Manchuria.

This was not the end of the Khitan. Some of them – the so-called Kara-Khitan, the 'black Khitan' – fled westwards, re-establishing themselves south of Lake Balkhash, on the edge of Islam, where almost a century later, they would be crushed by Chingis Khan's armies.

Almost all of this happened unnoticed by Europeans at the time (and later as well, because Liao history was suppressed by the Manchu dynasty in the 18th century to downplay alien involvement in Chinese affairs). But the Khitans left one small mark on European history. When the survivors of Liao moved west, they referred to China by their own name, Khitai, as if it had all been theirs. Muslim historians followed suit. So in due course did the Mongols: 'Khiatad' is still Mongolian for China. From these sources came the late medieval European names for China: Kitaia in Italian, Cathay in English. Columbus said he was aiming for 'Catayo' when he discovered America. By then, of course, the original Cathay – which had never been China proper – had been defunct for over 300 years.

The Roots of Mongol Greatness

Far to the north, beyond the borders of Liao, in the valley of the Onon river, lived a small group of nomadic clans known to the Chinese as the Meng-wu. They would later be better known as the Mongols. There was no sign then, around 1000, that this insignificant people would ever amount to anything.

A young outcast, Bodonchar, was considered so stupid and dull by his four brothers that they excluded him from his share of the property left by his mother, Alanqoa. As the tribal foundation epic, The Secret History of the Mongols, tells it, Bodonchar built himself a grass hut and lived alone, hunting with a tame hawk, living on wolves' leftover scraps, and begging airag *– fermented mare's milk – from neighbours.*

Eventually, an elder brother tracked him down, and was impressed by what he found. At Bodonchar's suggestion, the brothers raided the neighbouring tribe, 'and so came into livestock, property and people for servants with which they settled down'.

And the significance of this? Bodonchar was the ancestor of the Borjigin clan, into which Chingis Khan was born 150 years later. It was the sudden emergence of the world's greatest land empire that inspired the Mongols to seek their origins in myth and anecdote, and have them recorded in the mid 13th century by the anonymous author of The Secret History.

4 | Hsi-hsia: 'The Great State of White and High'

In 982, the region between the Gobi and Tibet – today the immense western Chinese province of Xinjiang – became the core of a kingdom that rivalled both Sung and Liao.

Some 300 years before the millennium, the Tanguts, a mix of Tibetan, Burmese and Chinese blood, had emerged from the ever-shifting tribes, clans and lineage groups of Central Asia as semi-nomadic stockbreeders fiercely independent of their neighbours: the Chinese, the Tibetans and the Liao. In the 10th century, their base lay in the middle of the Ordos, the sweep of territory within the bend of the Yellow River. Here, around the citadel of Hsia-Chou, they specialized in breeding horses, which they drove in vast herds for sale in the Tang (and later the Sung) capital, K'ai-feng. Both Tang and Sung sought to control them by a combination of trade, bribery and force.

As it happened, the Sung dynasty came to power as the Tanguts and the Liao were also on the rise. With all three jockeying for power, the Tanguts split. One faction surrendered to the Sung. Another, under the command of a minor Chingis Khan figure named Li Chi-ch'ien, took off to the north-west into the pasturelands of present-day Inner Mongolia, controlling territory spanning the Yellow River. Li set about welding nomadic groups into an alliance, promising protection against the Sung.

In building his power-base in this no-man's-land, Li tried a variety of tactics to deal with his powerful neighbour: gifts, trade, warfare, diplomacy. The Sung – facing war on two fronts (Liao to the north, Tanguts to the west) – tried to exert control with sanctions, ordering trade by barter, banning cash because the Tanguts melted down copper coins to make weapons. In 985, Li responded by seizing back some of the land from which he had fled. In 994 the Sung hit back, razing Hsia-chou. But Li, with an army 50,000 strong, struck west, taking Ling-chou, which became his first capital in the spring of 1002. Within a year, Li had repaired its old canal system, renaming the city Hsi-p'ing Fu.

But Li also had to reckon with the rising power of the Liao. At first he sought to buy time with diplomacy, seeking a Liao princess as his wife. In 989 the Liao agreed, acknowledging Li as a king, if less than equal, gaining a useful breathing space

for both while the Liao and Sung fought and talked their way to the accommodation finally reached in the treaty of 1005 (p. 95).

By then Li was dead, aged 41, slain in an ambush by Tibetans while trying to extend Tangut authority into the Tibetan province of Tsung-ko on his south-west borders (p. 93). His son, Li Te-ming, negotiated his own treaty with the Sung in 1006, which in effect acknowledged him as an independent sovereign.

This proved significant the following year, when Li's mother died. She had adopted Buddhism, long established in China proper, but with only one significant temple in these outlying regions: the Dayun Temple in Lanzhou. Li requested permission to make offerings at ten temples on Mt Wutai, a great pilgrimage centre (then and now) in the north of Shanxi province. Mt Wutai was associated with a cult of Manjusri, a *boddhisattva*, one of whose functions was to protect states. Li's pilgrimage and his patronage of the site could have been an important assertion of his emerging identity, and it also sanctioned the growth of Buddhism.

In 1020, assured of political and economic security, Li chose a strategic position between the Yellow River and the Gobi, and began building a new capital. It went by several successive names, including Ningxia (now the name of the province) and then finally Yin-chuan, which it remains today.

A Hsi-hsia coin displays the Tangut script. The 6,600 characters were invented, using Chinese as a model, to write the culture's now extinct Tibeto-Burman language, which is still only partly deciphered.

From here, the next ruler, Li Yüan-hao, drove westward into two small Uighur states, Sha-chou (today's Dunhuang) and Kan-chou in 1028–36, then south into Tibetan territory. It was this ambitious and talented khan who stamped Tangut authority on the region. He did so by giving himself a new royal name (Wei-ming instead of Li), and by imposing a new look, something that set the Tanguts apart from their neighbours. His subjects were instructed to shave the top of their heads, in typically nomad style, leaving a fringe over the forehead and at the sides, to adopt uniforms, and to write with a newly devised 6,000-character Tangut script.

In 1038, Wei-ming had himself crowned emperor of the realm now formally re-titled The Great State of White and High, making his chieftains swear oaths of loyalty sealed with libations

of blood and wine poured from a cup made from a human skull. His empire – best known by its Chinese name of Hsi-hsia (Xi-xia in the more recent Pinyin transliteration), or Western Hsia – ran from the strategic borderland of the Ordos, across grassland and desert, spanning the corridor between the Gobi and the Tibetan highlands.

The Sung had little option but to accept this new arrival, signing a treaty in 1044 by which they paid an annual tribute of 135,000 rolls of silk, 2 tonnes of silver and 13 tonnes of tea (proof that even the nomadic cattle-raisers of the steppes had by then taken up the Chinese habit of tea-drinking).

Central Asia had acquired a new political entity that would last for another two centuries, until Chingis Khan descended from north of the Gobi and wiped it out.

5 Korea: Struggle for Unity, Wealth and Independence

Towards 1000, Korea's elitist class system, sustained by a cosy relation-ship with China, was confronted by two problems, one old, one new: internal rivalries and an ambitious kingdom on its northern borders.

Over the previous thousand years, Korea had been several kingdoms, then three, then, for 300 years, a unified nation. In 918, Wang Kon, better known by his posthumous temple-name of T'aejo, established the Koryŏ dynasty, from which the country derives its modern name, with a new capital, Kaesŏng (Kaegyong as it was then).

Among their problems, T'aejo and his heirs faced a paradox: how to absorb and resist Chinese influence. Chinese culture, imports, literature and language permeated every aspect of Korean life. Border areas had often fallen under direct Chinese control. Those in power devoted much energy to striking a balance between independence and sub-servience. This was not easy. Chinese writing and social concepts did not match well with Korea's language and social structure (Koreans, for instance, gave higher status to women than the Chinese: brothers and sisters inherited equally). And national unity, a prerequisite of Korean independence, was not easily preserved. Local warlords and army commanders challenged T'aejo's five successive heirs, of whom two were assassinated.

But there were firm foundations. In this neatly confined area, Korea's tightly knit society, with a population roughly estimated at 2 million, was well adapted for centralized control. Buddhism, made the state religion by T'aejo, combined with Confucianism to imbue a sense of civic respons-ibility. In the words of an eminent scholar, Ch'oe Sung-no,

Carrying out the teachings of Buddha
Is the basis for cultivation of the self;
Carrying out the teachings of Confucius
Is the source for regulating the state.

A rigid class system rested on the shoulders of free peasant farmers and fishermen, and of 'out-castes' – enslaved criminals and prisoners of war – who were owned both by the state and by individuals.

On these foundations, T'aejo's successors, in particular Sŏngjong (reigned 981 – 97), built a new power structure, with wide-ranging effects on Korean society. Their aim was a compliant elite controlling a compliant population. The aristo-cratic elite received power and wealth from a combination of land grants and civil service jobs. From 958, officials, traditionally aristocrats whose posts were a hereditary right, were also recruited by examination, Chinese style. This demanded a high level of education, to which Sŏngjong responded by founding a National University,

This seated boddhisattva was carved in granite in the late 10th century for a Buddhist temple in Koryong, central south Korea.

with six colleges for Chinese studies, and three others for Law, Calligraphy and Accounting. But the exams were not open to all. Recruits, who had to prove that they had had no 'outcaste' rela-tions for eight generations, were the sons of gentry who had themselves secured wealth from land, which was nominally granted to them and their heirs by the state. Wealth, power, land, inheritance patterns, marriage arrangements, the law, the family – all the mainsprings of Koryŏ society interacted, locking king, the ruling class, peasants and slaves into an intricate system designed to ensure control and continuity.

All roads led to the new capital, Kaesŏng, its site carefully chosen according to the principles of geomancy with a mountain backing the palace and a river to the south. With its government build-ings for the four chancelleries and six ministries, its aristocratic houses, its monasteries and its 70 temples, all surrounded by the thatched houses of ordinary people, Kaesŏng was the fount of authority, the centre-point of society, the heart of trade. With a population of over 100,000, the city was alive with merchants, especially at the great Buddhist festivals, like the autumn Harvest festi-val and the springtime Lantern Festival. Merchant ships – mostly Chinese, with the addition of a few Arab ships from southern Asia – linked Korea to the Chinese coast and to Japan. On arrival, cap-tains could follow beacon fires up the Yesong river, and then stay and pray at Buddhist temples.

From Kaesŏng, power flowed outwards. Ten provinces and two frontier districts under military administration – a hierarchy different from the civilian one, and of a lower status – gave Kaesŏng centralized control, with funding from taxes. All male commoners between 16 and 59 could be called upon for labour, building and rebuilding irrigation schemes, city walls or roads. A 36,000-man army defended the capital and maintained a nationwide network of fire beacons to signal the approach of invaders. A pony-express service with 500 relay stations ensured that information flowed rapidly. Ten state granaries controlled the distribution and price of grain.

All of this was set at risk by the rise of two new powers: the Sung in China proper, and the Khitan of Liao on the northern frontiers. Liao's seizure of Po-hai (Parhae) in 926 drove Jürchen refugees southwards and brought Liao to the Korean bor-der. A few years later, the Sung offered to buy Korean horses for their armies, not an offer that could be refused. Liao now had two causes for complaint – the presence of Jürchen rebels on Korean soil, and the horses being supplied to Liao's great rival. War was virtually inevitable.

It came in October 993 when some 800,000 Khitan crossed the Yalu river, ostensibly to crush

ng-ching
capital)

Yalu

• Kuju
(Kusong)

Pukkye

• Anbuk-pu

ong (Pyonggyang) ■
(western capital)

Anbyon-pu •

Kyoju-mok ○

Hwangju-mok ○

Sohae

Kyoju

Sea
of
Japan

• Anso-pu

Kyonggi
■ Kaegyong
(Kaesong)

Myongju-mok •

Tonggang

K O R Y O

Yellow
Sea

■ Namgyong

Kwangju-mok ○

Han

Ch'ungju-mok ○

Yanggwang

Ch'ongju-mok ○

• Andong-pu

○ Sangju-mok

Naktong

—36—

Chonju-mok ○

Kum

Annam-pu

Tonggyong ■

Kyongsang

Cholla

○ Chinju-mok

○ Naju-mok

Korea

	Koryo
– – –	district border
⌐⌐⌐	wall (built 1033–44)
— —	northern border 1019
■	capital
•	garrison
○	district administrative headquarters

Liao campaigns

first invasion, 993

second invasion, 1011–12

third invasion, 1018–19

course, to become the kingmaker.

Such instability was a problem to Liao. Koreans had begun to arm themselves more effectively, recruiting two new armies and setting up five regional military centres. Besides, they were still selling horses to the Sung, and much else besides – maritime trade with the Sung boomed, with the Koreans exporting raw copper, silks, paper and furs in exchange for tea, lacquerware, dyes, cosmetics and medicines. And an attempt to control their wild borderlands had ended in the massacre of 95 Jürchen, whom Liao considered its subjects. Liao, which had secured its own position with the 1005 Treaty of Shan-yan, now turned its attention again to Korea.

In the winter of 1010/11 Liao cavalry swept across the frozen Yalu, ostensibly to punish the Koreans for regicide, overwhelmed the Korean army, put an abrupt end to Kang Cho, and sacked Kaesŏng. The terrified court fled south, and sued for peace, handing over those responsible for the massacre of the Jürchen. A brief peace gained a respite.

But only a small one. The Koreans still had hopes of winning Sung aid, and Liao mounted a third invasion in 1018. This time, the Koreans were better prepared. An ambush at the border town of Kwiju (Kuju) forced the Liao to negotiate, and peace followed at last in 1022, with Korea happy to avoid further trouble by conceding tributary status.

Assured of peace, the court set about putting its house in order. Forced labour contingents – some 300,000 men – worked for seven years rebuilding the shattered capital. Other contingents were set to work on a wall across the northern border. Begun in 1033, it took 11 years to complete.

As it happened, Korea, with trade on the rise and some businesses already using newly introduced coins, could well afford these works. At last, Korea regained the security and national unity established by T'aejo a century before. There would be no more foreign incursions for two more centuries, and Korea entered a century noted for its artistic glories.

the Jürchen. They then made several unpleasant demands of the Koreans: pay tribute, exert control over your own borderlands, and break off diplomatic relations – and horse-trading – with the Sung. Sŏngjong had little option but to comply.

In these difficult circumstances, Korea's top men, and one strong woman, brought on a crisis. A new king, Mokchong, succeeded in 997. But he was still a teenager, and the real power lay with his mother, the queen dowager. She had an illegitimate son by a lover, who had ambitions that the child should inherit the throne. In 1009, Mokchong appealed to the country's most powerful general, Kang Cho, the military commander in Pyongyang. This proved to be a mistake. Kang Cho marched south, as requested, but then turned on both the king and his mother, murdered them, and placed his own puppet on the throne, Hyonjong (ruled 1010 – 31). His idea was, of

6 Japan: The Rise and Rise of Michinaga

From Japan's dominant family there emerged a master of intrigue who held the reins of power for almost 30 years. In character and background, Michinaga was uniquely qualified, and he presided over a unique period.

Michinaga, the dominant personality in Japanese politics in 1000, came to power, like his predecessors, because he had the right family connection with the emperor: a maternal relative.

For a Fujiwara leader, the prime aim was to pair off a daughter with the emperor, as wife or consort, in the fervent hope that she would bear a son who would be an heir to the throne and become another Fujiwara puppet. Thus, if cards were played right, family and imperial line protected each other. But this was not an easy balance. Court and capital were hotbeds of rivalry, often degenerating into Montague *v.* Capulet street fights. And the granting of office depended crucially on who admired whom at court.

Michinaga owed his position to his father, Kaneie. One of Kaneie's other children was a daughter, Akiko, an imperial concubine, who had a son, Ichijo, who was heir to the throne. When Ichijo came to the throne at the age of 7 in 986, Kaneie became his regent and his daughter became the dowager empress. Akiko developed into a formidable character of towering prestige. Kaneie's three sons became regents in sequence. Two of them died, leaving Michinaga as the natural successor – if he could asssert his claim.

Michinaga, then 30, was a young man of unusual skills. Japanese politics was a game as complex and subtle as three-dimensional chess, with overtones of soap opera. In this game, Michinaga was a grand master, with a scriptwriter's assured ability to manipulate character, temperament, ambition and statecraft. He began to work his way to dictatorial power by intrigue, aided by his sister, Akiko.

One of his rivals was a brilliant young nephew, Korechika, a favourite with the ladies of the palace, noted for for his poetry, charm and gorgeous clothes. Michinaga sidelined Korechika with skill and ruthlessness, deployed with discretion. It happened that Korechika had a mistress, who, unluckily for him, he shared with a former emperor, Kazan, who had been forced to take early retirement and become a monk. This did not inhibit his night-time assignations. On one such occasion, a Korechika gang-member just happened to spot his master's rival, and shot an arrow, which, by another astonishing coincidence, merely touched the ex-emperor's sleeve. If Michinaga had been accused of involvement in this drama, he could easily have denied it. But the slight to such a revered figure was enough, after a long court case, to have Korechika banished, leaving Michinaga closer to supreme power.

It was Akiko who had her brother Michinaga confirmed in office in 995. At the time, he could not claim the regency because he had no maternal relative linked to the emperor. He put matters right by deploying his five daughters as consorts both for the emperor (Michinaga's nephew) and his children. By the time of Michinaga's death, the imperial line consisted largely of young men who had married their aunts. The heir could not help but be a Fujiwara.

Map labels

Rebun
Riishiri
Sea of Okhotsk
Kunashiri
Shibotsu
Habomai Is.
144°
140°
44°
A I N U
Hokkaido
c. 1000
40°
E Z O
Idewa 709
Kuriyagawa 1062
Okachi 759
c. 800
Momuno 769
Nakayama 804
Iwafune 648
Sado
Hokurikudo
Tosando
San yodo
Tokaido
Honshu
36°
Oshima
Niishima
Kozushima
Mishima
Tsushima
Shimono
San indo
Shoda
Awaji
Nankai
Shikoku
Korea Strait
Iki
Inland Sea
Nakadori
Fukae
Dazaifu
Kyushu
Saikaido
East China Sea
Amakusa Shima
Koshiki Retto
Tanegashima
PACIFIC OCEAN
Heian (Kyoto)
capital from 794
136°
132°
32°

0   100 km
0   100 miles

N

Japan

——	major highway
▬▬	northern frontier, with date
◣	fortress, with date
⌂	Ainu hillfort

Major shoen (private estate)
- ● imperial family
- ● Fujiwara family
- ● Todaiji monastery
- ○ other

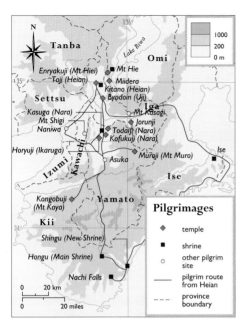

nine ranks, each divided into senior and junior grades, with the lower six divided again into an upper and lower class. Official ranks were equally complex. A man might hold a position in both court and government. To know how to assess anyone demanded a knowledge of his ranks and positions. These subtleties were compounded by a name taboo. People were referred to by their places of residence: Third Avenue Counsellor, Minister of Fortune Lane, Mistress of the Wardrobe.

The system suited Michinaga. Prestige could be granted, power withheld. Michinaga himself was so powerful he scarcely needed offices. His honor-ific title of Nairan, which he held from 995, gave him access to all palace documents. Regent in everything but name, he accepted a formal appointment as regent only in 1016. That pre-ceded his retirement in favour of his son and his retreat into a monastery. But he remained the power behind the throne and regency until his death in 1027.

All this was accomplished with panache. Michinaga claimed to be as flawless as the full moon riding the skies, with good reason. He was superb at archery, riding and poetry. Respectful of religion, etiquette and ritual, he knew how to cloak his intrigues with the proper language and behaviour, preferring to charm rather than fight.

He could afford charm, because his estates were the largest and his palaces the grandest. 'All the land in the Empire belongs to the First Family', complained one of Michinaga's less well-to-do kinsmen. 'There is not a pinpoint where they are not owners.' He, more than any other family head, benefited from Japan's peculiar form of feudalism. Once, all land had been subject to taxation by the state. But over two centuries, the state had honoured religious orders and rewarded officials with tax-exempt land, thus creating landed estates (shoen) comparable to those in medieval Europe. Peasants then found it expedient to hand over, or 'commend', their smallholdings to local landowners in exchange for protection, mostly against Japan's major curse – bandits. Technically, the land itself belonged to the state. But the system ensured the steady erosion of central authority and the growth in power and influence of great families and religious institu-tions – always, though, with the nominal blessing of the emperor.

The result was a sort of benign dictatorship, exercised through the few thousand state officers, court officials and churchmen, all obsessed with prestige. It was a constrained world, in which wealth was to be displayed within the bounds of a rigid hierarchy. At court, for instance, there were

The Tale of Genji: The World's First Novel

The Fujiwara age was one of literary and cultural brilliance. With a weak emperor and a lavish court governed by intrigue, cre-ative energy focused on artistry and the intricacies of human behaviour and feeling. By 1000, Japanese prose had reached a peak of maturity: intimate, heart-felt, polished, yet using ordinary speech, very dif-ferent from the stiff, formal Chinese still used in offi-cial documents, in philo-sophy, in religion. The best works were court diaries and stories, many written by women, giving detailed insights into the court's aristocratic coterie.

The work acknowledged as the greatest was The Tale of Genji, all the more remarkable since it is also famed as the world's first novel. It was written by a woman known as 'Murasaki Shikibu'. Her real name is unknown: 'Murasaki' is a character in her novel, and Shikibu, the Ministry of Ceremonial, her sponsor. In any event, she was herself a Fujiwara, born in about 978. Genji was probably started in 1001, when Murasaki's husband died, and written over a period of years, from 1004 onwards when she served the empress Akiko.

With emperors, princesses and state officers making appearances, The Tale of Genji was clearly intended in part as a realistic por-trayal of life. For instance, when Genji goes into exile, he benefits from the im-munity enjoyed by country estates, handing over the deeds of his lands, gran-aries and warehouses to a trusted friend.

The story deals with Genji's life, mainly his love life: his youthful affairs, his wives, his mistresses. Like his two possible models, the young and tragic Korechika and the brilliant intriguer Michinaga, Genji is an ideal of excellence: noble, wealthy, handsome, witty, irresistible, a heart-breaker. But the focus is on his inner life, his longings and regrets. Murasaki avoids explicit sexuality, which had no more place in liter-ature than nudity in art, and emphasizes refinement. After a wild youth, Genji, haunted by melancholy, acquires compassion and wisdom, his pessimism relieved by an awareness and love of beauty: colours, shapes, perfumes, poetry, calligraphy. One of many images captures the book's spirit of sadness and hope. Among a group of flower-ing trees in spring, Murasaki writes, 'it was the plum trees that gave the surest promise, for already their blossoms were uncurl-ing, like lips parted in a faint smile.'

Murasaki's later fate is unknown. She probably died between 1025 and 1031.

The Khmers: The First of Angkor's Wonders

By 1000, the Khmers were masters of an empire that dominated the south-east Asian mainland. Already they had begun to build one of the wonders of the world: Angkor.

In 1860, a French naturalist, Henri Mouhot, came across ruins in the Cambodian jungle, a vast and mysterious archipelago of temples carved from sandstone. For centuries the jungle had grown over them, until roots, branches and creepers had encased the stones and prised them apart. For Mouhot, it was like stumbling upon an artefact built by alien beings. A few years later, the French novelist Pierre Loti was so taken with the 'mystery' of these ruins, with their thousands of Buddhist statues, that he spun wonderfully romantic notions about their creators, the Khmers. They were the product of some great migration from India, he said, a 'detached branch of the great Aryan race, who settled here by chance' – and then vanished.

Well, no. When found, Angkor was not completely abandoned – it had a working monastery. Even then, historians knew that Cambodia's medieval empire had deep local roots, on which Hinduism and Buddhism had grown after their spread from India. Chinese travellers and historians had written about the Khmers from the 3rd century. The air of mystery was a reflection of European ignorance and romanticism. As France established and then lost its empire across south-east Asia, the ruins and their history have been revealed.

In 802 Cambodia was united by a Khmer king, Jayavarman II, the 'universal monarch', who seems to have declared independence from Javanese overlords and named his kingdom Kambuja after an early north Indian state, and introduced the cult of the god-king, the earthly counterpart of the Hindu god Shiva. Kambuja

absorbed the less powerful Mon states to the north and west, eventually expanding to include present-day Thailand, half of Laos and the southernmost part of Vietnam, imposing tributes that funded grandiose building projects. Its capital, Yasodhapura, became better known by its later name of Angkor (from the Sanskrit for 'city'). The dynasty, and the cult, lasted some 600 years, each king adding temples, palaces and carvings in honour of his ancestors, his gods and himself. Angkor itself became the prime focus for this extended building spree, which in 300 years would produce over 100 temples, most notably the 12th-century glory, Angkor Wat ('city-temple') itself. Over this time it underwent a shift of religious focus when, during the 12th century, the worship of Shiva gave way to tantric Buddhism, a local form of the cult that had already spread to Tibet and offshore south-east Asia.

Angkor, the capital of this inward-looking, riverine empire, was built just north of the great lake of Tonle Sap. The lake's waters could be used for two purposes, practical and mystical. The gentle, shallow monsoon floods, which had long made the Cambodians rice-rich, were used to fill huge reservoirs. These supplied domestic water in the dry season, and also framed the 'temple mountains' that represented Shiva's mythical sea-girt dwelling-place, Mt Meru. They also acted as royal tombs (and in some cases served astronomical purposes).

Cambodia's god-king apparently served several functions. He was the embodiment of Shiva, spirit of the ancestors and the earth and the fount of fertility. As a national hero, he was a personification of all virtues: bravery, artistry, sexuality, spirituality. After he died, his temple became his body, a being animated by ritual, connecting past to future. The cult guaranteed not only a king's authority but also that of the elite below him, ensuring an upward flow of wealth from the land into the temples, their statues, and the inscriptions that provide highly selective details to back up the scanty sources of Cambodia's history.

Initially, in the 9th and 10th centuries, the tower of the 'temple mountain' was the temple's dominant feature, with a causeway leading to a tiered base topped by a summit sanctuary opening to the east, and three false doors to the north, west and south. In later designs, the tower was surrounded by courtyards, galleries, colonnades, and corner-towers, all wreathed in statuary, all executed with an underlying compactness, for Cambodian architects could not build proper arches, only narrow lintels.

By the mid 9th century, Angkor already had two vast reservoirs, 4 km (2.5 miles) and 6.5 km (4 miles) long, and a dozen temples and temple-mountains. In 968, Jayavarman V inherited the throne. This shadowy figure, about whom little

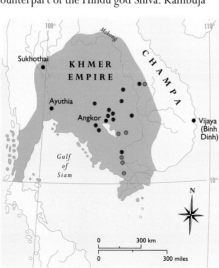

Khmer Empire

- ● pre-Angkor site
- ● Angkor site

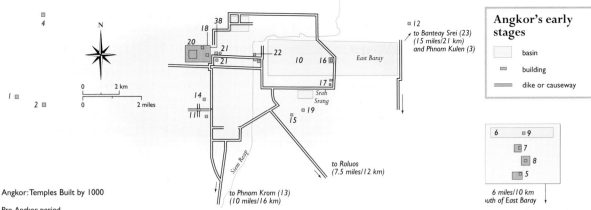

to Banteay Srei (23)
(15 miles/21 km)
and Phnom Kulen (3)

East Baray

Srah
Srang

to Roluos
(7.5 miles/12 km)

to Phnom Krom (13)
(10 miles/16 km)

Siem Reap

Angkor's early stages

- basin
- building
- dike or causeway

6 miles/10 km
outh of East Baray

Angkor: Temples Built by 1000

Pre-Angkor period
1 Prasat Prei Kmeng
2 Prasat Ak Yum

Reign of Jayavarman II (802—50)
3 Phnom Kulen

Reign of Jayavarman III (850—77)
4 Prasat Kok Po
5 Prasat Prei Monti

Reign of Indravarman (877—89)
6 Baray of Roluos
7 Preah Ko
8 Bakong

Reign of Yashovarman I (889—910)
9 Lolei
10 Eastern baray
11 Phnom Bakheng
12 Phnom Bok
13 Phnom Krom

Reign of Harshavarmann I (910—28)
14 Baksei Chamkrong
15 Prasat Kravan

Reign of Rajendravarman I (944—68)
16 East Mebon
17 Pre Rup
18 Phimeanakas (pyramid)?
19 Prasat Bat Chum

Reign of Jayavarman V (968—1001)
20 Royal Palace
21 North and South Khleang
22 Ta Keo (early)?
23 Banteay Srei

Reign of Jayaviravarman (1001—2)
22 Ta Keo (late)?

was recorded, was a boy when he succeeded. He spent some years closely supervised by relatives and officials, which indicates a time of peace in which Kambuja's intricate social hierarchy worked effectively without strong leadership. The role of his supervisors is recalled in the inscriptions of one of Angkor's finest temples, Banteay Srei (Fortress of Women), named after the female figures decorating its towers. A small, delicate temple of pink sandstone, it was recovered from the jungle only in 1916. Standing some 20 km (30 miles) apart from Angkor's temple complex, it was dedicated in 967, a year before Jayavarman succeeded, by an official who became the young king's mentor.

Later, Jayavarman built the enclosure of the Royal Palace, 600 by 250 metres (2,000 by 800 feet), which overlooked a vast terrace and included more reservoirs, apartments and a small temple-mountain, the Phimeanakas; two rectangular buildings, North and South Khleang ('emporium'), the purpose of which is unknown; and a huge five-tiered temple-mountain, Ta Keo, which seems to have remained unfinished for unknown reasons.

Jayavarman has one other claim to fame. Although a Hindu Shaivite – a worshipper of Shiva – he was tolerant of Buddhism, which had first appeared in the area over two centuries before and had been making an increasing impact from the early 10th century. His apparently peaceful reign reinforced the tradition by which Buddhist elements fused with – and later dominated – Hindu ones, without conflict.

These temples were immense artistic and technical achievements, Asian equivalents of Gothic cathedrals (though without the architectural sophistication). The stones, each weighing between 1 and 8 tonnes, were cut in quarries to the north, dragged onto barges by elephants, floated downriver, dressed, and rubbed together until abrasion made them fit exactly. No two blocks are alike: every structure is an irregular patchwork. Then came the cutting of the windows, doors, bas-reliefs and inscriptions. Each temple demanded an army of workers and artists.

It was too much. The later, grander creations of Angkor, with their kilometres of bas-reliefs, scores of towers and thousands of statues, are unique syntheses of architecture and sculpture, of Hindu and Buddhist pantheons, but the immense effort inspired by the greatest of Cambodian kings, Angkor Wat's creator Jayavarman VII, seems to have drained the empire's economic life-blood. The tax burden was too great, and with Thai and Lao peoples sweeping down from the northern hills into present-day Thailand and Laos, tribute from outlying regions vanished. Cambodia shrank. In the 15th century, Thai invasions forced the court to the safety of Phnom Penh, and the abandoned temples of Angkor were left to the encroaching jungle.

Banteay Srei, the 'Fortress of Women', was completed in about 967 to honour the Hindu god Shiva. Standing 20 km (12.5 miles) apart from the main Angkor complex, its graceful bas-reliefs, carved in pink sandstone, make this the pinnacle of Khmer art and architecture.

8 India: Fleeting Power, Enduring Glory

The Chola dynasty sprang from the rice-rich plain of the River Kaveri, today's Tamil Nadu. They had ruled here as minor chieftains for 800 years when, in the middle of the 9th century, they emerged as heads of a small independent state. In the early 10th century they expanded southward, into the territory of the Pandyas. In the north they were constrained by ancient enemies, the Rashtrakutas, until in 972 the Rashtrakutas were defeated by enemies of their own, the Paramaras.

Into the power vacuum stepped Arulmoli, better known by his Chola title of Rajakesari, but best known by the name he gave himself in 1004: Rajaraja I (985–1014), 'king of kings', a title that made clear his imperial ambitions. He, together with his son Rajendra, wrote a new agenda for their dynasty and for all southern India.

Chola history was in part a history of the campaigns of father and son, whose reigns overlapped by two years (1012–14). Supremacy demanded control both of the Chalukya rulers of the Deccan highlands to the north and of Arab-dominated sea-routes linking the southern Indian coast and Ceylon. Numerous campaigns took Chola troops into the Deccan, across the sea to Ceylon, north-east to Bengal, south-west to the Maldive Islands, and finally – in an assault that might have led to a lasting Indian Empire in south-east Asia – to Sumatra. In its day, this empire was the lynchpin of Asia's maritime economies, sitting astride Arab routes to south-east Asia, and reaching out to China – in 1016, Rajendra sent a diplomatic and commercial mission to China (two others followed in 1033 and 1072).

The most effective of these assaults – the most devastating, from an opposite point of view – was Rajaraja's on Ceylon (Sri Lanka) in 992–3. Ceylon, which had once been powerful enough to rule some of southern India, had been a target for a brief Chola foray 50 years before. In the meantime, it had become easy prey. Its ruler, Mahinda (982–1029), was 'smitten with indolence', according to the later Ceylonese history, *Culavamsa*. He had failed to ensure a proper flow of taxes from his peasants, been unable to pay his troops and been chased from his ancient capital, Anuradhapura, to a smaller town, Rohana. A Chola horse-dealer returning from a trading trip told Rajaraja of the anarchy into which his old rival had fallen, and the emperor seized his chance.

An inscription in a temple on India's southern tip, Kanyakumari, memorializes the campaign by comparing it to the god Rama's legendary journey to the island. 'Rama built with the aid of monkeys a causeway across the sea and then with great difficulty slew the King of Lanka by means of sharp-edged arrows. But Rama was excelled by this king [Rajaraja] whose powerful army crossed the ocean by ships and burnt up the King of Lanka.' The Chola army destroyed Anuradhapura, turned an old military outpost, Polonnaruwa, into a new capital, and began to siphon off Ceylonese wealth. Mahinda fled to the unoccupied south.

With the booty, Rajaraja set about creating works of art that would glorify his name and achievements. Perhaps the most astonishing is the great temple of his capital, Thanjavur (Tanjore), probably built 1004–1010. Dedicated to Shiva, it is also a massive glorification of Rajaraja himself. It employed 850 people, 400 of them dancing girls chosen from lesser temples and housed in two adjoining streets. Its solid base raises the floor by 5 metres (16 feet), above which stone deities and representations of Shiva dance. Inside is an inner sanctum 7.5 metres (24 feet) square. Its pyramidal tower, the highest in India at the time, rises in 13 diminishing storeys to 65 metres (216 feet). Yet like all Indian temples this immense structure was built without cement, its granite blocks being so finely dressed that they fit as neatly and firmly as a three-dimensional jigsaw. Its building was so sensational that it inspired a play that was performed at a festival soon after the temple was completed.

Inside the shrine, a gallery contains relief sculptures of Shiva dancing. Frescoes portray representations of Shiva in action, destroying demonic forts, dancing, sending a white elephant to transport a devotee to heaven. Bronzes (now in the Tanjore Art Gallery and other collections) show off Chola artistry at its best – lithe Shivas and his consort Parvati, a slim-waisted, full-breasted figure, one hip seductively raised. These subtle and sexy figures have done more than any other works of Chola art to ensure Rajaraja's reputation as leader and patron.

On his succession in 1012, Rajendra displayed all the ambitions of his father. In 1017 he completed the conquest of Ceylon, persuading Mahinda to creep from his jungle hiding place by offering terms. Rajendra then seized the hapless Mahinda, together with his queen, his crown jewels, his Buddhist relics and the treasures of his monasteries.

Rajendra soon acquired the arrogance of a successful empire-builder. After leading a campaign on Bengal in 1023, he ordered a new capital 60 km (40 miles) north of Tanjore, naming it 'City of the Chola who conquered the Ganges', all compressed into one word: Gangaikondacholapuram. Here he built himself a palace, now almost totally destroyed over the centuries by locals using its

Among the most glorious of India's artistic wonders from around the year 1000 are the elegant and finely detailed bronzes created for the Hindu rulers and temples of the Chola empire of today's Tamil Nadu. This one is of Shiva dancing.

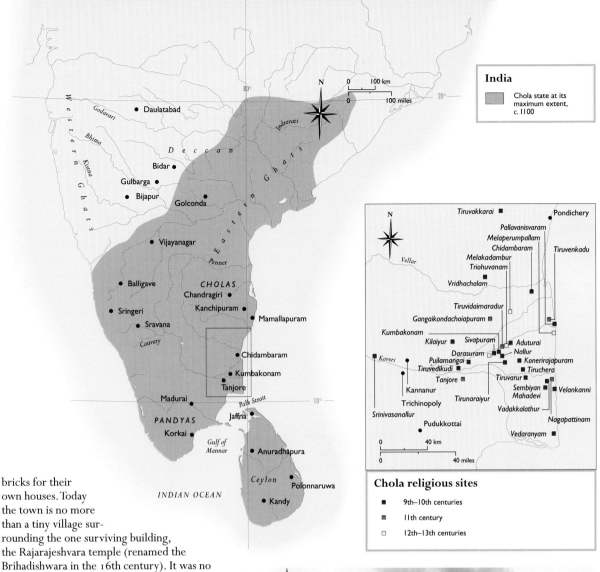

Map labels (main map):

Godavari · Daulatabad

Deccan

Indravati

Bhima

Krisna

Western Ghats

Bidar

Gulbarga

Bijapur

Golconda

Eastern Ghats

Vijayanagar

Penner

CHOLAS

Chandragiri

Balligave

Kanchipuram

Sringeri

Sravana

Cauvery

Mamallapuram

Chidambaram

Kumbakonam

Tanjore

Madurai

Palk Strait

PANDYAS

Jaffna

Korkai

Gulf of Mannar

Anuradhapura

Ceylon

Polonnaruwa

INDIAN OCEAN

Kandy

Inset map labels:

N

Tiruvakkarai · Pondichery

Pallavanisvaram

Melaperumpallam

Chidambaram

Melakadambur · Tiruvenkadu

Vellar

Triohuvanam

Vridhachalam

Tiruvidaimaradur

Gangaikondachoiapuram

Kumbakonam

Kilaiyur · Sivapuram

Aduturai

Kaveri

Darasuram · Nallur

Puilamangai · Konerirajapuram

Tiruvedikudi · Tiruchera

Kannanur

Tanjore · Tiruvarur

Sembiyan Mahadevi · Velankanni

Trichinopoly

Tirunaraiyur

Vadakkalathur

Srinivasanallur

Nagapattinam

Pudukkottai

Vedaranyam

Chola religious sites

■ 9th–10th centuries
▤ 11th century
□ 12th–13th centuries

bricks for their
own houses. Today
the town is no more
than a tiny village sur-
rounding the one surviving building,
the Rajarajeshvara temple (renamed the
Brihadishwara in the 16th century). It was no
challenge to that of his father in height, but the
concave sweep to its nine-storeyed roof is still an
architectural wonder. He ordered the defeated
princes of Bengal to carry holy water from the
Ganges, 1,600 km distant, all the way to his new
capital, where he built a vast tank to hold it – a
'liquid pillar of victory' – which no doubt was
used to anoint the huge shivalingam standing in
the temple's inner sanctum. Its statues were
adorned with jewels seized in wars; its lights were
fuelled by oil supplied by Ceylonese villagers.

Chola power endured for another century,
until, drained by incessant campaigning, it was
undermined by the Hoysolas from the Deccan,
and finally the empire fell to the Pandyas from the
south in the late 13th century. But the Cholas
ensured that no one who visits the area will forget
them. Dozens of their temples have vanished,
but enough remain to attract tourists by the
thousand along a temple-trail south and west of
Pondicherry.

The Brihadishwara temple in Thanjavur was built as a tribute to the power of its patron, Rajaraja I. It remains one of the greatest glories of Indian architecture.

9 Indonesia: Two Empires Built on Spices

While mainland cultures in south-east Asia built wealth from rice and tribute, two other states in Sumatra and Java built wealth from trade.

Mt Merapi's volcanic out-pourings gave central Java its rich soils. But when it exploded in the 10th century, it devastated the trading state of Mataram, forcing its people to re-establish further east.

For centuries, India and China had imported spices grown in the Moluccas, which would one day be known in Europe as the Spice Islands. It was a specialized trade, in several ways. The three main spices – cloves, nutmeg and mace – were produced by two tropical evergreens. So ordinary are spices today that few people know of their original source, or why they were once so extraordinary. Cloves are the dried unopened flower-buds of clove trees, which grew only on five tiny islands off Halmahera. Nutmegs, from the nutmeg tree, are dried kernels found inside the nutty seed, from the rind of which mace is derived; and nutmeg trees once grew only on the ten Banda Islands. The two species have to be carefully tended, and do not transplant easily. In 1000 the 'Spice Islands' had long been famous as sources of wealth (though not as famous as they would become when the Portuguese, Dutch and English started squabbling over them in the 17th century). Whoever controlled the trade had a licence to print money.

But getting to the Spice Islands was no easy task. International traders, dependent on seasonal winds, could reach Sumatra and Java and return in a season, but the final 1,500 km (1,000 miles) to the Banda Sea was beyond them. For their supplies they had to depend on locals, who not only possessed the seafaring skills of their Malayan–Polynesian ancestors, but also had a permanent head start on Westerners: they made the journey west from the Spice Islands on the same winds that carried the traders homewards. The two sets of traders did not coincide. The spice-treasure had to be handled by middlemen, hence the importance of Sumatra and Java in medieval maritime commerce.

The great Asian sea-trade boom, which lasted from the early 10th to the mid 13th century (and which eventually acted as a stimulus to European economies), had already begun to bring great wealth to two states in Indonesia: the empire of Śrīvijaya in the Malacca Straits, which was in a position to control the sea lanes, and the state of Mataram in Java, which dominated the trade in spices. Both responded to Indian influences in religion and architecture, absorbing both Hinduism and Buddhism, which shaped much of traditional Indonesian culture.

Śrīvijaya (Sanskrit for 'Auspicious Victory') is a name known to few, because it vanished from history in the late Middle Ages. Even its name was unknown until 1918, when archaeologists made known a handful of stone inscriptions, the earliest surviving records in Malay, from the forests of Sumatra and the small island of Bangka. With the name identified, researchers found other scattered references in Chinese records, southern Indian temple inscriptions, Buddhist literature, even travellers tales (Sinbad, the hero of *1001 Nights*, visited Śrīvijaya).

Śrīvijaya first arose on the east coast of Sumatra in the 7th century. Perched between sea and forest, its original capital may have been near present-day Palembang on the lower Musi river, where some of the earliest stone inscriptions were found. By 700, it controlled a swathe of territory along the Sumatran coast and on the Malay Peninsula opposite. It had become a major Buddhist centre: Chinese pilgrims stopped over to learn Sanskrit before travelling on to Sri Lanka and northern India. After a brief decline, mirroring the fate of the Tang dynasty and Palava Empire of India, trade bloomed again as China came under Sung control, south India blossomed under the Cholas, and the Fatimids reached out from Cairo across the Indian Ocean.

Around 1000, however, Śrīvijaya's political centre shifted to the now abandoned port of Muara Jambi, 30 km (20 miles) downstream from present-day Jambi on the Batang Hari river, where archaeologists have recently discovered Buddhist temple remains and residential debris stretching for 5 km (3 miles) through jungle along the riverbanks. Quantities of Chinese ceramics and Islamic glass speak eloquently of the wealth possessed by its rulers and handled by its merchants. Muara Jambi, too, was a major Buddhist centre. In 993, a wandering Chinese monk returning from India via 'San-fo-tsi' (Śrīvijaya) took a local Hindu monk with him to help in translation work; and the great Tibetan teacher Atisha is said to have studied in Śrīvijaya between 1011 and 1023.

Its success in trade was matched by diplomatic outreach. In 1006 its king, Chulamanivarnam, headed an embassy to the Cholas (p. 104), and was granted permission by the Hindu Rajaraja to dedicate a Buddhist temple in Nagapattinam, on the coast of Tanjore. But such contacts could not eradicate imperial rivalry. In 1025 the Chola navy attacked several Śrīvijayan ports. Apparently the attack had little lasting effect, because in 1028 Śrīvijaya sent another well-received trade mission to China, and trade links with China continued to strengthen for another two centuries.

Śrīvijaya had more than the Cholas to contend with. To the east lay Mataram, a Javanese state whose origins are equally obscure. It emerged in the early 8th century when an inland kingdom seized the coastal trading state known to the Chinese as Ho-ling. Mataram had two advantages:

rice and spice. Rice grew well on the volcanic soils of inland Java, which gave it a strong tax base; and it monopolized the cloves, nutmeg and mace of the Spice Islands and the sandalwood of Timor. With stability backed by its rice-and-spice economy, it rode out the downturn that affected Śrīvijaya, and its currency was copied in Sumatra, on the Malay Peninsula, even in the Philippines. Its rice surpluses fed the thousands of stonemasons and sculptors who built the magnificent 8th-century Buddhist complex at Borobudur, with its kilometres of bas-reliefs, as well as the dozens of other Buddhist and Hindu temples around Prambanan. By the mid 9th century, Mataram had spread eastwards, acquiring ports in the delta of the Brantas river.

But Mataram grew rich on borrowed time. In 928, its greatest volcano, Mount Merapi, the source of its wonderful soil, erupted suddenly and violently, spewing ash and rivers of hot mud down the valleys, burying temples and palaces. Merapi was a Javanese Etna, its towns local Pompeiis. One temple was drowned under 7 metres (23 feet) of mud. In Wonoboyo, near Prambanan, archaeologists have recently discovered a royal treasure of gold and jewels beneath 2 metres (6.5 feet) of volcanic mud. From this and other finds, it seems that the people had no time to collect their possessions before fleeing. Temples collapsed, rice fields vanished. Central Java became a wasteland. Many people moved east, and looked to sea trade to revive their fortunes.

In 1016, one of Mataram's minor neighbouring states destroyed the capital and killed most of its royal family, the Sailendras. One survivor, though, was a 16-year-old prince, Airlangga (c.991–c.1049), who according to tradition found refuge in a monastery on Mount Vanagiri. Three years later, he was offered the throne.

Tradition conferred divine status upon him as the earthly manifestation of the Indian god Vishnu who conquered his 'demon' enemies by pure mind-power. He ruled first from 'Kahuripari', an unidentified place probably near today's Surabaya, some 60–80 km (40–50 miles) up the River Brantas. Airlangga rebuilt fast, seizing Bali in about 1025, and creating an empire well able to withstand Śrīvijaya. By 1037, he ruled all central and eastern Java from a new base, Hujung Galah, probably the site that became today's Surabaya. According to tradition, he gave himself a secure economic base by damming the Brantas, controlling its floods, extending irrigated areas, drawing in population and expanding political control inland. He is also credited with a literary, artistic and social renaissance, for under his aegis Hindu epics were translated into Javanese, and regional codes of law were united into one Javanese code.

Mataram's elite sought private wealth, not public expressions of opulence. Their temples were smaller and less ornate. Clothing on statues shows that imports of Indian printed cotton inspired the Javanese to invent batik, the wax-and-dye technique of printing on cloth. Around the same time, Javanese also transplanted black pepper and safflower (a source of a gorgeous rose-red dye) from southern India, steadily becoming Asia's main supplier of both.

After Airlangga's death in about 1049, his empire was divided between two sons, and soon collapsed into civil war and a confusion of statelets. From the ruck, in the late 13th century, there would arise the great Javanese state of Majapahit, the first power to dominate most of Indonesia. Śrīvijaya and Mataram became the stuff of folk memory, until archaeologists resurrected them from the jungle and volcanic mud.

Śrīvijaya and
Mataram, c.1000

△   Hindu/Buddhist
     temple, 600–1300

AFRICA

Early States and Proto-Empires

In the 1890s the whole history of pre-colonial Africa south of the Sahara could be dismissed by an Oxford historian as 'blank, uninteresting, brutal barbarism'. A century later, the lack of written sources remains a problem. But increasingly, historians, anthropologists and archaeologists are revealing it to be almost exactly the opposite: teeming, fascinating and remarkably free of wilful destructiveness.

The best-documented African cultures around 1000 were those abutting the Sahara – principally ancient Ghana (not to be confused with modern Ghana) – because they were the first to be tightly linked to Islamic culture, and thus to scholars who wrote their histories (as best they could, from afar). The weight of Islamic sources once reinforced a prejudice that African states were somehow inspired by non-African influences. Now historians accept that this is not so. The 4,200-km (2,600-mile) sweep of the Niger, with its hugely varied patterns of rainfall, created an immensely productive though erratic ecosystem. Here, probably aided by a moister climate that prevailed a few centuries either side of the year 1000, a rich patchwork of peoples learned to adapt relatively peacefully to the region's complex and unpredictable demands. When people began to group together, they formed 'cities without citadels' and proto-states which (initially) were without central controls – collections of cooperatives that had worked out how best to live with their generous, demanding river. When Muslims from north of the Sahara made contact in the 8th century, they built trade links with well-founded indigenous cultures.

The course of African history in the rest of the continent has unique patterns, highlighted by the problem of its scanty population. In the year 1000, Africa, though possessing 22 per cent of the world's land surface and with equivalent ecological richness, had only about 15 per cent of its population (some 40 million out of about 250 million), most of whom lived in North Africa and the Nile Valley. Sub-Saharan Africa – over half the continent – supported a mere 10 million, a quarter of its population. Clearly, the region presented humans with problems.

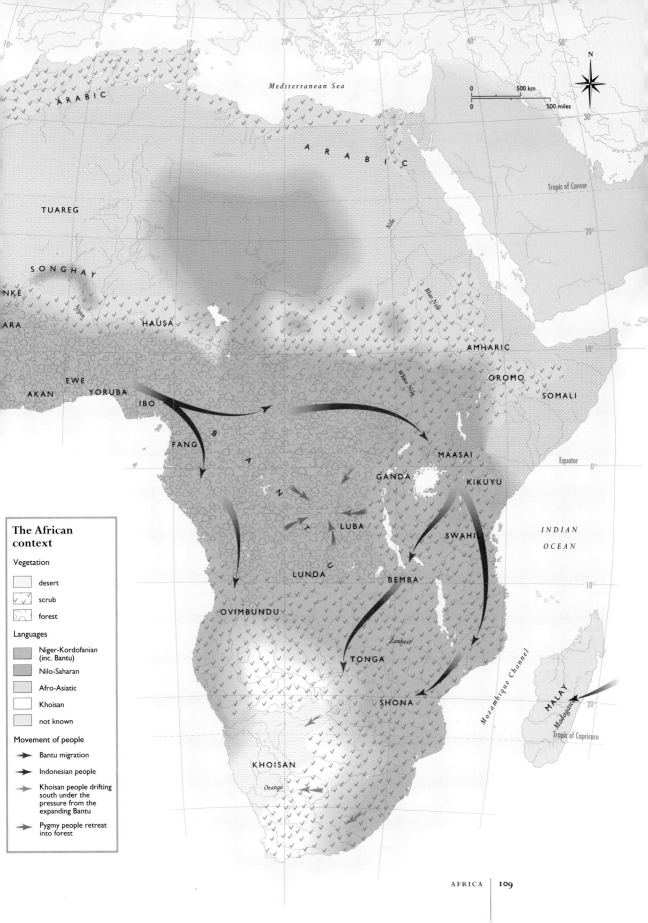

The African context

Vegetation

- ⠿ desert
- ⌄⌄ scrub
- forest

Languages

- Niger-Kordofanian (inc. Bantu)
- Nilo-Saharan
- Afro-Asiatic
- Khoisan
- not known

Movement of people

- → Bantu migration
- → Indonesian people
- → Khoisan people drifting south under the pressure from the expanding Bantu
- → Pygmy people retreat into forest

Mediterranean Sea

ARABIC

ARABIC

TUAREG

SONGHAY

NKÉ

ARA

HAUSA

AKAN

EWE

YORUBA

IBO

FANG

B

A

N

T

U

OVIMBUNDU

LUNDA

LUBA

TONGA

SHONA

KHOISAN

Orange

Zambezi

GANDA

MAASAI

KIKUYU

SWAHILI

BEMBA

AMHARIC

OROMO

SOMALI

Nile

Blue Nile

White Nile

Niger

Equator

Tropic of Cancer

Tropic of Capricorn

INDIAN OCEAN

Mozambique Channel

MALAY

Madagascar

N

0   500 km

0   500 miles

This 10th-century bronze, only 7.6 cm (3 inches) high, was found in Igbo-Ukwu, south-eastern Nigeria in 1959 – 60, along with many other bronze objects and 100,000 beads. The find underlines the importance of archaeology in the study of ancient sub-Saharan Africa. Since the area lacks bronze, the metal was probably brought by Arab traders. The face, perhaps a pendant, may have been that of a local priest-king, the Eze-Nri – facial scars like these were worn by the Eze-Nri until recently.

One major constraint unique to tropical Africa is disease. The tsetse fly, for example, infests some of the most potentially productive land of tropical Africa. Thriving in woodland areas with annual rainfalls of 500–700 mm (20 – 28 inches) and daytime temperatures of 15°C (60°F) or over, two species of the fly carry the parasites that cause sleeping sickness in humans, and also kill cattle (though indigenous animals like antelope have had time to evolve immunity). Sleeping sickness was joined by other fatal or debilitating parasitic diseases – billharzia, hookworm, malaria.

Together, such diseases produce a cascade of effects. For one thing, although African iron-using peoples could have made ploughs – and the technology was long practised in Ethiopia – they did not, partly because suitable domestic animals did not survive for long enough, partly because such diseases often strike harder where people form settled communities. In central and southern Africa towns were rare, and kingdoms unknown until about 1000. Without a need to administer large areas over long periods, there was no reason to keep records – hence the poverty of African historical sources and the vital importance of other types of evidence.

The absence of centralized states conferred on sub-Saharan Africa a unique trait. Without the intensity of competition that defined change in Europe, Asia and Central America, there was a surprising absence of warfare. While villages built enclosures to protect their cattle, they seldom made provision to protect themselves, because there was little danger of attack.

A major theme of the history of central, eastern and southern Africa was the coming of the Bantu farmers. During the first millennium, long-established pastoral nomads and hunter-gatherers were joined by the Bantu who, on the basis of linguistic analysis, are thought to have originated in eastern Nigeria and western Cameroon. They migrated slowly east and south, diversifying into groups with some 300–600 (depending on which classification is used) related languages, interacting with Nilotic peoples in vast, slow migrations, forming complex patterns the shape of which remain obscure and disputed. They carried with them knowledge of how to work iron, a skill probably imported across the Sahara in the first millennium BC, and related farming techniques.

The combination of skills and demands transformed much of sub-Saharan Africa. Iron-making needed trees for charcoal; forest felling opened lands for cultivation;

that provided more food, for more people, who felled more trees, a process intensified by more benign conditions that peaked between about 900 and 1300. Rich ecologies and iron-age technologies provided foundations for evolving cultures. In turn, these spawned power structures, kingdoms, trade links, towns.

But much that is now known, or believed to be true, about these proto-states owes its existence to European historical attitudes. Take, for example, the region between Lake Victoria and the lakes of the Western Rift. The first European explorers here, John Speke and James Grant, came in search of the source of the Nile in 1861 – 2. They found well-established kingdoms: Karagwe, Buganda, Bunyoro, Rwanda. To research the origins of these peoples, they asked a question suggested by their own culture: who were your kings? King-lists, after all, had always provided the key chronological narratives in the Bible and in European history. Lo and behold, king-lists appeared. Speke thus 'discovered' that the Karagwe royal line stretched back 20 generations, never mind that the first 10 of them were all named Ruhinda and Ntare, in sequence, or that he could not know what length of time a generation was. Later, other king-lists for other tribes were gathered, in particular by missionaries determined to make their would-be converts fit social and historical models derived from ancient Israel. The lists added little to historical knowledge. Yet the Karagwe and other 'interlacustrine' peoples had a clear sense of their own identity in time. How is their history to be pinned down, without imposing alien patterns of explanation?

One part of the answer lies in the ground. Here is hard evidence from the past, which at least shows something. This is hard-won history, for the evidence first has to be found. Even this effort may be influenced by attitude: the first archaeologists in the 1950s spent a good deal of time looking for royal tombs to confirm the king-lists. A grave, though, raises problems: was this individual royal? Who says, and why? Were the objects it contains contemporaneous, or placed there later? What exactly was being honoured – a person, a sacred place, a deity? Historians and archaeologists (for in Africa they are often one and the same) find themselves fighting through an intellectual fog, constantly working to be aware of current assumptions while also working towards saying something valid about the past.

This is, and will probably remain, a recipe for frustration and disappointment. Much of sub-Saharan African history will remain lost, or obscurely hinted at in folklore, or locked away undiscovered in the earth. Individuals will never leap from the past as they do from European and Asian records. But there *is* evidence, lots of it. More of it emerges from African soils every year. The past is not utterly beyond recall. The problem is one of understanding, which is what gives the African past such a challenging and exciting future.

Islam's Peaceful Trade with Realms of Gold

Indigenous sub-Saharan cultures acquired wealth enough to attract Islamic traders from the north, contacts that would permanently change their nature.

'It is said that beyond the source of the Nile is darkness,' wrote a Persian scholar, Ibn al-Faqih, in the early 10th century, 'and beyond the darkness are waters which make the gold grow… In the country of Ghana gold grows in the sand as carrots do, and is plucked by sunrise.'

By the turn of the millennium, this distant land of West Africa's Saharan fringes – ancient Ghana, as it is called, to set it apart from today's – was better known, for it had become a vital part of Islamic economy, a major source of their gold. Its heyday, coinciding with Islamic trade at its peak, reached a high point between about 800 and 1200. So significant was the Islamic influence on Ghana that into the 1970s it was commonly stated that the empire and its towns sprang from nowhere in response to the arrival of Muslim trans-Sahara traders. Then a series of archaeological finds revealed that the empire arose on the foundation of a patchwork of towns and trading cultures that date back a further 1,500 years, a foundation that was entirely Saharan or sub-Saharan. When the Muslim traders came, they were able to slot their new trade into ancient links within Africa itself.

There would have been no trade routes at all if Ghana had not had its own internal economic and political strength. That strength derived from the Niger. Fed by tributaries that run together to form a single stream near Timbuktu, the river typically floods a parched landscape in September, leaving low-lying areas covered for six months. The waters fuel an explosive growth in grass and rice, and spread fresh soil which, as the floods retreat, grows crops and pastures. The river produces tens of thousands of tonnes of fish. But this cornucopia is unpredictable. Quantity of rain, timing of rain, level of floods, crops, fish production – all vary wildly.

The inhabitants responded to such variations with a high degree of adaptability. Apparently, the strategy that worked best was cooperation among specialist communities of farmers, herders and fishermen. As John Reader writes in *Africa: A Biography of the Continent*, 'What distinguishes the delta throughout its 1,600 years of archaeologically recorded history is not the frequency of conflict, but the maintenance of peaceful and reciprocal relations.'

As a result, when people came together to make towns, they did so by choice, undirected by central authority. To the west lay two statelets, Takrur, at the mouth of the Senegal, and Awdaghost (probably today's Tegdaoust), dominated by nomadic Berbers. In ancient Ghana, several centres arose: Koumbi Saleh (then known as Ghana, which gave its name to the empire), Timbuktu, and Jenne-jeno, each with 10–20,000 inhabitants. Gao, of a similar size, had a ruler of its own. (Further east, in the Lake Chad region, nomads known as Zaghawa established a prototype empire, Kanem, about which little is clear at this time, except that it lacked towns.) In all these centres, traders and craftsmen produced and exchanged their products.

The links that arose were originally rooted in the trade of one main mineral: salt, cut from deposits in the north-east. The Sahara has vast deposits of salt, created when ancient lakes dried out. The greatest source is a great basin north of Bilma, where a 2,400-square-km (900-square-mile) lake left well over a million tonnes of salt. From here, salt had been traded into equatorial regions for centuries, much of it going some 1,500 km (1,000 miles) west to Timbuktu for transport up and down the Niger. By the 5th century, the introduction of camels from Arabia vastly extended the amount of salt exported and the range of the trade – thousands of tonnes every year, cut into 30-kg (65-lb) slabs and loaded on to camel trains. (In the 19th century, at the height of the trade, the trains stretched for 50 km (30 miles). It still continues, in a small way.) From Timbuktu, canoes carried the salt several hundred kilometres up- and downriver, from where it was taken cross-country by donkey or human porters. In exchange, traders received ivory and kola nuts, a bitter-tasting stimulant. By the time the salt reached the south coast, its value had risen 60-fold, while kola nuts underwent a comparable increase in value on their way north.

Some time after about 800, Berber traders known as Sanhadja from the north and west Sahara established a trans-Sahara link with Ghana, using the great caravan base of Sijilmasa in the Moroccan oasis of Tafilalt as their entry into the desert. Eventually, the trade involved many products: slaves, copper, salt, and primarily gold, which had begun to filter across the Sahara over the preceding centuries, after the introduction of camels made Sahara crossings more feasible. But the sources of the gold were outside Arab experience. It lay in the hills from which the Niger, Senegal, Volta and Gambia rivers flowed, and was spread downriver and over flood plains by erosion. Panned as gold-dust or tunnelled from 'reefs', West African gold was of remarkable purity, and much needed in the burgeoning Islamic economy.

For those living south of the Sahara, this demand introduced fundamental changes.

Traditionally, their most valued metal was copper, which they worked into religious objects and ornaments. They did not think much of gold, and never made gold coins (all the mints were Islamic, north of the Sahara). Although the evidence for the trade is almost all archaeological and hard to interpret, it seems that with the rise of the Fatimids in Egypt, demand for raw gold shot up, inspiring a whole new production industry of part-time gold-panners.

From about 900, according to one estimate, several hundred thousand people must have been working between 240,000 and 480,000 shafts, each producing 2.5–5 grams (0.1–0.2 ounces) of gold a year. This was enough to make the 2–3 tonnes a year needed to supply Fatimid mints. Increasingly from the mid 10th century, the Ummayads in Spain sought to hijack the gold trade, minting their own coins first in Córdoba, then in Sijilmasa, the town from which camel caravans set out on their two-month haul southwards. This route linked traders as sophisticated as any in the Muslim world. One writer, ibn Hawkal, himself a merchant, reported that when he was in Sijilmasa he saw a cheque written by a trader in Awdaghost for 40,000 dinars (some 170 kg (375 lb) of gold), for which a modern equivalent would be something like £1 million or $1.5 million).

But the trans-Saharan route was not a single track. Arabic writers, principally the 11th-century Andalusian al-Bakri, and the Sicilian al-Idrisi (1100–1166), mention a maze of routes and many placenames. Though few of these can be identified, it is clear that caravans followed both western tracks between the Senegal river and Sijilmasa, and eastern ones from Ghana and Kanem to Wargla (today's Ouargla in central Algeria).

The new trade changed sub-Saharan society. Unlike other areas within the reach of Islam, conquest played no role, perhaps because there was no violent resistance (at this early stage) to the spread of Islam. From the late 10th century, sophisticated Arab merchants elbowed out the Sanhadja, who had established the trade originally. The merchants came and settled, creating a sort of middle-class consumer market for wheat, dates, oil-lamps, glassware and silver. Their tastes spread to the locals.

Yet the source of the gold still remained obscure to Arabs, for the gold-fields and the points of exchange were controlled by black middlemen known both as Dyula (from the Soninke for 'trader') and Wangara, who seem to have formed a sort of guild, jealously guarding their trade. Once, some Arab merchants captured a local and tried to prise from him the source of the gold.

The Ghana empire

- Ghana empire, c. 1000
- Almoravid state, 1055
- Almoravid state, 1100
- trade route
- alluvial gold

Nigeria's Enigmatic Roots

Beyond the reach of Islam, in the savannahs and rain-forests of Nigeria, states were emerging around 1000 that would produce works of art to astonish the world: the bronzes of Benin, the masks of Ife, the regalia of Igbo Ukwu (p. 110).

But the process of state-formation — dating, social structure, trade relations — remains obscure. Walls survive, but each area displays a different settlement pattern, from Old Oyo's 50km of concentric mud-brick ramparts to Benin's bee-hive cluster of over 600 adjoining villages. On current evidence, it seems that by c. 1000 these varied societies were already ruled by kings, or priests, or priest-kings, or rich traders, presiding over farmers, smelters and craftsmen.

Ife, the 'holy city' of the Yorubas, is thought to be the oldest of these 'emergent kingdoms'. But an overgrown bulwark near Lagos may upset that belief. In the 1950s anthropologist Peter Lloyd revealed the rampart as a huge feature protecting the kingdom of Ijebu. In the mid-1990s, a freelance archaeological surveyor, Patrick Darling, collated the evidence and declared it Africa's largest monument — a 3-metre-wide (10-foot) ditch backed by a rampart, making a barrier up to 20 metres high (66 feet), which runs in a rough circle for 160 km (100 miles). After a partial survey, two carbon dates suggest that it was built in c. 850 – 1100.

Locals say the rampart was dug on the orders of Sungbo, the wealthy, childless wife of a king, or perhaps a rich trader in her own right. Giving a Christian gloss to their folk-memory, they also claim that Sungbo was none other than the Queen of Sheba. Whoever built 'Sungbo's Eredo (ditch)' had the power to mobilize workers to shift some 3.5 million cubic metres of earth, enough to fill the Great Pyramid, and more.

Why was it built? How did its people live? How were they governed? No one has any idea. But clearly this vast, little-known structure hints at the existence of states much earlier than had been believed, and also at mysteries still to be unearthed.

He died without saying a word, and the Wangara cut off trade for three years. As a result of this deliberate secrecy, 'Wangara' was long thought by Muslims to be a sort of African El Dorado. The 12th-century writer al-Idrisi said it was an island 500 km (300 miles) long surrounded by the waters of the Nile. Even the 18th-century explorer Mungo Park expected to be able to sail down the Nile to Wangara. An empty hope: not only had it never existed, but by then the goldfields themselves were almost exhausted.

Trade, a flow of wealth, economic control, the exercise of power: under these influences, the sub-Saharan states began to edge towards true statehood, with Ghana emerging as dominant. The name is a source of some confusion. Its inhabitants, the Soninke, called their country Wagadu (recalled by the town of Ouagadougou); Arabs picked up a term for the main town – 'gana' (chief) – and extended it to the empire as a whole, in memory of which Kwame Nkrumah renamed his newly independent country in 1957.

Ghana – the town – was probably today's Koumbi Saleh in Mauritania, the ruins of which cover some 250 hectares (620 acres). In the 1060s the Spanish–Arabic writer Abu Ubaid al-Bakri, one of half a dozen historians who reported on Ghana, gave a detailed if second-hand description of the town and its ruler. The town, mostly of straw-thatched clay huts, also had stone buildings, a slave market and a dozen mosques for its large Muslim population.

The king had long been an absolute ruler, living in a separate royal suburb 10 km (6 miles) from the main town, which was set in protective thorn-thickets. He communicated through ministers, and headed a religious cult with its own priesthood. Adorned with jewels and a golden headdress, he held court in a pavilion guarded by ten horses with gold trappings and dogs wearing collars and bells of silver and gold. Pages, vassal princes and officials attended him. His countrymen paid obeisance by pouring dust on their heads, Muslims by applauding him. His treasure included a gold nugget so large that he tethered his horse to it. When he died, he was buried with retainers beneath a great dome of timber and earth. Al-Bakri said he had an army of 200,000, of whom 40,000 were archers. This could well have been a huge exaggeration, but even an army one-tenth that size would have been enough to deter invasion, and enough also for slave-raids that provided one of Ghana's chief exports. The king controlled the supply of gold, seizing all nuggets for himself in order to prevent a glut and keep the price of gold up. He also controlled the export and import of copper, salt and manufactured goods, on which he imposed taxes.

As Ghana's power grew and became more centralized, its rulers sought to extend their interests rather more directly than before – shortly before 1000, Ghana seized control of neighbouring Awdaghost and put a Soninke governor in command, giving it control over the middle Niger,

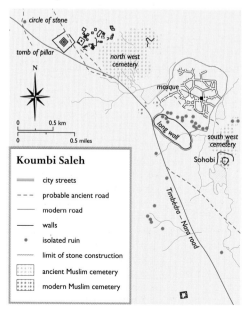

Koumbi Saleh

- ═══ city streets
- ╌╌╌ probable ancient road
- ─── modern road
- ▬▬▬ walls
- • isolated ruin
- ───── limit of stone construction
- ▦ ancient Muslim cemetery
- ▦ modern Muslim cemetery

circle of stone
tomb of pillar
north west cemetery
N
0   0.5 km
0   0.5 miles
mosque
long wall
south west cemetery
Sohobi
Timbédra – Nara road

Jenne-jeno: A Patchwork City

Near today's Jenne (Djenne), a town of mud-brick buildings on the Niger's floodplains about halfway between Mali's capital Bamako and Timbuktu, lies an enormous mound of eroded mud houses and trash: Jenne-jeno, one of the great cities of medieval sub-Saharan Africa.

This was not a city on the European model, with powerful rulers funding grand buildings and sturdy defences. It was a place made by and for ordinary people, one of the several great 'cities without citadels', in the words of two of Jenne-jeno's leading archaeologists, Susan and Roderick McIntosh, who undertook five excavations between 1977 and 1999. Radiocarbon dates show that people first settled here in about 250 BC. In 1000,

after over a millennium of occupation, this 33-hectare (82-acre) site on the river Bani consisted of a large tear-shaped mound surrounded by 69 hillocks, created by its people, which may have numbered up to 27,000, building and rebuilding their houses. The main area was a warren of narrow streets dividing small round and square houses, all surrounded by a wall 3.6 metres (12 feet) thick, made of mud-brick cylinders, possibly either to control floods or to separate domestic and market areas. A secondary mound was reached by a causeway.

In their surveys, the McIntoshes and their co-workers found that different areas, sometimes whole mounds, were homes to different trades or crafts. Fishers, metallurgists, potters and weavers left their products in the soil – bits of iron, slag, pottery, beads from north of the Sahara, grindstones, weights for fishing nets, even toy figures

of clay. Though set in marshy land, the town was well placed for traders to communicate by river with Timbuktu, and overland to the sources of gold and kola nuts to the south.

Apparently, these specialists, drawn from a wide area, settled as neighbours, but without losing their original identities. They must have bartered their services for rice, fish, oil and cattle-products from those living out in the countryside. Jenne-jeno must have a been an intriguing example of social symbiosis, where each family made its own specialist contribution to a wide range of goods and services, without sacrificing ethnic identity.

It was a system that worked well for centuries, and then, from the 12th century, fell into decline, possibly because the climate changed and its surroundings could no longer supply the food it needed. Jenne-jeno was abandoned around 1400.

Mud-brick walls [TOP] reveal patterns of life, work and defence in medieval Jenne-jeno, while the remains of a smith's work shop with three exterior furnaces [BELOW] show the importance of metal-working.

the headwaters of the Senegal and the southern end of the trans-Saharan caravan routes.

Where trade led, religion and government followed, for local rulers would have seen the benefits of peaceful links with Islam, as peoples on Europe's eastern fringes saw the advantages of Christianity. The first recorded ruler to become a Muslim was the 15th *dya* ('ruler') of Gao, Kosoy, who converted in 1009–10, and (according to al-Bakri) was sent a copy of the Koran by the Caliph to mark the occasion. Several other rulers followed suit. A certain War Dyabi of Takrur on the lower Senegal converted around the same time. Ghana (the town, Koumbi Saleh) had its mosques, and although the king was not himself a Muslim, he chose Muslims as his interpreters and ministers. Away to the east, according to a 14th-century history, Kanem's ruler became a Muslim in the 1060s (intriguingly, there is a possibility that the ruler concerned may have been a woman named Hawwa, the brevity of whose reign – c. 1067–71 – suggests a crisis associated with religious and dynastic strife).

Ghana fell into decline, giving way in later

medieval times to other empires: Mali and Kanem-Bornu. Why? Military conquest is one possibility. In the mid 11th century, the Sanhaja Berbers staged a dramatic comeback, acquiring a sudden enthusiasm for Sunni orthodoxy and uniting with other Berber groups to conquer for themselves an empire in the western Sahara. Known as the Almoravids, they drove north into Spain, and south along the Saharan trade routes, seizing Awdaghost.

Under Almoravid influence, Ghana became Muslim. But there is no evidence of a military conquest of Ghana itself, at least not yet. Its decline remains a historical puzzle. Possibly, the kingdom was undermined in part by its own success, in part by a change in climate. Perhaps wealth spawned more people, more animals, and greater pressure on the countryside at a time when rainfall declined. Whatever the explanation, in the 13th century, Mande-speaking invaders took over, and Ghana's heyday was a thing of the past, leaving one enduring change: the borders of Islam had spread southwards, to the very edge of the African heartland, where they remain.

2

The Rich Land of the Great lakes

Arab traders were pressing down the east coast, but their presence had no impact inland. In the region of the Great Lakes a culture developed in total independence.

Uganda is commonly called 'the pearl of Africa' for its astonishing fertility. It and the rest of the Great Lakes region has been a pearl almost since the arrival of the Bantu in the first millennium AD. It became so partly because it is blessedly free from the tsetse fly, partly because of the emergence of two revolutionary products: bananas and cattle.

During the first millennium, the forests were cleared to provide charcoal for iron-smelting, and open spaces for agriculture and livestock. Meanwhile, bananas had been introduced to the coastal regions from south-east Asia. Edible bananas are seedless, and can be propagated only by transplantation. They could not survive in East Africa's plains and the Rift Valley highlands of Kenya. Yet somehow, by about 800, bananas had spread from the coast, via the pastoralists and hill cultivators of the Rift Valley, to the Great Lakes, and evolved (perhaps under cultivation) a great range of varieties. The change was reflected in the growth of new terms for bananas, banana gardens and billhooks for pruning banana trees. By 1000, the areas covered by today's north-west Tanzania, Uganda, Rwanda and Burundi had bananas as a year-round staple.

Simultaneously, herders were using the new grasslands to develop wealth of a different kind: cattle, in particular the long-horned, humped zebu cattle. These were people seeking not to exploit marginal resources, but to maximize a lush environment. In brief, from grass sprang cattle, wealth, power, a whole new culture. Linguistic analysis by David Schoenbrun (then at UCLA, now at the University of Georgia) reveals what he calls 'an astonishing explosion of interest in pastoral pursuits' between 800 and 1450 – six new terms referring to horn shapes and at least 17 new terms for cattle colour. Cattle, bred for size and variety of horn shape, acquired mythical and religious status as gods, heroes and ancestors.

This revolution apparently produced the beginnings of a culture which evolved in the late Middle Ages with elements of urbanization and statehood. Did such a state exist? Perhaps. In 1863, John Speke told another Nile explorer, Samuel Baker, that much of this region had formerly been 'all united in one vast kingdom called Kittara'. The name was adopted by later historians as a sort of catch-all which, in the words of the archaeologist John Sutton, reflected 'a notion of a cultural region with elements of a shared history of considerable depth'. This culture supposedly consisted of societies which were linked by a common language, each defined by common traits: a monarch, a court, an administration, and a mixed agricultural and cattle economy. 'Kitara' is sometimes credited with a royal dynasty known as 'Chwezi'. But *chwezi* means something like 'spirit', and may be no more than a religious term co-opted to give a gloss of authenticity to an invented dynasty. Whether 'Kitara' actually existed is an open question. But, as Sutton argues, it, or its constituent societies, had precedents dating back at least to the year 1000.

One line of research looks at ancient iron-working sites. Iron was as significant a material here as elsewhere. Hammers and anvils were preserved in shrines and tombs, ancient iron-working sites venerated in *chwezi* cults honouring the spirits of ancestors. Other sites are earthworks and settlements. One hill, Mubende, 100 km (60 miles) north-west of Lake Victoria Nyanza, was a shrine in the 19th century, but pottery finds suggest that it too was in use (though not necessarily as a shrine) by 1000.

Possibly Mubende formed part of a network of sites, of which two main ones have been unearthed. One is at Ntusi (The Mounds, as the place is known today), 200 km (125 miles) west of Kampala. It is said that the mounds are the work of *chwezi*, or the Chwezi, but that may be just a recently invented 'tradition'. Probably, the site was an ancient one that combined iron-rich rocks and fertile soils. Here, huge numbers of cattle bones, pottery, grindstones, and the

Gateways to the Interior

By 1000, Arab sailors had established links with the East African coast from Somaliland, 'the land of the Barbar', southwards to the islands of Pemba and Zanzibar, and beyond to Sofala (p. 121). Though many of these were occasional bases, a few — Shanga, Pemba, Zanzibar (Unguja, as the Bantu called it) — were already permanent Arab settlements, as they had long been for local inhabitants. At Shanga in the Lamu archipelago a mosque, built of wood in about 800, was rebuilt in stone in the 10th century. One port, possibly Pemba, named as 'Qanbalu' by al-Masudi, the historian and geographer who claimed to have journeyed down the coast in the early 10th century, had a Muslim ruler who had gained power by conquest. But Islam remained a religion of outsiders for centuries. The 'Zanj' had their own rulers, and the harbours had their own cosmopolitan coastal culture, which acquired its own Bantu-based lingua franca, Swahili (from the Arabic sahil, 'coast').

Initially, the Arabs were drawn mainly by gold and ivory, supplied by elephant-hunters. This was a wide-ranging trade. 'The tusks usually go to Oman, and from there are sent to China and India,' reported al-Masudi. 'This is the chief trade route, and were it not so, ivory would be more plentiful in Muslim lands.' Other products were tortoiseshell, ambergris, iron and animal skins.

The east African coast was also a source of slaves. One account describes how Omani Arabs lured children into slavery by offering them dates, another how a Zanj 'king' was captured. But some historians suggest that the numbers were not great. Slave-raiding would have undermined other trades, and possibly demand for Zanj slaves decreased after the great slave revolt in lower Iraq in the late 9th century.

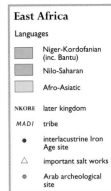

East Africa

Languages

▢ Niger-Kordofanian (inc. Bantu)

▢ Nilo-Saharan

▢ Afro-Asiatic

NKORE later kingdom

MADI tribe

● interlacustrine Iron Age site

△ important salt works

● Arab archeological site

remains of smelting and iron-ore deposits are all evidence of an economy that supported thousands who, according to radiocarbon dating, started to settle there soon after 1000. Their descendants stayed for over 400 years. Reservoirs (*bwogero*) dug out to provide water for cattle and rubbish burned in communal dumps – forming two great mounds known as 'male' and 'female' – suggest large-scale urban administration. Ash, meat-waste and dung could well have been used to intensify the growing of sorghum, the staple crop.

At Bigo ('Defended Place'), 13 km (8 miles) north-east of Ntusi, mounds, earth ramparts and 10 km (6 miles) of ditches, some hacked 4 metres (13 feet) into rock, rear up beside a swamp, a source of fresh water. This site, occupied later than Ntusi but overlapping in time, made a 300-hectare (750-acre) refuge for cattle-owners, who could clearly mobilize a mass of workers well equipped with iron digging tools – which may well have been manufactured at Ntusi. Gaps, sometimes protected by an outer earthwork, suggest gateways with guard-walls.

It is hard to avoid speculation that Ntusi and Bigo were fortresses, or at least refuges, with a ditched and banked central area for the elite; or that they were successive 'capitals' from which 'Kitara' was administered. But at present little seems clear, except that cattle-herding had inspired something of a slow revolution in living habits and social organization. Neither site has the trade goods that would indicate links with Arab traders on the east coast. This was apparently a culture evolving in virtual isolation, interacting only with distant pastoral people like the Maasai and perhaps surviving Khoisan.

Both places seem to have been abandoned in the 16th century, perhaps as a result of over-use. 'Never again,' as Sutton writes, 'was there a settlement as concentrated and permanent as Ntusi; never again were massive earthworks constructed, or enclosures of the size and complexity of Bigo.' But it is likely that here lie the roots of later Ugandan kingdoms like Bunyoro, Toro, Ankole and Buganda, which existed into this century, and whose traditions form a part of Uganda today.

Ethiopia: A World Apart

For well over 1,000 years, Ethiopia had dominated the Red Sea, trading from its port, Adulis, with the Islamic world, India, even China. Traditions spoke of a ruling dynasty founded in the 10th century BC by Menelik, son of Solomon and the Queen of Sheba, who is also credited with stealing the Ark of the Covenant and placing it in the imperial capital, Aksum. A Jewish sect, the Falashas, still look back to these ancient links with Judaism. It had minted its own coins. It had its own written language, Ge'ez, making Ethiopians Africa's only literate non-Islamic people. From Aksum, it had had contact with Christianity for almost 700 years, with a fully fledged offshoot of the Egyptian Coptic Church for over 400 years. The Ethiopic Bible, begun in about 350, was one of the earliest translations.

But in the 7th century, Adulis was destroyed by Arabs. With control of the coast gone, the empire slipped into decline, then fragmented. Obscurity followed. Coins were no longer minted, inscriptions in stone no longer made. In the words of the 18th-century historian Edward Gibbon, 'Encompassed on all sides by the enemies of their religion, the Ethiopians slept near 1,000 years, forgetful of the world, by whom they were forgotten.' Later accounts of these hidden years drew on conflicting traditions. King-lists were more concerned to establish genealogies back to Solomon and Sheba than to root fact from fiction.

To attempt an account of this period is to enter a world as obscure and contradictory as that of Arthurian Britain.

According to some sources, Aksum's decline was hastened after about 950 by a queen called Judith, or Gudit. She was perhaps Jewish, and/or a member of the Zagwe tribe, and/or the wife of a Syrian, and/or ruler of an independent kingdom against which the Ethiopian king mounted an unsuccessful expedition – the range of options make it almost impossible to say anything about her that is certain. In one of the most dramatic tales, Judith is said to have been as beautiful as the Queen of Sheba and of royal blood. In this account, she is inspired by a desire for revenge after becoming the victim of blatant injustice. A young priest falls in love with her and asks to sleep with her.

'You are a priest and I am from the royal family,' she says. 'How dare you sleep with me?'

'State and church are equal,' replies the ardent young man. 'Tell me what I should bring you.'

Judith names her price: golden shoes. The young man tears fabric from a sacred golden curtain, and has them made into shoes. People see the damage, and notice that the hole is foot-sized. Judith's feet match the hole. She produces the shoes, and names the culprit.

So the elders and learned people of the country assemble to pass correct judgement and they say, 'What can a boy under 20 years do when he sees such beauty? She is the one who put him under temptation to do that. He is innocent of guilt and his age will protect him. She is the only one solely responsible for the desecration.' She is condemned to have her right breast cut off, and is chased into exile to the north, to Syria perhaps. There, a local Jewish prince learns of her fate, sympathizes, and marries her. All this while she longs for vengeance against her oppressors and their religion. Her new husband grants her wish, and sends in his troops, taking captives, destroying churches, driving the king, Anbessa Wudem, into exile in Lasta province, 250 km (150 miles) to the south.

There is other evidence that the vengeful 'Judith' actually existed and that these were chaotic times. The patriarch of the Coptic Church in Alexandria had refused to appoint a head (*abuna*) of the Ethiopian Church since the early 10th century. Around 1000, an unnamed king of Ethiopia, possibly Anbessa Wudem, wrote to his neighbour, George (or Girgis), king of Nubia, asking him to use to his influence with the patriarch, Philotheus (in office 979–1004) to have an *abuna* appointed to strengthen his hand against 'a woman, a queen' who 'had revolted against him and his country'. The Arabic historian ibn Hawkal wrote in about 977, 'Regarding the land of the

This church hewn from solid rock was supposedly destroyed by the vengeful Judith. When Christianity returned under a later Zagwe ruler, the tradition was revived and developed to brilliant effect in the rock-churches of Lalibela.

Abyssinians, it has been governed for many years now by a woman. She killed the king of Abyssinia [and] continues to this day to dominate her own country and the neighbouring regions.'

After Judith's death, there followed a brief period of peace. An *abuna*, Daniel, was appointed. Anbessa Wudem's son, Dil Ne'ad, returned from exile, restored Christianity, and had churches built. But his dynasty had been too weakened by war to survive long. A legend relates how Dil Ne'ad had a beloved daughter, Mesobe Werq, of whom it was said that whoever married her would seize the kingdom. For this reason the king kept her under lock and key, until a trusted commander, Mera Tekle Haimanot, saw her, fell in love with her and by a trick married her. In another version of the story, the daughter is thrown into a ditch, where Mera finds her, and raises her as his daughter until she is old enough to become his wife.

In any event, Aksum fell for the second and final time. The focus of Ethiopian culture shifted south, to the Lasta province. Mera founded a new dynasty, known as Zagwe, for reasons that remain obscure. The name perhaps derives from the new king's first names, Zewge Michael; or from his tribe, the Agaw; or from a word meaning 'to pursue' or 'persecute'.

After this possibly apocryphal start in about 1030–50, the Zagwe kings – different lists name a dozen or more – ruled from their capital, Roha, for over 200 years, until a new dynasty claiming Solomonic descent seized power in about 1270. The Zagwe remains an obscure dynasty, because it was never regarded as legitimate by subsequent rulers. But one king in particular stood out: Lalibela (1160–c.1211), who inspired the creation of one of the wonders of the medieval world – a dozen churches carved from solid rock. With

their glorious wall-paintings, these extraordinary churches seem to have continued a tradition established by Dil Ne'ad in Aksum. They survive as tributes to the sturdiness of Ethiopian Christianity, drawing tourists to Roha, later renamed Lalibela in honour of the greatest Zagwe leader.

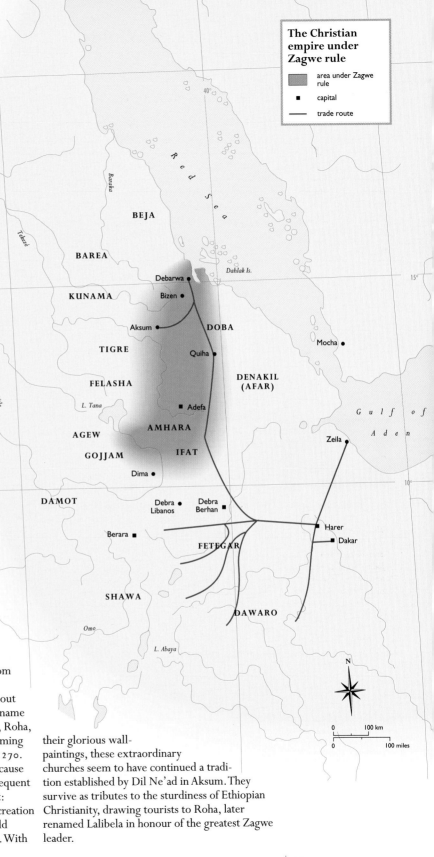

The Christian empire under Zagwe rule

- area under Zagwe rule
- ■ capital
- — trade route

4 The South: The Golden Meadows of Zimbabwe's First Capital

On the borders of present-day Zimbabwe and South Africa, dry-stone ruins on a flat-topped hill offer the earliest evidence of stability and wealth.

This rhinoceros, 15.2 cm (6 inches) long, was one one of many golden objects found on Mapungubwe. It is made of hammered gold sheets folded and tacked to a carved wooden base.

In the 1890s, in the wilds of the northern Transvaal, a white loner named Lotrie took to the wild and began living as a hermit. His sanctuary was an elongated sandstone mesa, one of many on the southern bank of the Limpopo, a remote spot where lions roamed and elephants waded across to feed on malala palms. Lotrie chose well, for the locals dreaded the hill – Mapungubwe, the Hill of the Jackals – and avoided it. Lotrie somehow scaled the 60-metre (200-foot) cliffs, found himself on a treeless platform 320 metres (350 yards) long, and saw strange things – stones, walls, pottery, graves. He brought down a large earthenware pot, which he eventually gave to a local.

Years later, in the late 1920s, this man, now very old, told the story of how he came by the pot to a farmer and prospector named van Graan. Intrigued, van Graan, his son and three other companions came looking for the hill in late December 1932. A local, Mowena, promised to act as guide, but as they approached, Mowena's courage failed him. He refused even to point out the hill. His son, trembling with fright, did so, but refused to go further. Forced forward by van Graan and his companions, he showed them the way up – a narrow cleft, about 30 cm (12 inches) wide. On either side of the cleft were holes. Once

these had held bits of wood, making the rungs of a ladder. At the summit, the explorers found heaps of boulders, apparently placed so that they could be rolled onto intruders. They had stumbled on a fortress.

Earthenware pots buried to the neck in the sandy soil had served as a reservoir. There were rusted iron tools, copper wire, glass beads and, to the astonishment of the Afrikaners, gold beads, bangles and little gold-plated rhinoceroses. A grave revealed a skeleton with iron and gold bangles. The five men realized they had a treasure trove on their hands. They divided the gold between them, and wondered what to do next. Luckily, van Graan junior had as a student at Pretoria University become interested in pre-history. He recognized the importance of the site and consulted his old professor. A month later, a university archaeological expedition arrived, just in time to prevent an invasion from hundreds of treasure-seekers.

The work, initially marred by inexperience and haste, was only resumed seriously in 1968 by Professor J.F. Gloff and continued by his former student Andrie Meyer of the University of Pretoria's Anthropology Department. The results, published in 1998, at last throw light on the origins of the people who dug for gold in dozens of mines across Zimbabwe, left ruins at scores of sites, and whose successors built southern Africa's best-known example of drystone architecture, Great Zimbabwe itself.

Mapungubwe presents many enigmas. It is an ancient site, occupied before the arrival of Bantu people, probably by Khoisan (which would mean that they too had developed a settled culture before fleeing the Bantu). Perhaps Khoisan and Bantu fought over this prime site for centuries before permanent Bantu occupation. Research on Mapungubwe and related sites suggests that in the warm, moist climate that dominated the Limpopo river area around 1000, the ancestors of today's Shona developed a cattle-rich culture productive and stable enough to inspire a new power structure, new ways of controlling wealth, something that could be called a kingdom, even a state.

These cattle-herders would have lived in small homesteads flanking the larger byre of the chief. Wealth was measured in cattle, which could be lent, borrowed and given in exchange for other goods, and wives. The consequence can be seen at Mapungubwe and other sites. The principal ones are at the bottom of Mapungubwe Hill, a place known simply as K2, Mapungubwe itself, and other nearby sites of the region, known as the Greefswald.

At K2, some local 10th-century leader had built, and prospered, in part from Arab traders

Hunter-Gatherers of the Western Deserts

As the Bantu advanced southwards, favouring the wetter eastern areas, they tended to assimilate or drive out the original inhabitants, two copper-coloured small-statured peoples, the Khoikhoi (once known as Hottentots) pastoralists and the San (or Bushmen) hunter-gatherers. The two are commonly referred to together as Khoisan, as is their language group. This is notable for its complex of

click-sounds, one of which is represented in the first letter of their best-known tribe, the !Kung.

Once scattered over all of southern Africa, most Khoisan were by 1000 already surviving only in the more arid regions of the western Cape and the Kalahari Desert. Not all of them: Khoisan hunter-gatherers probably still inhabited much of western and south-eastern Tanzania.

Elsewhere, the Khoisan must already have been falling back on the specialist skills that had, for more than 20,000 years, enabled them to live in the relatively barren lands of the Kalahari and the

Karoo. A study in the 1960s, during a severe drought that placed 180,000 on a UN relief programme, showed that the !Kung, foraging and hunting for a mere 19 hours a week each, could supply themselves with 8.3 per cent more calories and 55 per cent more protein than the UN's recommended daily allowance. This was not luxury – the !Kung lacked fats, and birthrates were low. But the findings explained how the Khoisan had survived the ever harsher conditions and ever smaller ranges imposed on them by the spread of the Bantu.

For some three centuries, the natural fortress of Mapungubwe was a city-state, and the heart of a kingdom that preceded – and perhaps inspired – the Shona culture of Great Zimbabwe.

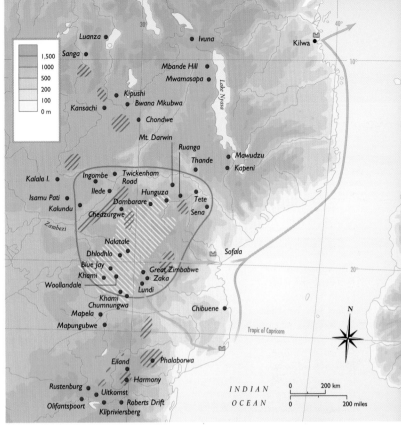

Mapungubwe and Zimbabwe

- ● Iron Age site
- Islamic fort
- copper mining and working area
- gold mining and working area
- → major route of the gold trade
- ◯ area under control of the Shona monarchy based at Great Zimbabwe

from the established ports of east Africa to the north who made occasional landings on the Mozambique coast, and exchanged their goods for slaves, leopard skins (which were used to make saddles), tortoiseshell and ivory. They called this region by the name of their anchorage: Sofala, from the Arabic for 'shoal'. The place had 'meadows of gold', according to the 12th-century Sicilian geographer al-Idrisi. By al-Idrisi's day, the inland plateau between the Limpopo and the Zambezi was a gold-rich empire, and it seems likely that Africans, who had long known how to extract iron and copper, had begun to use gold in the 10th century, probably in response to Arab interest in it.

Traditionally, wealth had been based on cattle. Now, wealth of a different kind worked a revolution. Gold panned from the hills to the north, ivory, glass beads and cloth could be hoarded as cattle could not, for that would destroy the culture's ecological base. For the first time, there emerged a society that was recognizably urban, defined by the acquisition of material goods. Beads and pottery from India, Egypt, China and the Middle East found at Mapungubwe suggest that around 1000 the Greefswald region was integrated into Arabic trade patterns across the Indian Ocean. Growing wealth also supported specialists: potters, iron-workers, weavers, makers of ivory bracelets and bone tools

As power and wealth grew, so too did the central court's impact on its surroundings. In about 1020, the central house had produced so much rubbish that its midden swamped the cattle byre. There was nothing for it but to move the cattle out, and create more space for people.

Two generations passed, and growth continued, until the site could hold no more. The king moved his HQ onto the natural fortress itself. An emerging class structure received outward and visible expression. On the hillside above he built a stone residence, as if (in the words of one archaeologist) to assert 'an association between the majesty of hills and the majesty of kingship'.

Within a few years, Mapungubwe expressed the new social stratification: a scattering of stone-built residences probably owned by brothers and uncles of the chief – in effect, the town houses of district leaders – and a densely packed enclosure for commoners. The ladder was not the only point of entry. A staircase cut into the rock, with supports as bannisters, led up to the king's own drystone enclosure, with separate buildings for his wives – indicated by the presence of grindstones – and a burial ground for the elite. It was an arrangement reflected in four other hilltop sites discovered within 100 km (60 miles). One of these, Mapela, 85 km (53 miles) to the north-west, was a 100-metre-high (330-foot-high) hill entirely terraced to provide level building sites all the way round, and all the way up.

Mapungubwe's heyday was over by about 1250, perhaps because the climate became drier, perhaps because its inhabitants were cut off from their Arab trading partners by the opening of richer sources of gold further north. The people dispersed, some perhaps even migrating north, taking their cattle-rich culture, their trade, their religion and their social hierarchies with them. In areas where lower temperatures limited the virulence of the tsetse fly, they built new *dzimba dzemabwe*, 'houses of stone', a term that provided a name for a new capital that would become the greatest in medieval sub-Saharan Africa: Zimbabwe.

OCEANIA

Remote Worlds Linked by Polynesian Voyages

The southern hemisphere, which is mainly water, offers fewer niches for social evolution than the northern. Oceania, though, had two neighbouring cultures that could hardly be more different: the Polynesians and the Australian Aboriginals.

The contrast between Polynesia and Australia could hardly be more extreme. About the only thing they had in common was space. One, a world of small-scale settlements in immensities of water, had for over 1,000 years been thrusting, restless, outward looking. The other, small-scale settlements in immensities of desert, had found stability in post-glacial times, some 15,000–18,000 years ago.

Australia's original inhabitants crossed by boat from south-east Asia some time between 50,000 and 60,000 years ago according to the most widely accepted estimates. It is as well to be reminded of how ancient aboriginal culture is. In 1969, Jim Bowler of the Australian National University was studying sediments in Lake Mungo, one of the many ancient, dried-up Willandra Lakes in western New South Wales which have since yielded 135 skeletal remains over 15,000 years old. He found human remains of a slender young woman. After death, she had been cremated, her bones smashed, and the remains gathered carefully into a small depression beside the funeral pyre. The cremation took place some 17,000–20,000 years ago. The same reverential ritual was used continuously right on through the millennia, through the year 1000, until recent times in eastern Australia and Tasmania.

Confronted by such a timescale it seems presumptious to expect a a few decades to reveal significant change. The little period that is the subject of this book is dictated by distant developments that had no conceivable impact on this ancient land at the time. Yet, of course, they did later. Aboriginal ecological expertise would have no chance against the technological culture beginning to emerge in Europe in 1000. That year is a good a time as any to examine the strengths and weaknesses of Australia's indigenous cultures.

On the immense timescale of Australian history, this was not a static environment, and the presence of humans contributed to change. Dozens of species of large animals died out under the double pressure of increasing aridity and human predation (including a 7-metre (23-foot) lizard, a giant kangaroo, a giant wombat and a flightless bird). As the continental heartland reached its present-day aridity, the end of the last Ice Age flooded vast areas of coast. Some time before 2000 BC, dingoes arrived, probably as pets that escaped into the wild. Cultures evolved hundreds of local variants, and some 250 separate languages. As the population rose, the pace of change quickened, with change being measured over single millennia rather than in tens. From the timbered Blue Mountains to the grasslands of Arnhem Land, fire was used to modify environments and drive animals from cover. New foods were developed, some of which show astonishing ingenuity. In the south-east, Aboriginals somehow learned to process the poisonous nuts of the fern-like Macrozamia. The nuts are a wonderful food source – easy to harvest, high in carbohydrate and protein – but they have a severe drawback: unprocessed, they are not only toxic, sometimes fatally, but also contain a powerful carcinogen. Learning how to prepare them must have involved many trials and many unfortunate errors. Other groups became expert engineers, building traps and canals to catch eels, or took up fishing. All of this was accompanied by an extraordinary cultural depth, expressed in art, ritual and legend.

Yet Aboriginals lacked a number of elements which elsewhere have led on to urbanization, among them horticulture. This was not because of any lack of information or plants, like sugar cane and bananas. Had they wished, Aboriginals could have imported them from Indonesia (from around 1000, right up until 1907, people from the Indonesian island of Sulawesi visited north-west Australia every year to collect sea cucumbers, which were prized in China for making aphrodisiacs and soups). Nor was there total lack of opportunity for horticulture locally, since Aboriginals gathered and processed wild millet. Nor did they lack the ability to store foods.

One possible answer is that horticulture offered them no benefits. Instead, they turned their skills to maximizing the use of their surroundings as hunter-gatherers. In effect, all Australia was their farm and their store-house. Just as farmers refrain from eating seed-grain, so Aboriginals learned to use their environment to the full, enshrining knowledge in legend and ritual. Emus, for instance, were protected by taboos: one tribe in the south-eastern highlands forbade young men from eating emu flesh, another banned the gathering of emu eggs. What need was there to store fruit, when sun-dried fruit could be found lying on the ground, preserved by desiccation? Tilling, planting, harvesting and storing are immense labours, and Aboriginals had no need to undertake any of them. They were well off without.

Captain Cook's judgement of the Aboriginals in 1770 was sound: 'They may appear to some to be the most wretched people upon Earth, but in reality they are far more happier than we Europeans. They live in a Tranquillity which is not disturb'd by the Inequality of Condition. The Earth and the sea of their own accord furnishes [sic] them with all things necessary for life.'

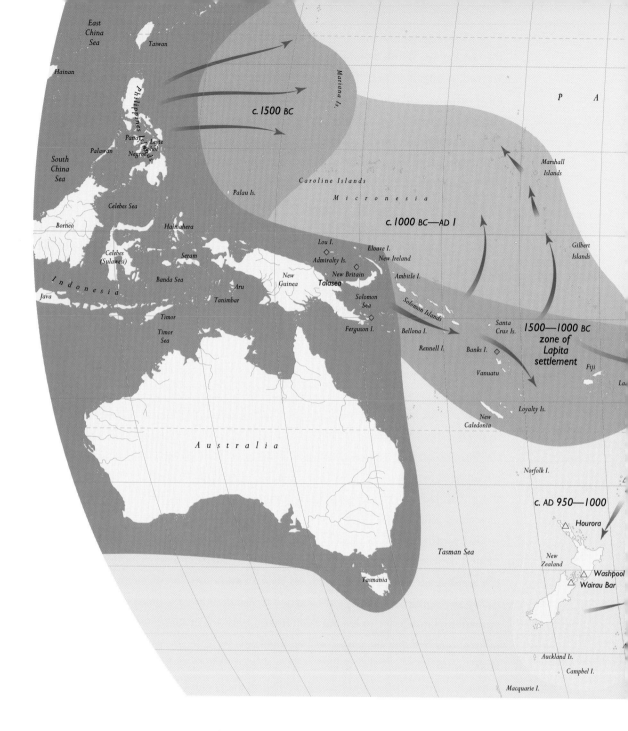

It was around 1000 that the world's most extensive culture reached its geographical
limits. For 3,000 years the Polynesians had been hopping from eastern Indonesia
along the 38 island groups and several hundred habitable islands that form a broad
belt spattering the Pacific. By the mid 10th century, they had marked out an immense
triangle of occupation, its corners on Fiji, Hawaii and Easter Island. The south, in the
direction of New Zealand, was as yet unexplored.

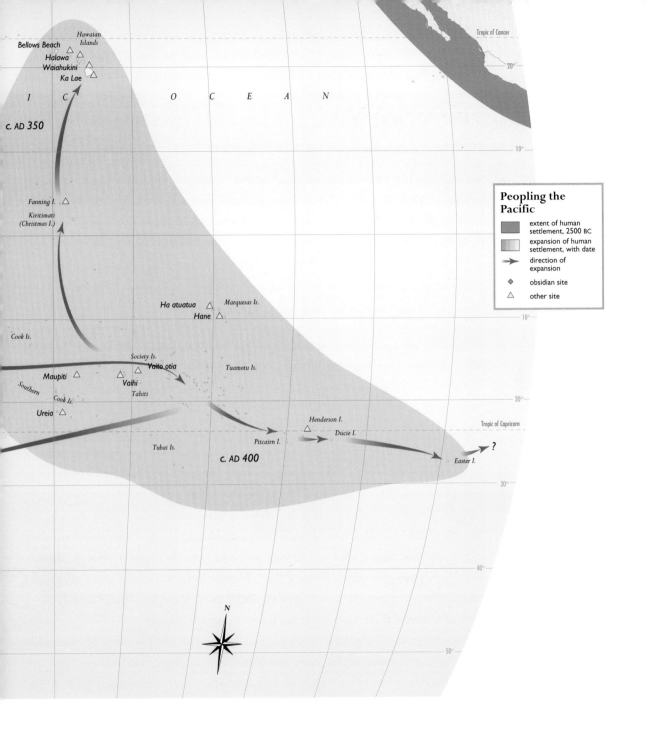

Hawaian
Islands

Bellows Beach
Halawa △
Waiahukini △
Ka Lae △

I   C   O   C   E   A   N

c. AD 350

Fanning I. △

Kiritimati
(Christmas I.)

Ha atuatua △   Marquesas Is.
Hane △

Cook Is.

Society Is.
Vaito otia
Maupiti △   △   Tuamotu Is.
Vaihi
Southern
Cook Is.   Tahiti
Ureia △

Henderson I.
△   Ducie I.

Tubai Is.   Pitcairn I.   ?
c. AD 400   Easter I.

Tropic of Capricorn

N

**Peopling the
Pacific**

extent of human
settlement, 2500 BC

expansion of human
settlement, with date

direction of
expansion

◆   obsidian site

△   other site

From the arrival of the first European scientists in Pacific waters in the 18th century, it was clear that these volcanic pinpoints and coral atolls had all been colonized by people of the same stock. Polynesians, of course, had always known this. But to Europeans it was an astonishing discovery. At a time when European and Chinese sailors warily hugged coastlines, Polynesians had been voyaging across hundreds of kilometres of open ocean, and on occasion over 1,500 km (1,000 miles). How had these feats been accomplished? That question led to others – did the first arrivals stay? Did they send word back? Would there have been a fleet of later arrivals? Long-drawn-out controversies divided academics. Many – like the great part-Maori historian Te Rangi Hiroa, or Sir Peter Buck to give him his Pakeha (white) name – portrayed Polynesians as the most expert colonizing seafarers in world history, ranging up to 5,000 km (3,000 miles) in their huge and fast double-hulled yachts. To landlubbers, it is almost beyond belief that such minute dots can be found at all, even given the Polynesian expertise at using stars for guidance. Yet there are many indications of an island, even when it lies over the horizon. Shallows create their own wave patterns, clouds hint at hidden land, birds range far from home – these effects and many more give an island an aura, magnifying a kilometre of sand and palms into a target up to 60 km (40 miles) across. Others disclaimed all this, saying that discovery had all been the result of accident, each island being discovered by random drifters.

The 'random drift' idea steadily lost ground. A computer analysis in 1973 simulated over 100,000 random-drift voyages, and failed to deliver any 'virtual' settlers to east Polynesia, let alone Hawaii, Easter Island or New Zealand. In 1985, the issue was settled to the satisfaction of almost everyone when Ben Finney, Professor of Anthropology in Hawaii, and his students sailed a 19-metre (62-foot) double-hulled canoe, the *Hokulea*, from Hawaii to New Zealand, guided only by a Micronesian expert in traditional navigation. The journey confirmed the view that there was nothing physically impossible about sailing intentionally between any of the Pacific islands.

But Finney and his crew had one supreme advantage: they knew that New Zealand existed. The first colonists, whether in New Zealand or anywhere else, did not. They departed with their families, animals and plants simply on the assumption that they would find land before they had to turn for home. Having found it, though, their skills were enough to allow them, if they chose, to return with the news, and invite others (though with very remote places, like New Zealand and Easter Island, the issue of whether there were multiple journeys remains open).

But why go at all? Perhaps tensions created by population pressure, or diminishing resources, or disease, or war were enough to inspire exploration in some cases. Yet many journeys seem to have been undertaken when no such pressures existed. And when the great days of exploration were over, the journeys ceased, and islanders proved quite capable of living within their island confines.

The best reason to explore was a reason common to all humanity: to find a good life in a rich and easy environment. A large Pacific island which had never had a large predator was a treasure. Oceania before humans arrived may have had 9,000 species of bird, more than all surviving species in the world today. A new island could offer undergrowth teeming with birds, shorelines rich in turtles and shallows packed with fish, all often protected by a coral reef. No wonder the uninhabited coral island is such a romantic ideal. As a paper on the settlement of New Zealand puts it, 'the uninhabited island was the prehistoric equivalent of winning a lottery'. Finding one meant peace and well-being for many generations. In brief, colonization was not a matter of wave-battered survivors struggling ashore after being lost at sea. It was fast, systematic, two-way and rewarding enough to make the risks worth taking.

One mystery that remains unsolved is that of the origin of the sweet potato, which Polynesians began to cultivate sometime in the first millennium. This is a South American plant, which has suggested the idea that some Andean seafarers were responsible for delivering sweet potatoes to Polynesia. The problem with this suggestion is that no South American culture is known to have produced such expert sailors. But Polynesia did. Could it be that around AD 400 a reconnaissance canoe actually made it all the way to South America, picked up some food-plants and returned to Polynesia? If so, perhaps these hypothetical explorers discovered Easter Island on the way, returning not only with sweet potatoes but also with news of yet another uninhabited island far to the east, the last in the line.

Of the many consequences of colonization, two stand out. The first is true of colonization everywhere. Habitats that had evolved an astonishing wealth and complexity were degraded as settlers assumed the role of top predators, consuming birds, turtles and shellfish.

The second consequence was true only of this scattered culture. Some 50 separate societies evolved, each governed as a chiefdom, a social structure ranked as intermediate between tribe and state. Polynesian chiefdoms ranged from the simple, in which chiefs were hardly more than respected elders, to highly complex and stratified societies like Hawaii, whose chiefs set themselves utterly apart from their subjects by surrounding themselves with possessions, hierarchies and rituals, even marrying their sisters to maintain the bloodline.

The opening up of New Zealand marked the end of the great days of exploration. Any island on the Pacific frontier would know that there was nothing else over the horizon (though there was one final, challenging step south-east of New Zealand, to the subarctic Chatham Islands, colonized in about 1400). Polynesian societies turned in on themselves, becoming more separate, evolving as island universes until the arrival of Europeans.

The Moth-Eaters of the Australian Alps

To most people, Aboriginal culture means outback culture. But Aboriginals had long lived in the cooler, damper south-east. They were even familiar with the uplands of the Great Dividing Range, and around 1000 they were making regular climbs into the heights of the Snowy Mountains.

For millennia, Aboriginal cultures had been rarefied by wilderness: a million people in 7.5 million square kilometres (3 million square miles). But at the turn of the millennium, many of these diffuse tribes were in some respects connected by trade. Pearl shells from the coast of the Kimberleys in the north-west were exchanged right across the continent and worn by people 1,600 km (2,600 miles) away in the Great Australian Bight. Baler shells from Cape York, chipped and perforated into ornaments, found their way to the south coast. Heavy-duty stone axes from a quarry on Mt William, Victoria, were used as currency over at least 300 km (200 miles). Ochre, extracted from several mines, in particular a huge one at Wilgie Mia, Western Australia, was particularly valuable. Turned to powder, dampened and worked into balls, it was then ready to be traded for use in ceremonies and rock painting as far as Queensland, some 2,500 km (1,500 miles) away. Wooden wedges in Wilgie Mia date mining, and probably trading as well, from around 1000.

These activities, combined with rituals and superb rock art, hint at the variety, depth and cooperative abilities of Aboriginal societies. But there is little here that allows for narrative history, little that indicates significant change on a scale less than centuries.

But in south-east Australia, in the Snowy Mountains, something new did develop. Rising to 2,230 metres (7,320 feet), the Snowy Mountains live up to their name for half the year, not the sort of area normally associated with Aboriginals. But by the 1970s several stone axes had been found near mountain peaks. Something had inspired local Aboriginals to become mountaineers.

The answer lies with a species of moth, *Agrotis infusa*, commonly known by its Aboriginal name, bogong. These moths evolved in cooler times, and do not like the summer heat of their homelands to the north and west of New South Wales's uplands. Relatively recently, they adopted the sensible habit of commuting to the mountains to aestivate (as opposed to hibernate) in high, cool crevices. Though they are less common now, perhaps due to the impact of grazing or insecticides, they used to arrive in clouds in early summer, between September and November. They settled on vertical surfaces in caves and fissures, forming huge mats, overlapping one another like miniature roof tiles. There they stayed until the weather cooled, then they left for home.

The moths' abdomens are over 50 per cent fat, and make a wonderfully nutritious food. This is what drew Aboriginals to the heights

Australia

- major rock art area
- axe-head distribution area
- major trade route for pearl and baler shells

Cape York
Laura
Victoria River
Kimberley
Burrup Peninsula
Pilbara
Central Australia
Carnarvon Ranges
Broken Hill
Cobar
Flinders Ranges
Olary
Great Australian Bight
Mt William
Grampians
Great Dividing Range
Sydney Hawkesbury area
N
0   400 km
0   400 miles
West-coast engravings
SW Tasmanian stencils

prospect of a feast inspired intertribal cooperation. From October on, several hundred Aboriginals from half a dozen different highland tribes – a sort of 'highland confederacy' that excluded coast-dwellers – would assemble for the 2–3 months of festivities, or 'corroborees'. Warned of the arrival of the moths by circling ravens, the tribes would first hold a corroboree at the foot of the hills, where bull-roarers and songs would drive away evil spirits. Then everyone would make the gruelling ascent to gather moths, and eat and socialize – trading, initiating young men into manhood, arranging marriages.

After a six-hour climb, the people would have been met by a heartening sight, as an 1865 expedition led by Robert Vyner discovered: 'On both sides of the chasms the face of the stone was literally covered with these insects, packed closely side by side, over head and under, presenting a dark surface of a scale-like pattern … So numerous were these moths that six bushels of them [about 200 litres] could easily have been gathered by the party at this one peak; so abundant were the remains of the former occupants that a stick was thrust into the debris on the floor to a depth of four feet [1.2 metres].'

Then came the preparations for the first of a series of feasts. An instruction leaflet for moth paté would run as follows: lay a kangaroo skin on the floor; run a stick under the bottom edge of the moth-tapestry, so that the somnolent moths fall en masse; collect moths in skin; take them outside; having previously prepared a fire and removed the embers, pour moths onto hot ashes, taking care not to burn them; sift off ashes; winnow in a net so that the singed heads drop off; place bodies in a hollow piece of bark, and grind them into a paté with a smooth stone; to serve, make into plum-sized cakes.

The result was delicious. The 1865 expedition leader, Robert Vyner, ate a quart of moths cooked by his Aboriginal guide 'and found them exceedingly nice and sweet, with a flavour of walnut'. Weeks of feasting ended as the remaining moths dispersed, and everyone descended in terrific shape. As another late-19th-century anthropologist noted, 'when they returned from the mountains their skins looked glossy and most of them were fat'.

During the summer months, bogong moths still form luscious hangings like this on the walls and ceilings of caves in the Bogong Hills.

of the Snowy Mountains around 1000, and kept them coming until the late 19th century, to five main ranges spanning the arc of the Australian Alps, but most notably to the region named after them, the Bogong Mountains. A bogong cave was discovered in the mountains in the 1970s by Jim Webb of the Botany Department, Australian National University, and described by the archaeologist Josephine Flood in 1981. This 'excellent overnight sleeping place', with a large floor area protected by an overhang, lies at the top of a knoll above the headwaters of the Tidbinbilla river. Here lay the evidence for the presence of moth-eaters: a few stone knives, a river stone that had been carried up to act as a pestle, and charcoal from a fire which, according to radiocarbon dating, had been used in about 1000. Of course, the moth-eaters may have discovered this item of diet long before, but there is no evidence so far.

On the basis of this and eyewitness accounts of 19th-century observers, it is possible to build up a picture of what went on here around the turn of the millennium.

If later practices are a guide to former ones, the

2 Colonists of the 'Long White Cloud'

The first arrivals in New Zealand were seafarers to match the Vikings. Like the Vikings, they discovered a new world. Unlike the Vikings, they stayed, and made it their own.

In the early 10th century, New Zealand was the world's last uninhabited land mass (discounting Antarctica). It lay isolated from human contact, as it had been for all human history, occupied only by birds and coastal mammals. But it is quite possible that eastern Polynesians guessed its existence from the streams of migrating shearwaters and petrels heading south to breed between late September and early November. Somewhere over the horizon there had to be land.

According to tradition as adapted by modern historians, in about 950 a catamaran captain named Kupe set out on a voyage of exploration from a base in southern Polynesia traditionally known as 'Hawaiiki'. There are strong similarities between recent archaeological finds in New Zealand and others in the Marquesas and the Society Islands, but 'Hawaiiki' might equally have been the Cook Islands or French Polynesia. Historians theorize that, like other Polynesian

explorers before him, Kupe took along enough to establish a colony in case he found new land: at least 20 men and women, dogs, and plants and seeds, perhaps in more than one canoe.

He and his expedition undertook something astonishing: a voyage of several weeks into the unknown. Not that the length of the voyage would have been a novelty for any of them, for many of Kupe's ancestors had made similar journeys. But all had been within the well-understood limits of the predictable trade winds. Kupe was heading south into chilly and stormy waters, without knowing what he would find.

Perhaps he and his crew were aware that it was a good time to travel. Climatologists have identified 950–1000 as a warm period, with strong winds blowing from the north-east towards New Zealand. Some 2–4 weeks' sailing south-west of Rarotonga, they would have seen the first indication that their journey was not in vain – circling birds, a distant cloud. Arriving on the north coast of Aotearoa – the Land of the Long White Cloud – they beached, and stayed.

Kupe must have been well prepared in case no one made the return journey. His people would have had all the expertise they needed to live well, with specialist knowledge of woodworking, horticulture, stone-working for tools and weapons, fishing, and food-preserving. He would

New Zealand

Vegetation

- alpine and sub-alpine
- forest
- shrub and fern
- tussock grassland
- swamp

→ *Hokulea's track (1985)*

Bay of Islands

North Island

South Island

Canterbury Plains

Otago Peninsula

N

| 0 | | 100 km |
| 0 | | 100 miles |

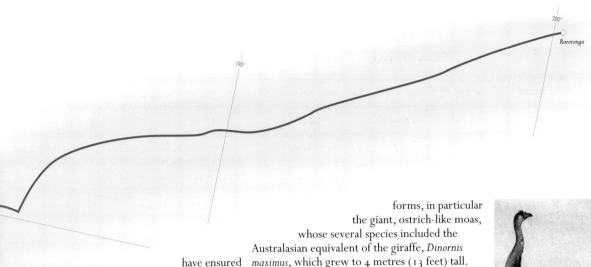

forms, in particular
the giant, ostrich-like moas,
whose several species included the
Australasian equivalent of the giraffe, *Dinornis
maximus*, which grew to 4 metres (13 feet) tall.

There is a belief among urbanized romantics
that idealizes hunter-gatherers as embodiments of
ecological wisdom, carefully preserving their food
sources from overuse. It is hard to find evidence
to support this belief. On the contrary, many pre-
urban societies exploited their resources to the
limit of their abilities, and continued to do so
when some new technique emerged. The Easter
Islanders were one example, the buffalo-hunters
of the North American plains another. New
Zealand's first settlers were no different. As their
numbers increased, their habits had dramatic
effects on the region's ecology.

Soil samples with charcoal particles, and
increasing amounts of grass pollen and decreasing
forest pollen, reveal that forests were burned to
encourage the growth of starch-rich edible
bracken. The drier, rolling country, like that in
Central Otago on the South Island, was burned
first. Moas, with no experience of predators, were
prime targets for spears and snares, and were
hunted out of their preferred browsing ranges
into remoter areas (the last ones may have survived into the late 18th century). Polynesian rats
thrived on birds' eggs, and many species were
driven rapidly towards extinction.

In these cooler regions, tropical horticulture
was not the best way to ensure a good life. Maoris
remained devoted to wild foods, even in the
balmier climate of the North Island's northern
regions where sweet potatoes could be grown.
Once the initial feeding frenzy in the south was
over, it was the north that sustained the greater
population. But agriculture was never a complete
answer, and wild resources were limited. After
some 400 years, the settlers gradually adopted a
new lifestyle in fortified villages. It seems that
diminishing resources in this once rich land led to
the rise of the small-scale warrior societies that
the Europeans found when they arrived in the
18th century.

have ensured
he had plants and
seeds to grow coconuts, paper
mulberry, yam and sweet potato.

The place he found exceeded all
expectation. This was no island, in the
Polynesian sense. It was a miniature continent,
entirely untouched, and packed with food
sources. Glorious forests. Swarms of birds throng-
ing the seas, coasts and forests. Seals galore. A
cornucopia, ripe for exploitation.

What followed was no routine colonization,
however. New Zealand's temperate climate made
it unsuitable for established tropical crops, like
coconut, banana and breadfruit. Sweet potato
could be made to grow, but only in the north, and
only in the right conditions. Polynesian pigs would
lack food, and could easily destroy a sweet potato
crop before it could be harvested. If pigs were
brought, they were not bred. More surprisingly,
nor were chickens. Perhaps the first colonists, surrounded by a such a wealth of winged alternatives,
saw no need for them.

Soon, perhaps, a crew was on its way back
home to report. Researchers guess that this would
have been the only way for the colonists to build
up the numbers they needed to spread so far
and so fast. Experienced sailors like these would
have been able to make a quick survey of the
entire coastline within one summer, if they
wished. After a few decades, one or two generations, there may have been as many as 500 people
busily exploring and exploiting their new-found
land.

The colonists would have discovered that the
South Island was even more of a treasure than the
mountainous and densely forested north. Shallow
lagoons and gently flowing rivers were rich in fish.
The open forests, shrublands and grasslands of the
Canterbury Plains were home to a range of new
delicacies. With no indigenous mammals and few
reptiles, birds had evolved impressive flightless

*Lacking predators, the
ostrich-like moas of New
Zealand evolved into at
least 13 species. Several —
including the 4-metre (12-
foot) Dinornis maximus,
portrayed here — co-existed
with Maoris, who hunted
them to extinction.*

Easter Island: The Message of the Statues

Around 1000, the people on this pin-point of land, the world's remotest inhabited spot, had achieved notable success. But success in-spired an obses-sion that would lead to catastrophe – a catastrophe of peculiar relevance to the world a millennium later.

After a five-hour flight west over the Pacific from Chile, the vast expanse of ocean is broken by a bleak triangle: Easter Island, the world's remotest inhabited place, 2,250 km (1,400 miles) from its closest inhabited neighbour, Pitcairn Island, and 3,765 km (2,340 miles) from the mainland. Its three volcanoes make it a spectacular place, but it is no tropical paradise. Too far south for coral, it has no reefs, no expanses of sandy beach, no waving palms. It would have little to recommend it were it not for the hundreds of massive stone faces scattered over its grassy slopes.

The place posed mysteries from the first visit by an outsider, a Dutch admiral, Jacob Roggeveen, on an Easter day in 1722. He was greeted by a man in a flimsy canoe, 'quite naked, without having the least covering in front of what modesty forbids being named more clearly'. On the island were some 3,000 people living in elongated reed huts, engaged in perpetual warfare and perhaps cannibalism. The place, he noted, was 'destitute of large trees'.

Yet the island, Rapa Nui to its inhabitants, had not always been so poverty-stricken, as its iconic statues indicate – over 800 of these *moai*, with their beetling brows, thin retrousse noses and distended earlobes. Some stare blankly across the grassy slopes, some are toppled, some lie un-finished in the Rano Raraku crater where they were carved from volcanic rock. Most are 2–10 metres (7 – 33 feet) high, and weigh up to 10 tonnes. The islanders Roggeveen saw could not have carved or raised them. Something very strange had happened here. A number of authors revelled in the mystery, proclaiming the statues as evidence of lost civilizations or alien visitations. Now, after four decades of research, archae-ologists have a rather more rational explanation, one that has disturbing implications.

The key is the lack of palms. There is no reason why they should not grow here, for the Chilean wine palm (*Jubaea chilensis*) grows several degrees further south on the mainland. In the late 1970s and early 1980s, scientist John Flenley took core samples from a swampy lake in the crater of Rano Raraku, and found that the island's lowlands had once been covered by palms. Other evidence con-firms this: post-holes made by tree trunks, palm nuts found in caves, rock carvings of large canoes made of tree trunks. This had once been a temper-ate Eden. Yet by the late 18th century there were no trees and hardly any canoes – indeed, the islanders preferred to swim, and the word for tree had come to mean 'wealth'. What had happened?

Legend speaks of an ancestral colonizer, Hotu Matua, arriving in a 30-metre (100-foot) canoe with scores of people and a survival package of plants and animals. Where did he come from? In the late 1940s, the Norwegian explorer-scientist Thor Heyerdahl made an epic voyage on his raft, the *Kon Tiki*, in an attempt to prove that the islanders came from South America. His drifting raft did indeed reach the Tuamotos after three months at sea – but he had managed to start the journey only by being towed 80 km (50 miles) away from shore to avoid being swept northwards instead of westwards. In fact, the strongest evid-ence points overwhelmingly to a Polynesian ori-gin. As with all Polynesian islands, settlement probably occurred by a combination of luck and judgement. Seeking new lands, Hotu Matua and his clan happened on this empty forested island, and stayed. An island tradition claims 57 genera-tions of kings from that first landing, which suggests that it occurred in the 5th century. According to one of about 30 radiocarbon dates obtained by archaeologists, people were well established by about 700.

By 1000, after perhaps six cen-turies of isolation, the islanders were prospering, despite their impoverished environment. The pigs had died quickly, and the island was too cold for other tropical plants. But they had enough: bananas, sweet pota-toes, sugar cane, fish and chickens. By then there would

Vai M

Maitake te M

Matari

Ahu Tepeu

Vai Tapa Er

N

Hanga Roa
(Cook's Bay)

Hanga
Roa
Village

Pu
Pa

Ana Kai Tangata

Mt Orito

Vinapu

Rano
Kau

Orongo Village
Mata Ngarau

Motu Iti
Motu Nui

have been a hierarchical society of several clans, with chiefs, an aristocracy and high-ranking specialist workers. It seems that those in the north-west specialized in fishing, while those in the south-east were the farmers. There was palm-wood for canoes, obsidian for knives, stones to act as foundations for the houses of chiefs and priests. Families lived in 12-metre (40-foot) boat-shaped houses, with entry tunnels that protected against the elements and stone-lined earth ovens in which they cooked their chickens.

Palm-wood was crucial to their economy, both for seafaring and house-building. The slopes of Mount Terevaka (meaning 'to pull out canoes') were covered in palm-forest, harvested by wood-cutters who lived in nearby houses. The foundations of some 400 have been found, dating from 800 to 1300 — 500 stable years of tree-felling and canoe-building.

obsidian picks from the volcanic rock of the Rano Raraku crater. They emerged face-up, attached to bedrock by a thin spine until they were broken off and moved. This was no simple matter. Experiments have shown that to haul statues of this size, even if rollers were used, would have taken up to 150 people and hundreds of metres of rope, woven from the inner bark of an island shrub, the Triumffeta. Once in position, the statues were then levered upright – another long, slow process – and placed on platforms with their backs to the sea. Probably they were commissioned and left *in situ* while the subject was still alive, and given their spiritual power (*mana*) after death by the addition of white coral eyes – the statues were not 'blind' as they are today – and by being set in position on a platform.

It was all an immense labour. The 20 craftsmen working for a year or so to make a statue would have needed to be fed by ordinary fishermen and farmers. A whole community would have been involved in dragging the statue to its platform (*ahu*). To make an *ahu* was another massive engineering project, demanding the moving of

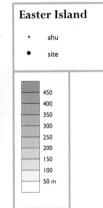

Easter Island

- ahu

• site

	450
	400
	350
	300
	250
	200
	150
	100
	50 m

Anakena
Ahu Ature Huke
Ovane
Ava Okiri
Te Pito te Kura
Mt Terevaka
La Pérouse Bay
Ahu Hekii
Ana o Keke
Rano Aroi
Poike
Vaitea
ivi
Rano Raraku
Tongariki
Hanga Te Tanga
Akahanga

By 1000 — according to radio-carbon dates — they had begun to carve their statues, a new way to express the religious beliefs they had brought with them centuries before. As elsewhere in Polynesia, the beliefs focus on ancestor figures. On Easter Island, these *aringa ora* ('living faces') were carved with

300–500 tonnes of rock. The biggest standing statue was 9.75 metres (32 feet) tall, and weighed 82 tonnes.

Why go to all this trouble? Almost certainly because these mighty figures asserted territorial rights on behalf of their clan. Staring inland, they watched over their descendants, conferring a sense of security. Probably from the start there was an element of competition behind this new art form. Early statues and platforms were small. But pressures grew. The island's natural wealth sustained a rise in population, which was probably at least 7,000 and may have been much more. As the forests were being cut back and the best land was used up, the work intensified. The bigger the statue, the more powerful the *mana*, the greater the clan's power and sense of security.

But without knowing it, the Easter Islanders had made for themselves a social vortex from which there was no escape. A high population put pressure on the land and intensified forest destruction. The coming crisis provoked by the competition for resources might with different leadership have inspired new thinking, new agricultural techniques, a cooperative determination to strike out beyond the encircling ocean. Instead, the society turned in upon itself, developing a mania for statues and platforms. This increased the need for rope, and for wood to make canoes and rollers and houses, which meant more trees felled, more Triumfetta bushes used, increased pressure, ever more statues. And no new trees – rats introduced by the first colonists gnawed the palm nuts, making regeneration impossible.

At some moment in the 17th century, someone cut the last tree, and the whole social machine collapsed. The largest statue of all, El Gigante – 20 metres (65 feet) tall and 270 tonnes – was left lying unfinished. Archaeologists doubt the islanders could ever have moved it.

A core of pollen drilled from Rano Kau crater confirms the timescale. Until 750, trees and shrubs predominate. Then comes a steady decline, over 450 years. By 1400, the Rano Kau area was barren. Two centuries later, so was everywhere else, with catastrophic results recorded by archaeologists in the island's so-called Decadent Phase. There was nothing left with which to make canoes, or ropes, or rollers, or houses. A community that had lived in peace for 1,400 years was thrown into a violent struggle for declining resources. Without canoes, there could be no fish, and little protein. People took to living in caves, reed huts and stone shelters. Soil erosion increased, crops declined. Chickens became treasures, guarded in dry-stone safes as solid as little Fort Knoxes. There was no spare labour now for making statues. Flaked obsidian spearheads suddenly appear in the archaeological record. Clan attacked clan, toppled their enemies' statues, and ripped up *ahus* to fortify their outposts.

Easter Islanders forgot their own past. When Europeans arrived, the locals no longer remembered how the statues had been transported, claiming they had 'walked' across the island. Thus one of the most ingenious, complex and sophisticated of Pacific societies was reduced to barbarism, surrounded by memorials to former grandeur – the end result of a test-tube experiment with population growth, misdirected effort and finite resources.

Statues abandoned in the Rano Raraku crater remain as forlorn memorials to a culture that unwittingly engineered its own collapse.

A Millennial Gazetteer

A selection of sites that recall a century: 950 – 1050

AFGHANISTAN

Ghazni. For those who risk the journey, ruins a few km to the north of Ghazni include a tower and mosque that were once part of Mahmud's great capital.

AUSTRIA

Werfen. 40 km south of Salzburg is the 11th-century fortress of Hohenwerfen.

BOLIVIA

Tiahuanaco (Tiwanaku). The site is 72 km from La Paz. Museum. Also the Archaeological Museum of Tiahuanaco in La Paz.

CAMBODIA

Angkor. Banteay Srei (Fortress of Women), the enclosure of the Royal Palace, the Phimenakas, North and South Khleang, and the Ta Keo temple-mountain.

CANADA

L'Anse aux Meadows, Newfoundland. National Historic Site (PO Box 70, St Lunaire-Griquet, Newfoundland AOK 2X0). UNESCO World Heritage site. Closest town: St Anthony. Visitor Centre and Viking Encampment (summer only).

Head Smashed-In, Alberta. Buffalo (bison) jump. 18 km north-west of Fort Mcleod. Interpretive Centre (May–October, tel. +1 403 553-2731).

CHINA

Kaifeng, Henan. Iron Pagoda, 11th century, of bricks made to look like iron.

TIBET

Reting. The monastery, associated with Atisha, was dynamited in the Cultural Revolution in 1966, but the main hall has been rebuilt.

Thöling (Toling). The monastic complex founded in the early 11th century was also ruined, but some parts remain intact.

ENGLAND

Barton-upon-Humber. St Peter's, a 10th-century church.

Kirk Hammerton, nr York. St John the Baptist church, dating from 951.

Maldon. The battleground. Northey Island is a National Trust nature reserve. Visits by appointment with the warden (tel. +44 621 853142). Causeway above water for two hours either side of low tide.

York. Jorvik Viking Centre. A widely praised reconstruction of 10th-century buildings and an archaeological site (tel. +44 1904 643211).

EGYPT

Cairo. Al-Azhar Mosque, founded in 970 and claimed as the world's oldest university. Al-Hakim's Mosque was restored in 1980 by Ismaili Shi'ites from Brunei.

GERMANY

Gernrode. St Cyriakus, Germany's best-preserved 10th-century church, and a fine example of Romanesque architecture. The first triforium north of the Alps, perhaps in deference to presence of the Byzantine princess Theophano in nearby Quedlinburg. It also contains the oldest (11th century) representation of the Holy Sepulchre. Guided tours daily at 3 p.m.

Hildesheim. St Michael's. A superb Romanesque church built by Bernward, bishop of Hildesheim, in 993–1022. A glorious ceiling of 1300 painted oak panels, three-quarters of them original.

Paderborn. The Ottonische Kaiserpfalz (Ottonian Royal Palace) is a meticulous reconstruction of the original destroyed by fire in 1165.

GREENLAND

Brattahlid (present-day Qassiarsuk). Norse ruins, including church built by Erik the Red's wife Thjodhild in c. 1000.

INDIA

Somnath. The museum preserves a few statues and friezes that survived Mahmud's attack.

Gangaikondacholapuram, Tamil Nadu. Rajendra's capital has his grand Brihadishwara temple. The remains of his palace are an archaeological site.

INDONESIA

Bali. The temple complex of Besakih, founded at the end of the 8th century, was extended in the 10th (and many more times since). Images, dance-dramas, masks and carvings recall history and legend dating back to the birth of Erlangga in c. 1001.

IRELAND

Monasterboice. Three of the finest of Ireland's many High Crosses (including the intricate Muiredach) and one of the best round towers.

Killaloe. By Lough Derg stands the mound of Béal Boru, near the possible site of Brian Boru's palace, Kincora.

Dublin. The Viking Centre (tel. +353 1 6796040) recalls a time when Dublin was a Viking capital.

ITALY

Venice. The Ascension Day ceremony known as the Marriage of the Sea commemorates Pietro Orseolo's departure in 1000, prior to his victory over the Dalmatian pirates.

JAPAN

Uji. Byodo-in, the one-time villa of Fujiwara Michinaga, then in the mid 11th century converted into a temple dedicated to Amida, Buddha of the Western Paradise. Now known as Phoenix Hall. Settings recall the time of Murasaki Shikibu, who drew inspiration here for the *Tale of Genji.* Open daily. Tourist information (tel. +81 774 23 3334).

MAURITANIA

Koumbi Saleh. 65 km south of Timbedgha, this is West Africa's most important and largest medieval site. Entry is free, if you can get there.

MEXICO

Chichén Itzá. Mexico's most popular site. Old Chichén is Maya, Chichén is Toltec from 1000 onwards. The site is open daily, 08.00–17.00.

Tollan (Tula). Ceremonial centre, partly restored and including temple and Atlantes. Site open daily, 10.00–17.00.

NORWAY

Oslo. Vikingskiphuset (Viking Ship Museum). Three oak ships unearthed from burial mounds. The Historical Museum houses Viking material.

Trondheim. Nidaros Domkirche, cathedral of Nidaros (Trondheim's original name). An 11th-century basilica, but overlaid by later additions.

SCOTLAND

Innerleithen. Traquair House. A 10th-century castle, with later additions. Scotland's oldest inhabited house. Open Easter–end September.

SPAIN

Córdoba. The Great Mosque (Mezquita). Look for al-Mansur's addition – seven rows of columns along the east side. 7 km north-west are the ruins of Medina al-Zahra, where al-Mansur kept Hisham.

Santiago de Compostela. The Cathedral. Rebuilding started in the 11th century, after the building was destroyed by al-Mansur in 977.

SOUTH AFRICA

Mapungubwe. Work in progress on a new national park and tourist facilities. Check status on website: http://mapungubwe.up.ac.za.

SRI LANKA

Polonnaruwa. Shiva temple built by Rajaraja after his conquest of northern Ceylon in 992–3.

UNITED STATES

Cahokia, Illinois. Cahokia Mounds State Historic Site (tel. +1 618 346 5160). UNESCO World Heritage Site. Open daily. Interpretive centre. Website: www.cahokiamounds.com.

THE SOUTH-WEST

Of several Anasazi sites, the best are:

Canyon de Chelly, Arizona. Entry only with a Navajo guide. National Monument Visitor Center (tel. +1 520 674 5500).

Chaco Canyon, New Mexico. National Historic Park Visitor Center (tel. +1 505 786 7014). Website: http://www.nps.gov. and click on Chaco.

Mesa Verde National Park, Colorado. The only national park devoted exclusively to archaeology. Visitor Center (tel. +1 305 529 4461).

THE NORTH-WEST

Scowlitz. For a site visit, or a cultural tour of the Harrison region, contact The Band Manager, Scowlitz First Nation, PO Box 76, Lake Erock, BC, Canada V0N 1N0 (tel. +1 604 826 5813).

UZBEKISTAN

Bukhara. Ismail Samani Mausoleum. 10th-century architectural gem.

Bibliography

INTRODUCTION

Gould, Stephen Jay. *Questioning the Millennium*. London, 1997.

1. THE AMERICAS

Coe, Michael, Dean Snow and Elizabeth Benson. *Atlas of Ancient North America*. New York, Oxford, 1986.

Fagan, Brian. *Ancient North America: The Archaeology of a Continent*. London, 1995.

Davies, Nigel. *Ancient Kingdoms of Peru*. London, 1997.

Davies, Nigel. *Ancient Kingdoms of Mexico*. London, 1982.

Hagen, Adriana von, and Craig Morris. *The Cities of the Ancient Andes*. London, 1998

Ingstad, Helge. *The Norse Discovery of America*. Norwegian University Press, 1985.

2. EUROPE

Alexander, Michael. *The Earliest English Poems*. London, 1991.

Bartlett, Robert. *The Making of Europe: Conquest, Colonization and Cultural Change, 950–1350*. London, 1994.

Duncan, Archibald. *Scotland: The Making of the Kingdom (The Edinburgh History of Scotland, Vol. 1)*. Edinburgh, 1975.

Fisher, Douglas. *The Anglo-Saxon Age*. London, 1973.

Fletcher, Richard. *The Conversion of Europe: From Paganism to Christianity, 371–1386*. London, 1997.

Focillon, Henri. *The Year 1000*. New York, San Francisco, London, 1971.

Golb, Norman. *The Jews in Medieval Normandy*. Cambridge, 1997.

Holmes, George (ed.). *The Oxford Illustrated History of Medieval Europe*. Oxford, 1988, 1996.

Jones, Gwyn. *A History of the Vikings*. London, 1984.

Lacy, Robert, and Danny Danziger. *The Year 1000*. London, 1999.

Newman, Roger. *Brian Boru*. Dublin, 1983.

Norwich, John Julius. *Byzantium: The Apogee*. London, 1991.

Norwich, John Julius. *Venice: The Rise to Empire*. London, 1977.

Otway-Ruthven, A.J. *A History of Medieval Ireland*. New York, 1993.

Roesdahl, Else. *The Vikings*. London, 1998.

Runciman, Steven. *A History of the First Bulgarian Empire*. London, 1930.

Smyth, Alfred. *Warlords and Holy Men: Scotland, AD 80–1000*. London, 1984.

Whitelock, Dorothy. *The Beginnings of English Society*. London, 1952, 1991.

3. ISLAM

Barthold, W. *Turkestan down to the Mongol Invasions*. Oxford, 1928.

Frye, Richard. *Bukhara: The Medieval Achievement*. University of Oklahoma, 1965.

Hitti, Philip. *History of the Arabs*. New York, 1970 (10th edition).

Lombard, Maurice. *The Golden Age of Islam*. Amsterdam, 1975.

Nazim, Muhammad. *Sultan Mahmud of Ghazna*. Cambridge, 1931.

Saunders, J.J. *A History of Medieval Islam*. London and New York, 1965.

4. ASIA

Chandler, David. *A History of Cambodia*. Boulder, Colorado, and Oxford, 1996.

Coedes, George. *The Indianized States of Southeast Asia*. Honolulu, 1975.

Dehejia, Vidya. *Art of the Imperial Cholas*. New York, 1990.

Deuchler, Martina. *The Confucian Transformation of Korea: A Study of Society and Ideology*. Cambridge (Mass.) and London, 1992

Dunnell, Ruth. *The Great State of White and High: Buddhism and State Formation in 11th-Century Xia*. Honolulu, 1996.

Eckert, Carter J., et al. *Korea Old and New: A History*. Seoul, Cambridge (Mass.) and London, 1990.

Franke, Herbert, and Denis Twitchett (eds.). *The Cambridge History of China, Vol. 6: Alien Regimes and Border States, 907–1368*. Cambridge, 1994.

Gernet, Jacques. *A History of Chinese Civilization*. Cambridge, 1996

Henthorn, William. *A History of Korea*. New York, 1971.

Kwanten, Luc. *Imperial Nomads*. Leicester, 1979.

Mason, R.H.P. and J.G. Caiger. *A History of Japan*. Rutland, Vermont and Tokyo, 1997.

Murasaki Shikibu. *The Tale of Genji* (trans. Arthur Waley). Many editions.

Nahm, Andrew. *Korea: Tradition and Transformation*. New Jersey, 1988.

Nilakanta Sastri, K.A. *History of Sri Vijaya*. Madras, 1949.

Ray, H.C. (ed.). *History of Ceylon. (Vol. 1, Part 1)*. Colombo, 1959.

Sinor, Denis (ed.). *The Cambridge History of Early Inner Asia*. Cambridge, 1990.

Tarling, Nicholas (ed.). *The Cambridge History of Southeast Asia*. Cambridge, 1992.

Wittfogel, Karl A., and Feng Chia-sheng. *History of Chinese Society: Liao (907–1125)*. Philadelphia, 1949.

Zephir, Thierry. *Khmer: Lost Empire of Cambodia*. London, 1998.

5. AFRICA

Budge, Wallace. *History of Ethiopia, Nubia and Abyssinia*. London, 1928

Bovill, E.W. *The Golden Trade of the Moors*. Oxford, 1968.

Connah, Graham. *African Civilizations*. Cambridge, 1987.

Davidson, Basil. *Africa in History*. London, 1992.

Fage, J.D. *A History of Africa*. London, 1995.

Fouché, Leo. *Mapungubwe: Ancient Bantu Civilization on the Limpopo*. Cambridge, 1937. [cf. Gardner]

Gardner, Guy A. *Mapungubwe, Vol. II: Report on Excavations, 1935–40*. Pretoria, 1963.

Hall, M. *The Changing Past: Farmers, Kings and Traders in Southern Africa, 200–1860*. Cape Town, 1987.

Hrbek, I. (ed.). *UNESCO General History of Africa, Vol. III: Africa from the Seventh to the Eleventh Century*. California, 1992.

Meyer, Andrie. *The Archaeological Sites of Greefswald*. Pretoria, 1998.

Phillipson, David. *African Archaeology*. Cambridge, 1985.

Reader, John. *Africa: A Biography of the Continent*. London, 1997.

Selassie, Sergew Hable. *Ancient and Medieval Ethiopian History to 1270*. Addis Ababa, 1972.

Sutton, John. *A Thousand Years of East Africa*. Nairobi, 1990; and 'The Antecedents of the Interlacustrine Kingdoms'. *Journal of African History*, 1993.

6. OCEANIA

Bahn, Peter, and John Flenley. *Easter Island, Earth Island*. London, 1992.

Bellwood, Peter. *The Polynesians: Prehistory of an Island People*. London, 1987.

Davidson, Janet. *The Prehistory of New Zealand*. Auckland, 1984.

Flood, Josephine. *Archaeology of the Dreamtime*. London, 1995.

Flood, Josephine. *The Moth Hunters*. Canberra, 1980.

Kirch, Patrick. *The Evolution of the Polynesian Chiefdoms*. Cambridge, 1984.

Mulvaney, D.J., and J. Golson (eds.). *Aboriginal Man and Environment in Australia*. Australian National University Press, Canberra, 1971.

Sutton, Douglas (ed.). *The Origins of the First New Zealanders*. Auckland, 1994.

Acknowledgements

My thanks to the following for their generosity, expertise and patience

1. THE AMERICAS

North America: David Wilcox, Museum of Northern Arizona [*South-West*]; Dr William Fitzhugh, Director of Arctic Archaeology, Smithsonian Institution, Washington [*Far North*]; Dana Lepofsky, Department of Archaeology, Simon Fraser University, British Columbia (with thanks also to Nicole Oakes, Natasha Lyons and Doug Brown) [*West Coast*]; Professor Dean Snow, Department of Archaeology, Pennsylvania State University [*Plains*]; William Iseminger, Cahokia Mounds Historic Site [*Mississippi*].

South America: Warwick Bray, Emeritus Professor of South American Archaeology, Institute of Archaeology, London.

2. EUROPE

Prof. Robert Moore, University of Newcastle.

Ireland and Scotland: Professor Alfred Smyth, St George's House, Windsor Castle.

3. ISLAM

David Morgan, Department of History, School of Oriental and African Studies, London.

Judaism: Dr Stefan Reif, Taylor–Schechter Genizah Research Unit, Cambridge.

4. ASIA

China: Dr Naomi Standen, Assistant Professor of Asian History, University of Wisconsin-Superior.

Japan: Dr Philip Harries, Oriental Institute, Oxford.

India: Dr Daud Ali, Department of History, School of Oriental and African Studies, London.

Korea: Dr Martina Deuchler, Professor of Korean Studies, School of Oriental and African Studies, London.

Tibet: Dr T. Skorupski, Department of Religious Studies, School of Oriental and African Studies, London.

South-East Asia: Prof. Jan Christie, Centre of South-East Asian Studies, University of Hull.

5. AFRICA

David Anderson, Department of History, School of Oriental and African Studies, London.

West Africa: Professor Roderick McIntosh, Department of Anthropology, Rice University, Texas.

South Africa: Prof. Andrie Meyer, Department of Anthropology and Archaeology, University of Pretoria; Ray Inskeep, formerly Professor of Archaeology, University of Cape Town.

East Africa: John Sutton, The British Institute in Eastern Africa, Nairobi.

6. OCEANIA

Graham Ward, Australian Institute of Aboriginal and Torres Straits Studies, Canberra; Dr Josephine Flood, formerly Director, Aboriginal Environment Section at the Australian Heritage Commission.

FOR THE PENGUIN PRESS

Martin Toseland, *Commissioning Editor*; John Woodruff and Mark Handsley, *Editorial*; Cecilia Mackay, *Picture Research*; Richard Marston, *Design*.

MAPS

Malcolm Swanston, Arcadia Editions.

PHOTOGRAPHS

AKG London: 37 *left* (Real Biblioteca, Escorial), 52, 56 (Bayerische Staatsbibliothek, Munich), 68 (Bibliothèque Nationale, Paris). Ancient Art and Architecture, Harrow: 43. Beth Hatefutsoth, the Nahum Goldmann Museum of the Jewish Diaspora, Tel Aviv: 59 (Cambridge University Library/Taylor–Schechter Genizah Research Unit, T–S Misc.35.90). Bodleian Library, Oxford: 42 (MS. Junius 11, fol. 54). Bridgeman Art Library, London: 33 (British Library), 37 *right* (Musée de l'Œuvre de Notre Dame, Strasbourg), 48, 61 (Hungarian National Gallery, Budapest), 77, 87 (Freer Gallery, Smithsonian Institution, Washington), 90 (Arthur M. Sackler Museum, Harvard University, Cambridge MA/Bequest of Grenville L. Winthrop), 95 (Oriental Bronzes Ltd, London), 98 (Kaep'o-dong, Koryong, Korea), 104 (National Museum of India, New Delhi). British Museum, London: 96. Cahokia Mounds State Historic Site, Collinsville: 21 (W. Iseminger). Cambridge University Library, by permission of the Syndics/Taylor–Schechter Research Unit: 82 (T–S K.5.13), 83. Camerapix: 118 (D. Willetts). Canadian Museum of Civilization, Hull: 28. Corbis, London: 22, 24 *left* (Museum of Man and Nature, Winnipeg), 24 *right*, 103. C. M. Dixon, Canterbury: 38 *left* (Universitets Oldsaksamling, Oslo), 38 *right*. E. T. Archive, London: 72 (Bibliothèque Nationale, Paris). Dr Josephine Flood: 129. Werner Forman Archive, London: 19 *upper* (Museum für Volkskunde, Vienna), 40, 64 (Biblioteca Nazionale, Venice), 75 (Museum für Islamische Kunst, Berlin), 91 (Beijing Museum, Beijing). Sonia Halliday Photographs, Weston Turville: 65, 78. Robert Harding Picture Library, London: 93, 134. Prof. Dana Lepofsky: 27. Dr Roderick McIntosh: 115 *upper/lower*. National Commission for Museums and Monuments, Lagos: 110 (D. Bakker). National Park Service and Chaco Culture National Historical Park, Albuquerque: 13. Natural History Museum, London: 131. Santa Barbara Museum of Natural History: 26. South American Pictures, Woodbridge: 17, 19 *lower*. TRIP Photo Library, Cheam: 29, 44, 70, 81, 105, 106. University of Pretoria, Dept of Anthropology and Archaeology: 120, 121.

Index

*Page references in italics
refer to maps*

Aachen 35, 36, 55, 58, 61
Abbas 67
Abbasids 67, 68, 70–71, 74, 76, 79
Abodrites 39
Aboriginals 122–3, 128–9
Abu-al-Misk Kafur 73
abuna 118, 119
Ackin 107
Adalbero, Archbishop of Reims 48, 56
Adalbert of Prague 57
Adam of Bremen 31
Adefa 119
Aden 67, 71, 73, 82
Adena 21
Adrianople 63, 65
Adriatic Sea 58
Adud al-Dowlah 70–71
Adulis 118
Aduturai 105
Aethelred (Ethelred) 42–3, 51
Afghanistan 68, 78, 80
Africa 108, 110, 112–15, 116
    slaves from 72
    sub-Saharan 108–21
Afro-Asiatic 109
Agadir 66, 70, 72, 82
Agew 119
Agra 92
agriculture
    Africa 110
    Americas 12
    Europe 34–5
Agrotis infusa 128–9
Aguada 16
Aguila 75
Ahmadabad 81
ahu 133
Aidhab 75
Ainu 100
Airlangga 107
Aix 36, 49, 55
Ajnadain 67
Akan 109
    goldfields 113
Akapana 17
Akiko 100
Aksum 118, 119, 119
Aland 39
Alans 67
Alba 46
Albania 64
Albuquerque petroglyphs 23
alchemy 69
Aleppo 63, 64, 65
Alessandria 55
Aleutian Islands 28
Alexandria 63, 65, 67, 71, 73, 75, 82
Ali 67, 74
Alicante 76
Alkali Ridge 23
Allahabad 81
Allier 50
Almería 76
Almoravids 115
Alp-tigin 80
Alpuente 76
Altai Mountains 94
Altenburg 55
Alto Ramírez 16
Alwa 67

Amalfi 36
Amasia 63, 65
Amboina 107
Amdo 92, 92
American Bottom 20, 21
Americas 12, 12–31
Amhara 119
Amharic 109
Amida 63, 65
Amiens 50
Amritsar 81
Amu Darya 67, 71, 73, 79, 82
Amur 89
Anagni 55
Anangula 28
Anasazi 22, 23, 23
Anbessa Wudem 118
Anbuk-pu 99
Anbyon-pu 99
An-ch'ing 89
Ancona 55, 55, 63, 65
Ancyra 63, 65
Andalus, al- (Andalusia) 70, 72, 76, 76–7, 82
Andes 16
Andong-pu 99
Angkor 102, 102–3, 103
Angkor Wat 102, 103
Angles 46
Anglesey 42
Angmagssalik 30, 40
Angoulême 49
Anjou 49, 50, 51
Ankole 117
Anlaf 43
Anna 52, 53, 64, 65
Annam 89
Annam-pu 99
Anse 49
Anso-pu 99
An-te fu 94
Antioch 67, 71, 73, 82
Antiochia 63, 65
Antwerp 55
Anuradhapura 104, 105
Aosta 55
A-pao-chi (T'ai-tsu) 94
Aquileia 36, 55, 55, 62, 65
Aquincum 62
Aquitaine 48
Arabia 66, 67
Arabian Sea 71
Aragón 35, 76
Aral Sea 71, 79
Arch Canyon 23
Arctic 28–9
Ardabil 67, 71, 73, 82
Arikara Indians 25
Arizona 23
Ark of the Covenant 118
Arklow 45
Armagh 36, 44, 45, 47
Armenia 53, 65, 67
Arnhem Land 128
Arpads 60
Arran 46
Arras 49, 50
Arulmoli (Rajaraja I) 104, 106
Arzachel 76
Ashkenazim 58–9
Asti 55
Astrakhan 53
Asuka 101
Aswan 73, 75
Athens 63, 65
Atisha 93, 106

Atjeh 107
Atlatl 22
Attalia 63, 65
Atto, Bishop of Verceil 37
Auch 36, 49
Augsburg 55, 61
Aures 51
Australia 122–3, 128, 128–9
Austria 109
Autun 50
Auvergne 49
Auxerre 49, 50
Avalona 65
Avicenna 79
Avignon 35, 36, 55
Avranches 49, 51
Avre 51
Awaji 100
Awdaghost 112, 113, 113, 115
Axum 67
Aymara 16
Ayuthia 102
Azelik 113
Azerbaijan 67
Azhar, al- 74
Aztecs 19, 23, 23

Babylon 82
Bacon Farm 21
Badajoz 76
Badr 67, 71, 73, 82
Baffin Island 28, 30
Baghdad 17, 67, 67, 70–71, 71, 73, 82, 82, 95
Baha al-Dowlah 71
Bahrain 67
Bahris 76
Baker, Samuel 116
Bakri, abu Ubaid al- (al-Bakri) 113, 114, 115
Balasaghu 79
Bali 107, 107
Balkans 54
Balkh 67, 71, 73, 79, 82
Balligave 105
Baltic peoples 53
Baltic Sea 39
Bambara 109
Bamberg 55
Bambuko 113
Bamburgh 42
bananas 116
Banda Sea 106
Bandar Abbas 81
Bandelier 23
Bangka 106
Bangladesh 81
banknotes 89
Banteay Srei 103
Bantu 109, 110, 116, 120
Baraka 119
Barca 119
Barcelona 36, 49, 49, 50, 58, 60, 76, 76, 77
Bardas Phocas 64–5
Bardas Sclerus 64, 65
Barea 119
Bargo 92
Bari 36, 62, 65
Barrow 28
Basasiri al- 71
Basil II 52, 57, 62, 64–5
Basle 55
Basra 67, 68, 71, 73, 82
Bath 42, 43
batik 107
Bavaria 54, 55, 61
Bay of Islands 130
Bayeux 35, 49, 51, 51

Bayonne 35
Beauvais 49, 50
Bec 51
Begrash 75
Begtuzun 79
Beirut 63
Beja 119
Belgrade 61
Bemba 109
Benares 81
Bengal 104
Beni Muzain 76
Benin 113, 114
Beothuk Indians 14, 31
Berara 119
Berbers 66, 112, 113, 115
Bergamo 55
Bergen 41
Bering Sea 28
Bering Straits 13, 28
Bern 55
Bernicia 46
Berno 37
Bertha 51
Besançon 35, 49, 50, 55
Beshbagowa 23
Bessin 51
Betatakin 23
Bethune 51
Bidar 105
Big Westwater 23
Bigo 117, 117
Bijapur 105
Bijistan 81
bilharzia 110
Bilbao 76
Birka 35, 36, 39
Birnirk 28
Biruni al- 80
bison-hunting 24, 25
bison-jumps 24
Bithynia 63, 65
Bito 113
Bizen 119
Black Duck Brook 31
Black Mesa 23
Black Sea 53, 82
Blois 49
Blue Jay 129
Blythe intaglios 23
Bodonchar 95
bogong moth 128–9
Bogong Mountains 129, 129
Bohemia 54, 55, 57
Boleslaw the Brave 38, 39, 57
Bolivia 16–17
Bologna 55
Bon 92, 93
Bordeaux 35, 36, 49, 58
Borg 39
Boris 63
Borjigin clan 95
Bornholm 39
Borobudur 107, 107
Borre 39
Bosnia 62, 64, 65
Bourbon 49
Bourges 36, 49, 49, 50
Bowler, Jim 122
Brabant 55
Braga 36
Brand 21
Brandenburg 55
Brantas 107
Bratislava 55
Brattahlid 41
Bremen 35, 36, 55
Brescia 55
Bretons 51

Brian Boru 44–7
Brihadishwara temple 105
Brindisi 36
Brittany, 36, 48, 49, 50, 51, 58
Brixen 55
Brodar 47
Broken Hill 128
Bromston 93
Bruges 34, 55
Brunei 107
Brunswick 55
Bryhtnoth, Earl of Essex 43
Bryhtwold 43
Buck, Sir Peter 126
Budapest 55
Buddhism 84, 86, 87
    Cambodia 102, 103
    China 91
    Hsi-hsia 96
    Indonesia 106, 107
    Korea 98
    Tibet 92–3
Buganda 111, 117, 117
Bughra 79
Bukhara 67, 68, 71, 73, 78–9, 79, 80, 81, 82
Bulgar 53
Bulgaria 33, 36, 53, 61, 63, 63–4, 65, 65
Bulgars 67
Bunyoro 111, 117, 117
Bure 113
Burgos 36
Burgundy 36, 49, 49, 51, 55, 58, 60
burial-mound culture 27
Burma 84
Burrup Peninsula 128
Burundi 116, 117
Bushmen 120
Busoga 117
Button Point 29
Buwayh, Ahmad ibn- 70
Buwayh abu Shuja 70
Buwayhid (Buyid) family 70–71, 78
Buwayhid Emirates 71, 73, 79, 82
Bwana Mkubwa 129
Byodoin (Uji) 101
Byzantine Empire 53, 61, 63, 65, 67, 71, 73, 75, 82
Byzantium 32, 57, 58, 62–5
    see also Constantinople

Caddoan Mississippian 21
Cádiz 58, 76
Caen 51
Caesarea 63, 65
Cahokia 13, 15, 20–21, 21
Cairo (al-Kahira) 71, 73, 74–5, 75, 82, 83, 106
calendars 10, 11
Calf Creek 23
Calloway Island 21
Cambodia (Kambuja) 84, 102–3
Cambrai 50, 55
Cambridge 42, 43
Camerino 55
Canons of Medicine 79
Canterbury 36, 42, 43
Canterbury Plains 130
Canton 89
Canute (Cnut) 43, 47
Canyon de Chelly 22, 23, 23
Canyonlands National Park 23
Cape Aston 30
Cape Bauld 30

Cape Chidley 29, 30
Cape Farewell 30, 40, 41
Cape Porcupine 30
Cape York 30, 128
Carana 63, 65
Carham 46, 47
Carinthia 55
Carnarvon Ranges 128
Carniola 55
Carnuntum 63
Carree 117
Carrier Mills 21
Cartagena 36, 58, 76
Carthage 66
Casa Chiquita 22
Casa Grande 23
Casa Rinconiada 22
Cashel 36, 44, 45
Caspian Sea 53, 78
castes 84
Castile 36, 58, 76, 76, 77
Catalonia 76
Catania 36, 58
cattle, in Africa 116, 117, 120
Cauvery 105
Celebes (Sulawesi) 107, 124
Celtic culture 44–7
Central Australia 128
Central Capital (Liao) 94
Central Plains 25
Ceylon 84, 104–5, 105
Chaco Canyon 13, 15, 22, 22–3, 23
Chaco Wash 22
Chalcedon 63, 65
Châlon 50
Chalons 49
Chalukaa 28
Champa 84, 85, 102
Champagne 49, 50, 51
Chandragiri 105
Chang Jiang 89
Ch'ang-an 85, 86, 88, 89
Chao-chou 94
Charentonne 51
Charlemagne 32, 36, 54, 57, 58, 62
Charroux 48
Chartres 49, 50, 51
Chatham Islands 124, 127
Chedzurgwe 129
Chen-chiang 89, 90
Chen-chou 94
Ch'eng-t'ien 95
Cheng-tsung 88
Cherbourg 51
Cherson (Korsun) 52, 53, 63, 65, 65
chert 20
Chester 42
Chetro Ketl 22
Chia-huan 89
Chiang-ling 89
Chiang-ning 89
Chiapa de Corzo 18
Chibuene 129
Chichén Itzá 18
Chichimecs 18, 19
Chidambaram 105
Chien-ning 89
Chih-shih chun 97
Chikoi 94
Chimu 17
China 66, 85–6, 88–91, 104, 106
   calendar 10
   Romanization of Chinese 90
Chi-nan 89
Chin-chou 94
Ch'ing-chou 89, 94, 97
Ch'ing-tang 93
Chinguetti 113
Ch'ing-yuan 89
Chinju-mok 99
Chin-ning chün 97
Chin-su 94

Chi-sang 97
Ch'itan see Khitan
Chola dynasty 84, 104–5, 105, 106
Cholla 99
Cholula 18
Chondwe 129
Ch'ongju-mok 99
Chonju-mok 99
Chou-chou 94
Chou K'uang-yin 88
Christianity 10
   Byzantium 62–3
   Church of Rome 36–7
   division in 33, 35
   Ethiopia 118, 119
   Hungary 60
   Iceland 40
   Rusian Orthodox 52–3
Chukchi Sea 28
Chulamanivarnam 106
Chumash 26, 26–7
Chumnungwa 129
Ch'ungju-mok 99
Chung-wei 97
Chur 55
Churchill 29
chwezi 116
Cimbalongus (Clidion) 64
Circesium 63, 65
Circle 28
Clermont 49
climate 33–4
Clontarf 45, 47
cloves 106
Cluny 37, 49, 50
Clyde 46
Clyde Inlet 30
Cnossus 63, 65
Cnut (Canute) 43, 47
Coba 18
Cobar 128
Codenra 62, 65
Cologne 35, 36, 50, 55, 58, 82
Colorado 25
Comacchio 55
Como 55
compass 91
Confucianism 98
Confucius 85
Connaught 44, 45
Constance 55
Constantine 64
Constantinople 33, 35, 52, 53, 53, 54, 61, 62, 63, 64, 65, 67, 71, 73, 82
Conza 36
Cook Islands 125
Coosa 21
Cordillera Real 16
Córdoba 36, 49, 58, 71, 72, 76, 76, 77, 77, 82, 83, 113
Cork 35, 44, 45
corn 13
corroboree 129
Corsica 55, 58
Cortés, Hernándo 19
Corunna 35
Cotentin 51, 51
Couesnon 51
Coutances 49, 51
Cracow 58, 61
Cremona 55
Cresap Mound 21
Crescentius 54, 56
Crete 63, 65
Crimea 52, 65
Croatia 35, 36, 60, 65, 62
Crooks Mounds 21
Ctesiphon 67
Cumberland 30
Cumbria 42, 46
Cushites 117
Cyprus 63, 65, 67
Cyrillic script 33
Czech Republic 57
Dai Co Viet 85

Dakar 119
Dalai Lamas 93
Dalriada 46
Daman 81
Damascus 63, 66, 67, 71, 73, 75, 82
Dambarare 129
Damot 119
Dane Law 35
Danegeld 38, 42–3
Daniel 119
Danube 53, 61, 65
Darasuram 105
Darazi, al- 75
Dar-es-Salaam 117
Darge-gonchen 92
Daud of Multan 81
Daulatabad 105
Davis Strait 30, 40
Dawaro 119
Dazaifu 100
Dean 42
Debarwa 119
Debra Berhan 119
Debra Libanos 119
Deccan 104, 105
Delhi 81
Denia 76
Denmark 35, 36, 38–9, 39, 55
Deols 27
Derbend 67, 71, 73, 82
Derby 42
Desmond 44
Desna 53
Detmold 55
Devon Islands 30
Dhlodlho 129
Diaspora 58, 83
Die 55
Digne 55
Dijon 49
Dil Ne'ad 119
Dima 119
dinar 69
dingo 123
Dioscurias 63
dirhem 69
Disco 30, 40
disease, in Africa 110
Disentis 55
Dives 51
Dnieper 52, 53
Dniester 53, 61
Doba 119
Doerschuk 21
Dominguez Escalante 23
Don 53
Donegal Bay 45
Donets 53
Dongola 67, 71, 73
Dorset people 28–9
Dortmund 55
Douve 51
Drava 65
Drobeta 63, 65
Dromtönpa 93
Druze 75
Dubh Linn see Dublin
Dublin 35, 36, 42, 44, 45, 47
Dubrava 57
Duisburg 55
Duklja 65
Dumbarton 46
Duncan 47
Dunhuang (Sha-chou) 97
Dura 63, 65
Durance 50
Durham 46, 47
Durostorum 63, 65
Dyrrhachum 65
Dyula 113
dzimba dzemabwe 121

East Anglia 42, 43
Easter Island 124, 125, 126, 127, 132–3, 132–4

Eastern Capital (Liao) 94
Eastern Settlement 30, 40, 40, 41
East Frankish Kingdom (see Germany)
East Kennet 42
Eaulne 51
Ebro 50
Echternach 37
Ecija 76
Edda 41
Edessa 63, 65, 67, 71, 73, 82
Edinburgh 46
Edward the Confessor 51
Edzina 97
Eger 55
Egill Skallagrimsson 41
Egypt 67, 75, 66, 74
Eichstatt 55
Eiland 129
Einar Jingle-scale 41
Eiriksfiord 30, 40
Ekven 28
El Morro 23
El Niño 26
Elburz Mts 81
Ellesmere Island 29, 30
Embrun 36, 49, 55
Emesa 63, 65
Emilia 55
Emma 51
Emona 62, 65
England 36, 42, 42, 61, 38, 42–3
Enryakuji (Mt Hiei) 101
Epaves Bay 31, 31
Ephesus 63, 65
Epte 51
Erik Bloodaxe 38, 41, 47
Erik Thorvaldsson (Erik the Red) 30, 41
Erzurum 67, 71, 73, 82
Escavada 22
Esslingen 55
Esztergom 55
Ethelred (Aethelred) 42–3, 51
Ethiopia 72, 118–19
Etowah 21
Euphrates 67, 70, 71, 73, 82
Eure 51
Europe 32–65, 34–5
   Islamic 76–7
Eva 21
Evansville 21
Evreux 51
Ewe 109
Exeter 42
Exilarch 83
Eze-Nri 110
Ezo 100

Faiyum 67, 71, 73, 82
Falaise 51
Falashas 118
Fang 109
Fanning Island 125
Fano 55
Faroes 41
Fars 67
Fatima 74
Fatimid Caliphate 70, 72, 82
Fatimids 67–8, 74–5, 106, 113
Fécamp 51
Felasha 119
Feng-hsiang 89
feohu 34
Ferghana 67
Ferrara 55
Fetegar 119
feudalism
   Europe 34, 51, 57
   Japan 101
Fez 72, 75, 82, 113
Fife 46
Fihl 67
Fiji 124, 124
Filioque Clause 35, 62

Finney, Ben 126
Finns 39
Flanders 48, 49, 55
Flenley, John 132
Flinders Ranges 128
Flood, Josephine 129
Florence 36, 55, 58, 60
Flores 107
Forez 49
Fort Ancien 21
France 35, 36, 48–52, 55, 58, 60, 61
   Judaism 58–9
Francia 48, 49, 51, 54
Franconia 55
Frankfurt 35, 55, 61
Fraser River 27
Fraxinelum 35
Freising 55
Fréjus 55
Freydis 31
Fribourg 55
Friendly Cove 26
Friesland 55
Frobisher Bay 30
Fu-chou 89
Fujiwara family 87, 100–101
Fustat 67, 74, 75, 83
   al-Fustat ('the ditch') 74

Gabes 75, 82
Gallagher Flint Station 28
Gallgeals 46
Gambia 113
Ganda 109, 81
Gangaikondacholapuram 104–5, 105
Ganges 81
Gao 112, 113
Garonne 50
Gartok 92
Gascony 49, 50
Gateway of the Sun 17, 17
Gatinais 49
Gdansk 57
Gedi 117
Ge'ez 118
Gelnhausen 55
Gelugpas 93
Geneva 55, 58, 60
genizah 83
Genoa 35, 36, 55, 58, 61, 82
geonim 82
George, king of Nubia 118
Georgian states 53
Gerbert of Aurillac 48, 51, 56, 60, 61
Germany 35, 36, 39, 49, 54–7, 55, 58, 60, 61
   Judaism 58–9
Gerona 36
Gershom ben Judah 59
Geza 60
Ghadamés 113
Ghana, ancient 108, 112–15
Gharshistan 81
Ghaznavid Empire 80–81, 81
Ghazni 71, 73, 81, 82, 80, 81
Ghur 81
Ghuzz 78
Gibson, Margaret 83
Gilgit 81
Gilla 23
Girgis, king of Nubia 118
Gisela 60
Gizur the White 40
Glaber, Radulf (Raoul/Rodolfus) 36, 37
Glamis 47
Glenn Mama 44, 47
Gniezno 36, 55, 57, 61
godar 40
Godthåb 30, 40, 41
Gojjam 119
Golconda 105
gold 69, 112–14, 121

Gormfhlaith 44, 47
Gortyn 63, 65
Goslar 55
Götar 39
Gothia 49
Gotland 39
Grado 36, 55
Graham Cave 21
Grampian *128*
Gran 36, 61
Gran Quivira 23
Granada (Gharnata) 76, 83, *113*
Grand Canal 89
Grand Gukh 23
Grand Plaza 20, 21
Grant, James *111*
Granville 51
Grasshopper 23
Grave Creek 21
Graz 55
Great Dividing Range *128*
Great Fear 34
Great Mosque (Córdoba) 77
Great Plains 24–5, *25*
Great Salt Spring 21
Great Sand Dunes 23
Greefswald *120*, *121*
Greenland 28, 29, *29*, 30, 31, 40, 40–41
Gregory V, pope 54
Gregory VII, pope 37
Gudit (Judith) 118–19
Gu-ge *92*, *93*
Guipuzcoa 76
Gulbarga 105
Gulf of Aden 119
Gulf of Bothnia 39
Gulf of Finland 39
Gulf of Riga 39
Gulf of St Lawrence 30
Gull Lake 24, *25*
Gumba 117
Gunnhild 43
gunpowder 90–91
Gurgan 67
Gurk 55
Gyanaste *92*

Hadhramaut 67
Hai ben Sherira 82
Hailar 94
Hainault 55
Hakam, al- 76
Hakemite Tables 75
Hakim, al- 74–5, 83
  mosque *74*
Hakon the Good 38
Halberstadt 55
Halthaway 21
Hàmadan 81
Hamburg 35, 55, 58, 60
Hamdanids 65
Hami (I-chou) *96*
Hamilton Inlet 30
Hamudids 75
Hamza ibn Ali 75
Han 99
Hananel ben Hushiel 83
Hangchow (Hangchou) 88, 89, *89*
Harald Bluetooth 38
Harald Greycloak 38
Hardaway 21
harems 72
Harer 119
Harfleur 51
Hariri, al- *72*
Harmony 129
Hatra 63
Hausa 109
Havelberg 55
Hawaian Islands *125*
Hawaii *124*, *127*
Hawaiiki *130*
Hawikuh 23
Hawkal, ibn 113, 118–19
Hawwa *115*

Hay Hollow Valley 23
Haytham, Ali al-Hasan ibn al- (Alhazen) 75
Head-Smashed-In 24, *25*
Hebrides 40
Hedeby 35, 38, 39
Heian (Kyoto) 86, *87*, 100
Heian Period 87
Heilbronn 55
Hejaz 67
Heliopolis 67, 71, 73, 82
Helmund 81
Henry I 54
Henry of Bavaria 62
Heraclea 63, 65
Herat 67, 71, 73, 79, 81, 82
Herjolfsson, Bjarni 30
Heyerdahl, Thor 132
High King of Ireland 44
Hilal 75
Hilarion 53
Hildesheim 55
Himalayas 85
Hinduism 84, 102, 103, 106, 107
Hisatsinom 22, 23
Hisdai ibn Shaprut 83
Hisham 76, 77
Ho-ch'ing 94
Ho-ch'ing chun 97
Ho-chou 97
Ho-chung 89
Hohenstaufen 55
Hohokam 22, 23
Hokkaido *100*
Hoko River 97
Hokulea's track *126*, *130*
Hokurikudo *100*
Ho-ling 106
Holstein 55
Holsteinsborg 30, 40
Holy Roman Empire 36, 48, 54–7
Holyhead 42
Ho-nan 89, 97
Hongu (Main Shrine) *101*
Honshu *100*
hookworm 110
Hopedale 29
Ho-pei 97
Hopewell 21
Ho-pung 94
Hortha-Land 39
Horyuji (Ikaruga) *101*
Hottentots 120
Hotu Matua 132
Hovenweep 23
Hoysolas 105
Hsia-chou 96, 97
Hsi-an chou 97
Hsi-chou 97
Hsi-hsia 86, 88, 89, 90, 94, 96–7, *97*
Hsi Liao 94
Hsi-liang fu 97
Hsing-ch'ing fu 97
Hsing-chung fu 94
Hsing-hua-chen 99
Hsi-ning 92, 97
Hsi-p'ing Fu 96
Huai-chou 97
Huai-te chün 97
Huan-chou 97
Huang Ho 89
Huang-chou 89
Huang-he 92
Huang-lung fu 94
Huang-shui 97
Huaxtecs *18*
Hudson Bay 29, 30
Hugh Capet 48
Hui-chou 97
Hujung Galah 107
Humahuaca 16
Humber 42
Hung Chou 94
Hung-chou 97
Hungary 35, 36, 53, 54, 55, 58,

60–61, *61*
Hungo Pavi 22
Hunguza 129
Hun-T'ung 94
Huo-shan chün 97
Hwang-ho 97
Hwangju-mok 99
Hyongjong 99

ibn-Sina (Avicenna) 79
Ibo 109
Icehouse Bottom 21
Iceland 30, 40, 40–41
Icelandic 41
Ichijo *101*
Iconium 63, 65
Idewa 100
Idrisi, al- 13, 113, 121
Ifat 119
Ifriqiya 67, 74
Iga *101*
Igbo-Ukwu 110, *113*, *114*
Igloolik 29
Iki 100
Ile-de-France 48
Ilek Khans 78
Incas 16
India 80–81, 84, 104–5, 106
  calendar 10
Indian Knoll 21
Indonesia 106–7, 123
Indravati 105
Indus 71, 73, 81
Ingombe 129
Innsbruck 55
Inscription House 23
Insulae Fortunatae 31
Inuit 13, 14, 28–9, 31, 41
Iona 46
Ipswich 42, 43
Iran 80
Iraq 66, 67, 70, 116
Ireland 44–5, 45, 47
Iringa 117
Irish kingdoms 35
iron, in Africa 116
Isamu Pati 129
Ise *101*
Isère 50
Isfahan 67, 71, 73, 81, 82
Islam 10, 66–83
  Africa 108, 112–15, 116
  calendar 10
  Spain 76–7
Islay 46
Isle of Man 42, 46
Isleif 40
Ismailis 74–5
Issoudun 49
Istakhr 67, 71, 73, 82
Italy 35, 49, 54, 55, 58
  see also specific cities
Itil 73, 82
Iton 51
ivory 112, 116
Ivrea 55
Ivuna 129
Iwafune 100
Iyalayet 28
Izamal 18
Izumi *101*

Jacob bar Jequthiel 59
Jaffna 105
Jaipal 80
Jalula 67, 71, 73, 82
Japan 10, 84, 85, 86–7, 100–101
jarls 38
Java 106
Jayavarman II 102
Jayavarman V 102–3
Jayavarman VII 103
Jelling 39
Jend 79
Jenne-jeno 112, *113*, 115
Jerusalem 67, 71, 73, 75, 82

Jewish quarter (Córdoba) 77
Jodhpur 81
John XII, pope 37
John Philagathos 54, 56
John Tzimesces 52, 54, 63–4
Jorunji *101*
Joshua ben Sira 83
Judaism 58–9
  calendar 10
  Europe 58–9
  Islamic world 82–3
Judith 118–19
Jui-an 89
Julianehåb 41
junks 91
Jürchens 95, 98–9, 99

Kabul 67, 71, 73, 79, 81, 82
Kaegyong 99
Kaesong 98, 99
Kaffa 65
Kagera 117
K'ai-feng 88, 89, *89*, 90, 91, 94, 96
Kairouan 66, 70, 73, 75, 82, 74, 83
Kakadu National Park *128*
Kalacakratantra 93
Kalasasaya 16
Kalenjin 117
Kalinjar 81, *81*
Kalossa 61
Kalundu 129
Kambuja 84, 102–3
Kampala 117
Kanchipuram 105
Kan'chou 97
Kan-chou (Hsuan-hua fu) 97
Kandy 105
Kaneie 100
Kanem 112, 113, 115
Kanem-Bornu 115
Kang Cho 99
Kannanur 105
Kannauj 81
Kansachi 129
Kanyakumari 104
Kaoli 89
Kapeni 129
Kara Khans 78
Karagwe 114, 117
Karaites 82–3
Kara-Khitan 95
Karluks 91
Karmatians 71, 73, 82
Kasenyi 117
Kashgar 79, 81
Kashmir 81, *81*
Kasuga (Nara) *101*
Katta *101*
Kattegat 39
Katwe 117
Kaupang 35, 36
Kawachi *101*
kayaks 28
Kazan 91
Kenneth mac Alpin 47
Kent 42
Kerbela 67, 71, 73, 82
Kermadec Islands *130*
Kerman 78
Kerulen 94
Khami 129
Khar Moron (Hsi Liao) 94
Khazars 53, 67, 71, 73, 82, *82*, 83
Kherson 82
Khirghiz 79
Khitan 86, 88, 90, 94–5, 98–9, 99
Khmer empire 102, 102–3
Khoikhoi 109
Khoisan 109, 117, *117*, 120
Khotan 81, 92
Khurasan 67, 78, 80, 81
Kiamtwara 117

Kiatuthlana 23
Kibengo 117
Kibiro 117
Kiet Siel 23
Kievan Rus 52–3
Kiev 38, 52, *53*, 53, 57, 61, 82
Kii *101*
Kikuyu 117
Kilaiyur 105
Kilipwa 117
Killaloe 44, 45
Kilwa 129
Kimberley *128*
Kin Kletso 22
Kin Klitzin 22
Kin Nahasbas 22
Kincora 44
king-lists, Africa 111
Kingigtorssuaq 30, 40
Kinishba 23
Kinkaid 21
Kinlichee 23
Kipushi 129
Kirgiz 91
Kirina 113
Kirman 67, 81
Kisigo 117
Kitano (Heian) *101*
Kitara 116, 117
kivas 23
Kiziba 117
Kliprivversberg 129
Klumes 93
Kofukuji (Nara) *101*
Kokand 79
Kokonor 91
kola nuts 112
Kolomoki 21
Kon Tiki 132
Konerirajapuram 105
Kongobuji (Mt Koya) *101*
Kopingsvirk 39
Koran 66, 68
Korcula 62
Korea (Koryo) 85, 95, 98–9, 99
Korechika 100, *101*
Korkai 105
Koshiki Retto *100*
Kosoy 115
Koster 21
Koukya 113
Koumbi Saleh 112, *113*, 114, *114*, 115
Kozelsk 53
Kozushima 100
Krivichians 53
Kua-chou 96
Kuawa 23
Kuei-te chou 94
Kufa 67
Kuhistan 81
Kuju (Kusong) 99
Kukulcan 19
Kum 99
Kumbakonam 105
Kunama 119
Kunashiri 100
Kung-chou 97
Kung Fu-tzu (Confucius) 85
Kupe *130*
Kuriyagawa 100
Ku-sso-lu 93
Ku-yu kuan 96
Kw'adza 117
Kwakiutl 26, *26*
Kwangju-mok 99
Kyoju 99
Kyoju-mok 99
Kyonggi 99
Kyongsang 99
Kyto 86
Kyushu 100

La Quemada 18
L'Anse aux Meadows 30, 31
Labrador 29, 30
Lace 21

Ladakh 92
Lahore 80, 81
Lake Melville 30
Lake Texcoco 18
Lake Titicaca 16, 17
Lalibela 118, 119
Lamaghan 81
Lamoka Lake 21
Lamtuna 113
Lamu Archipelago 117
Lan-chou 97
Langres 49, 50
Lang-shan Mtn 97
langue d'oc 48
Laon 50
Laos 102, 103
Lapita 124
Lapps 39
Larisa 63, 64, 65
Lasta 118, 119
Lastovo 62
Laura 128
Lausanne 55
Lausitz 55
Lavant 55
Le Croy 21
Le Puy 50
Lechfeld, Battle of 54
Legend of the Four Captives 83
Leif Erikson (Leif the Lucky)
   30, 31
Leinster 44, 45, 47
León 35, 36, 58, 76, 76, 77
Lewis 46
Lewis, Agnes 83
Lhasa 92
Li Chi-ch'ien 93, 96
Li Te-ming 96
Li Yüan-hao (Wei-ming) 97
Liao-chou 94
Liao Empire 86, 88, 90, 94,
   94–5, 96, 98–9
Liao river 94
Libya 67
Liège 50, 55
Limerick 44, 45
Limoges 49, 50
Limousin 49
Limpopo 120
Lin-chou 97
Lincoln 42
Lindisfarne 36
Ling-chou (Hsi-p'ing fu) 96, 97
Linz 55
Lisbon 76
Lisieux 49, 51
Little Salt Spring 21
lodestones 91
Lodi 55
Loire 50
London 21, 35, 36, 38, 42, 60
Lorch 35
Lorraine 49
Los Muertos 23
Loti, Pierre 102
Lotrie 120
Lough Corrib 45
Lough Derg 45
Lough Ree 45
Louis V 48
Lower Burgundy 35
Lower Lorraine 50, 55
Lowry 23
Luan-chou 94
Luanza 129
Luba 109
Lübeck 55
Lucena 76
Luna 55
Lund 35, 39
Lunda 109
Lundi 27
Lüneburg 55
Lung-chou 97
Lung-hsing 89
Lung-hsü 94–5
Luwu 107

Lyons 35, 36, 49, 50, 55, 58,
   60, 72

Maa 117
Ma'a 117
Maasai 109, 117
Macassar 107
Macbeth 47
mace 106
Macedonia 63, 64, 65
Mackenzie river 28
Mâcon 50
Madi 117
Madinah al-Zahira 77
Madinat al-Zahra 77
Madjapahit 107
Madurai 105
Magdeburg 36, 55
Maghreb 70, 72, 82
Magyars 54, 60
Mahadevi 105
Mahdi 67, 74
Mahdiyya 74, 75
Mahinda 104
Mahmud of Ghazni 71, 73, 79,
   79, 80–81, 84
Maine 49, 51
Mainz 36, 55, 58, 59
maize 13
Majapahit 107
Makakam 107
Makah 26
Makkura 71, 73
Makran 67
Malacca 107
Málaga 58, 76
Malagarasi 117
malaria 110
Malay 109
Malay Peninsula 107
Malayu (Jambi) 107
Malcolm II 47
Maldive Islands 104
Maldon 42
Maldon, Battle of 38, 43
Mali 115
Malinalco 18
Malindi 117
Malinke 113
Mamallapuram 105
Mamluks 73
Manchuria 95
Mande 109
Manjusri 96
Mansur, al- bi-Allah (Almanzor)
   70, 76–7
Mantua 55
Manú 16
Maoil Seachlainn 44
Maol Mordha 44, 47
Maoris 131
Mapela 129, 121
Mapungubwe 120–121, 129
Marcianopolis 63, 65
Marcia's Rincón 22
Marietta 21
Marne 50
Marrakesh 113
Marseilles 49, 55, 58, 60
Marshall Islands 124
Mar-yul 93
Masaka Hill 117
Maslamah al-Majriti 76
Masudi, al- 116
Mataram 106–7, 107
Mathgamain 44
Mathura 81, 81
Matlatzincas 18
Mawudzu 129
Maxon-Derby 21
Maya 19
Mayapán 18
Mbande Hill 129
Mbisha 117
McKeithen 21
Meath 44, 45, 47

Mecca 67, 71, 73, 75, 82
Mecklenburg 55
Medieval Warm Period 34
Medina 67, 71, 73, 75, 82
Mediterranean Sea 58
Meissen 55
Melakadambur 105
Melaperumpallam 105
Melitene 63, 65
Melville Bay 29, 30, 40
Menelik 118
Meng-wu (Mongols) 94
Mera Tekle Haimanot 119
Mercia 42
Merians 53
Merida 76
Merkid 94
Merseburg 55
Mertola 76
Merv 67, 71, 73, 78, 79
Mesa Grande 23
Mesa Verde 22, 23, 23
Mesobe Werq 119
Mesopotamia 67, 70
Messina 36, 62, 65
Metz 50, 55, 58, 60
Meuse 50
Mexico 18–19, 23
Meyer, Andrie 120
Michinaga 100–101
Middle Mississippian 21
Mieszko 57
Miidera 101
Milan 35, 36, 55, 58, 60
Miletus 63, 65
millenarians 34
millennium, dates and timing
   11
Mimbres Valley 23
Mindanao 107
Minden 55
Ming-sha 97
Minsk 53, 61
missionaries 36
Mississippi 20, 21, 25
Mississippian culture 20, 21
Missouri 20, 24, 25
Mkadini 117
moai 132
moas 131
Mocha 119
Moche pyramid 16
Modena 55
Modoc 21
Mogollan 23
Mogollon 22, 23
Mojave Desert 23
Mokchong 99
Moluccas (Spice Islands) 106,
   107, 107
Mombasa 117
Momuno 100
Mon 102
Mongolia 95, 96
Mongols 86, 91, 95
monks 36
Monks Mound 20–21
Monophysites 62
Monreale 36
Mont St Michel 51
Montana 25
Monte Albán 18
Montenegro 64
Montezuma Castle 23
Monument Valley 22, 23
Moravia 33, 55
Moray 46
Moray Firth 46
Morelos 18, 19
Moron 76
Moscow 53
Mossi 113
Mosul 67, 68, 71, 73, 82
Mouhot, Henri 102
Mound City 21
Moundville 21
Mt Arjuna 107

Mt Hie 101
Mt Kasagi 101
Mt Merapi 106, 107
Mt Meru 102
Mt Shigi 101
Mt Terevaka 133, 133
Mt Vanagiri 107
Mt William 128
Mt Wutai 96
Muara 107
Muara Jambi 106
Muhammad 66
Mühlhausen 55
Muizz, al- 74
Mukran 67
Mule Canyon 23
Mull 46
Multan 67, 71, 73, 82
Munich 55
Munster 44, 47, 45
Muntasir 79
Muqaddasi, al- 78
Murasaki Shikibu 101
Murchadh 44, 47
Murcia 76
Muroji (Mt Muro) 101
Mursa 62, 65
Muscat 67, 71, 73, 82
Mustakfi, al- 70
Mutasim, al- 70
Mwamasapa 129
Myongju-mok 99

Nachi Falls 101
Nagapattinam 105, 106
Nagarkot 80–81
Nagpur 81
Nain 30
Najran 67, 71, 73, 82
Naju-mok 99
Nakadori 100
Nakayama 100
Naknek 28
Naktong 99
Nalatale 129
Nallur 105
Namgyong 99
Nanchao 89
Nanjing 94
Nankaido 100
Nantes 49, 49
Naples 36, 58, 61, 62, 65
Narbonne 36, 49, 50
Narva 53
Nasr 79
Natchez 20, 21, 21
native Americans 14, 20–31
Natural Bridges 23
Naumburg 55
Navarre 35, 36, 49, 58, 76, 77
Nazca lines 16
Nebo Hill 21
Nebraska 25
Nehavend 67, 71, 73, 82
Neisse 55
Nepal 10
Nestor 52
Nevers 49
Neville 21
New Alto 22
New Mexico 22–3, 25
New Style calendar 11
New Zealand 124, 126, 127,
   130, 130–131
Newfoundland 13, 14, 30
Niamey 113
Niani 113
Nice 35, 49, 55
Nicomedia 63, 65
Nicopolis 63, 65
Nidaros 41
Niebla 76
Niemen 53
Niger 108, 112
Nijmegen 55

Nile 74
Nilotic peoples 110
Ning-chiang fu 94
Ning-kuo 89
Ning-pien chou 97
Nish 36, 61, 63, 65
Nishapur 67, 71, 73
Nisibis 63
Nissim ben Jacob ibn Shahin 83
Nizam al-Mulk 78
Nkore 117
Nodwell 21
Nootka 26
Normandy 48, 49, 50, 51, 51
Normans 51
North Africa 66, 68, 74–5, 77,
   83
North Dakota 25
North Island 130
Northumberland 35
Northumbria 42, 46, 47
North-west coast (US) 26
North-western Plains 25
Norton 28
Norway 35, 38–9, 39
Nottingham 42
Nova Scotia 30
Novae 63, 65
Novara 55
Novgorod 38, 52, 53, 53
Noviedunum 63, 65
Ntusi 116–17, 117
Nubians 67, 72
Nugdlit 29
Nuh 79, 80
Nuremberg 55
nutmeg 106

Oberwesel 55
O'Brien dynasty 47
obsidian 19
Oceania 122–34
Odense 39
Odilo 37
Odon 51
Oescus 63, 65
Oghuz 78
Oise 49
Okachi 100
Oklahoma 25
Okvik Island 28
Oland 39
Olary 128
Old Åsa 117
Old Oyo 113, 114
Old Style calendar 11
Oldenburg 55
Olga 52
Olifantspoort 129
Olomouc 55
Olympic Peninsula 27
Oman 67
Omi 101
O'Neills 44
Ongamo 117
Onion Portage 28
On-Ogur 60
Ontario 25
Opol and Ratibor 55
Oporto 35, 36, 58, 76
Ordos 96, 97
Orkneys 35, 36, 40, 41, 46, 47
Orléans 35, 49, 50
Orne 51
Oromo 109
Orseolo, Pietro 62
Osceola 21
Osconto 21
Oseberg 38
Oslo 39, 38
Osnabrück 55
Otago Peninsula 130
Otranto 36, 58, 61
Otrar 79
Otto I (the Great) 36, 54, 56,
   60
Otto II 54, 56, 60, 64

Otto III 32, 54–7, 62, 64
outcastes 98
Oviedo 76
Ovimbundu 109
Owen the Bald 47
Oxford 42, 43

Pachacamac 17
Pachuca 19
Paderborn 55
Padua 55
Pagan 84
Pai-ch'ih fortress 97
Pakistan 81
Palermo 36, 65
Palestine 64, 74, 82
Palk Strait 105
Pallavanisvaram 105
Palmer 21
Palmyra 63, 65
Pamplona 76
Pandang Lawas 107
Pandyas 104, 105, 105
Pangani 117
P'an-lo-chih 93
Pannonia 62, 65
Panticapaeum 63, 65
Pao-an chün 97
Pao-ch'ing 89
Pao-chou 94
Pao-te chün 97
papal states 35
paper 91
Paplios 63, 65
Paracas 16
Paramaras 104
Paris 35, 36, 49, 50, 51, 51, 58, 59, 60
Parma 55
Parvati 104
Passau 55
Patras 63, 65
Pawnee 25
Pays de Caux 51
Peace of God 48, 49, 51
Pechenegs 52, 53
Pecs 61
Peking 94
Pemba 116
Penasco Blanco 22
Penner 105
Pepin III 48
pepper 107
Perigord 49
Périgueux 50
Perlak 107
Persia 66, 67, 70, 80
Perugia 55
Perun 53
Peshawar 80, 81
Pest 61
Phalaborwa 129
Phasis 63
Philippi 63, 65
Philippopolis 63, 65
Phillips Spring 21
philosopher's stone 69
Philotheus 118
Phnom Penh 103
Piacenza 55
Picts 46, 47
Pilbara 128
pilgrimages, in Japan 101
Pinelawn Valley 23
P'ing-chiang 89
P'ing-chou 94
Pinsk 53
Pinyin 90
Pisa 36, 55
Pitcairn Island 125
Pityus 63, 65
'Plains Village' people 25
Plaquemine Mississippian 21
ploughs 35
poetry
    English 43
    Icelandic 41

Po-hai 94, 98
Point of Pines 23
Poitiers 49, 50
Poitou 49
Poland 36, 39, 53, 54, , 55, 57, 58, 61
Polonnaruwa 104, 105
Polotsk 53
Polyanians 53
Polynesia 122, 124–6
Pomerania 55
Pomo 26
Pondichery 105
Ponthieu 49
Port Mollet 28
Poverty Point 21
Poznan 57
Prague 55, 57, 58, 61, 82
Prambanan 107, 107
Pre-Asu 117
Prespa 64
printing 91
Provence 48, 50, 55
Prussia 55, 57
Prutul R. 65
Pskov 53
Pucara 17
Pudukkottai 105
Pueblo Alto 22, 23
Pueblo Bonito 22, 22–3
Pueblo del Arroyo 22
Pueblo Grande 23
Pueblo people 14, 22, 23
Puilamangai 105
Pukkye 99
Punjab 67, 80–81
Purang 93
Puye 23

Qadisiya 67
Qaim, al- 71
Qamdo 92
Qanbalu 116
Qinghai 92
Quanchou 89
Quarai 23
Quebec 30
Quetta 81
Quetzalcóatl 18, 19
Quiha 119
Qusdar 81

Rabbanites 83
Ragnarok 41
Ragusa 36, 61
Rahman, Abd al- 76, 83
Rai 67, 71, 73, 82
Rajaraja I (Rajakesari) 104, 106
Rajarajeshvara temple 105
Rajasthan 80
Rajendra 104–5
Rama 104
Ramla 82
Rano Raraku 132, 133, 133,134
Rapa Nui 132
Rarotonga 131
Ras 65
Ras Kipini 117
Rashi of Troyes 59
Rashtrakutas 104
Ratzeburg 55
Ravenna 36, 55, 58, 61
Rayy 78
Razi, al- 70
Rebun 100
Red Sea 82
Regensburg 55, 58
Reggio 36
Reigh 21
Reims 36, 49, 50, 55, 58, 48, 51, 59
Remagen 55
Rennes 49
Republican River 24, 25, 25
Resaina 63, 65
Resolute Bay 29

Resolution Islands 30
Reting 92, 93
Réville 51
Reykjanes 30, 40
Rhadanites 82
Rhegium 62, 65
Rhine 35, 36, 50, 58, 59, 61
Rhodes 67
Rhône 50
Ribagorza 49
Ribat 113
Ribe 39
Richard, Duke of Normandy 59
Riishiri 100
Rimini 65
Rinchen Zangpo 93
Rio Grande 25
Ripen 36, 58
Risle 51
Riverton 21
Robert the Magnificent 51
Robert the Pious 48, 51, 56
Roberts Drift 129
Robin Mound 21
Roden 21
Rodez 49
Rodgers Shelter 21
Roggeveen, Jacob 132
Roha 119
Rohana 104
Romagna 55
Romanization of Chinese 90
Rome 33, 35, 36, 36–7, 54, 55, 57, 58, 60, 62, 82
Ronda 76
Rose Island 131
Roskilde 35, 39
Rostov 53, 53
Rouen 36, 49, 50, 51, 51, 58
Rualin 16
Ruanga 129
Rufiji 117
Rügen 39
Ruin Island 29
Rumi, Jauhar al- 74
Rus 38, 52–3, 62
Rusha 117
Russia 38, 52–3
Russian Orthodox Church 52–3
Russian Primary Chronicle, The 52
Rustenburg 129
Rutara 117
Ruvu 117
Rwanda 111, 116, 117
Ryazan 53

Sabaki 117
Sabur ibn-Ardashir 71
Sackett 21
Sado 100
safflower 107
sagas 38, 41
Sahagún, Fray Bernadino de 18
Saikaido 100
Sailendras 107
St Adalbert the Martyr 57
St Andrews 46
St Benedict 36, 37
St Bertin 50
St Clair sur Epte 51
St Cyril 33, 53
St Davids 42
St Denis 49
St James the Apostle 77
St Lawrence Island 28
St Lô 51
St Louis 21, 21
St Mark 62
St Methodius 33
St Peter, Patrimony of 55
St Quentin 50
St Stephen see Stephen, king of Hungary
St Vladimir see Vladimir
Saintonge 49
Salamanca 76

Salamis 63, 65
Salerno 36
Salihan 26
Salish 26, 27, 27
Salmon 23
salt 112
Saluzzo 55
Salzburg 36, 55
Saman Khudat 78
Samanids 71, 73, 78–9, 79, 80
Samarkand 67, 68, 71, 73, 78, 79, 79, 81, 82
Samarra 70
Samosata 63, 65
Samuel 41
Samuel ha-Nagid 83
Samye 92, 93
Sana 129
Sancerre 49
Sandwich Bay 30
Sanga 129
Sangju-mok 99
Sangre de Cristo Mountains 25
Sanhadja 112, 113, 113, 115
San 120
San Marcos de León 76
San Pedro de Atacama 16
sandalwood 107
San'indo 100
Sant' Angelo 36
Santa Rita 18
Santabong 107
Santiago 76
Santiago de Compostela 76, 76, 77
San'yodo 100
Saône 50
Saragossa 58, 76, 82
Sarai 53
Sardes 63, 65
Sardinia 55, 58
Sasania 67
Satala 63, 65
Sava 62
Savoy 50, 55
Saxony 36, 55, 58, 60
Scandinavia 38–9
Schechter, Solomon 83
Scie 51
Scodra 62, 65
Scone 46
Scoresby Sound 40
Scotland 36, 44, 46, 47
Scottia 46
Scowlitz 27
Scupi 63, 65
sea cucumber 9, 123
Sebastopol 52
Sebuk-tigin 80
Seckau 55
Second Coming 34
Secret History of the Mongols, The 95
Sées 51
Seine 50, 51
Seistan 67
Sembiyan 105
Sena 129
Senegal 113
Sens 50, 50
Serbia 33, 65
Serpent Mound 21
Settsu 101
Seuta 117
Severn 42
Severyanians 53
Seville 76, 82
Shabik'eshchee Village 22
Sha-chou 96, 97
Shah-Nama 80
Shanga 116
Shang-ching 94
Shannon 45
Shan-yan, Treaty of 95, 99
Shao-hsing 89
Shawa 119
Sheng-kuei fortress 97

Sheng-tsung (Lung-hsü) 94–5
Shen-hua ch'eng 94
Shetlands 40, 41
Shigatse 92
Shih-chou 97
Shi'ite Muslims 66–7, 70, 71, 74
Shikoku 100
Shingu (New Shrine) 101
Shinto 87
Shiraz 81
Shiva 102, 103, 104
Shoda 100
shoguns 87
Shona 109, 120, 121
Shou-ch'un 89
Shun-ch'ang 89
Shun-chou 94, 97
Shun-hua crossing 97
Shuo-chou 94
Sicily 55, 58
Siena 36, 55
Sigtuna 39
Sigurd the Stout 47
Sijilmasa 112, 113, 113
Silesia 55
Silk Road 68, 79
silver 69
Silvester II, pope see Gerbert of Aurillac
Sind 67
Singara 63
Singhasari 107
Singidunum 63, 65
Sinope 63, 65
Siqilli, al- (Jauhar al-Rumi) 74
Siret 63, 65
Siscia 62, 65
Sistan 81
Sitric Silkenbeard 44, 47
Sitten 55
Sivapuram 105
Skagerrak 39
Skagit 26
skaldic verses 41
Skye 46
slavery 34, 58, 60, 68, 72–3, 98, 116
Slavinia 55
Slavs 35, 34, 54, 57, 58, 60, 62, 72
sleeping sickness 110
Slovakia 57
Slovianians 53
Smith Sound 30
Smolensk 53
Snaefelisnes 30, 40
Snaketown 23
Snowy Mountains 128–9
Soba 67, 71, 73, 82
Socotra 73, 82
Sofala 116, 121, 129
Sofia 63, 65, 64
Sogyony (Pyonggyang) 99
Sohae 99
Soissons 50
Sokoto 113
Solothurn 55
Somali 109
Somaliland 116
Somali slaves 72
Somme 51
Somnath 81, 81
Songhay 109, 113
Songjong 98–9
Soninke 113, 114
Sorento 36
Sosso 113
South Appalachian Mississippian 21
South China Sea 89
South Island 130
south-east Asia 85, 106–7
Southern Capital (Liao) 94
Southern Plains 25
Southhampton Island 29
Spain 66, 67, 76–7, 83

Sparta 63, 65
Speke, John 111, 116
Speyer 55, 58
Spice Islands 106, 107
spice trade 106, 107
Spiro 21
Spitzbergen 41
Split 62
Spoleto 55, 55
Sravana 105
Sri Lanka (see Ceylon)
Sringeri 105
Srinivasanallur 105
Srivijaya kingdom 84, 106, 107, 107
Srivijaya (Palembang) 107
Stad 40
Stamford 42
Stephen, king of Hungary 56, 60, 61
Stoan 21
Stobi 63, 65
Strait of Belle Isle 30
Strasbourg 55
Strathclyde 42, 46, 47
Styria 55
Subh 76, 77
sub-Saharan 108–21
Su-chou 97
Sudak 53
Sudanese slaves 72
Suhar 67, 71, 73, 82
Sui-te chün 97
Sukhothai 102
Sulaim 75
Sulawesi 123
Sumatra 84, 104, 106, 107
Sumbawa 107
Sung China 89
Sung Dynasty 86, 88–91, 94, 95, 96, 97, 98–9, 106
Sungari 94
Sungbo 114
Sungbo's Eredo 113, 114
Sunnah 66
Sunni Muslims 66, 70, 71, 78, 115
Supreme Capital (Liao) 94
Suquamish 26
Susa 67, 71, 73, 82
Sutri 55
Suzdal 53
Svear 39
Svein Forkbeard 38, 39, 42–3
Svolt, Battle of 39, 43
Svyatoslav 52, 63, 64
Swabia 54, 55
Swahili 109, 116
Sweden 35, 38–9, 39
sweet potato 127, 131
Syr Darya 67, 71, 73, 79, 82
Syracusae 65
Syria 66, 67, 74

Tabriz 67, 71, 73, 81, 82
Tabuk 67, 71, 73, 82
Tadmekka 113
T'aejo 98
Tafilalt 112
Taghaza 113
Tahiti 125
Tai, al- 71
T'ai-tsu 94
T'ai-Tsung 88
T'ai-yuan 89
Takama 117
Takas 107
takkanot 59
Takrur 112, 113
Talas 67, 71, 73, 82
Tale of Genji, The 101
Talmud 58, 59, 82, 83
Tamil Nadu 104
Tamils 84
Ta-ming 89
Tamuín 18
Tana 117

Tanba 101
T'an-chou 89, 94
Tangier 82
Tanguts 86, 88, 89, 90, 93, 95, 96–7
Tanjore
Tanjore (Thanjavur) 104, 105
Tanzania 116
T'ao-chou 97
Tara 44, 45
Taranto 36, 58
Tarentaise 36, 49, 55
Tarentum 65
Tarsus 63, 65, 67, 71, 73, 82
Tashi-gompa 92
Tato 117
Taylor, Charles 83
Taylor–Schechter Genizah Research Unit 83
Tbilisi 53
Te Rangi Hiroa 126
Tees 42
Tehuacán 18
Tenochtitlán 18, 19
Tento 23
Teotihuacán 18, 18–19
Ternate 107
Tete 129
Tha'alabi, al- 78
Thailand 102, 103
Thames 42
Thande 129
Thangbrand 40
Thanjavur 104
Thar Desert 81
Theodosia 63
Theophano 54, 64
Thérouanne 49
Thessalonica 63, 64, 65
Thetford 42
Thier 58
Thöling 92, 93
Thorarin the Black 41
Thorfinn Karlsefni 31
Thorgeir 40
Thorgilsson, Ari 40
Thorkell the Tall 43
Thorvald 31
Thousand and One Nights 69
three-field rotation 34
Three Kim Pueblo 23
Three Men of Khams 92
Thule people 28–9, 30, 40
Thunupa 17
Thuringia 55
Thyri 38, 39
Tiahuanaco (Tiwanaku) 16, 16–17, 17
Tiaret 82
Tiberias 82
Tibet 85, 89, 92, 92–3, 96, 92–3
Tidore 107
T'ieh-chou 94
T'ien-te 94
T'ien-te-chun 97
Tiflis 67, 71, 73, 81, 82
Tigre 119
Tigris river 70, 71
Timbuktu 112, 113
Ting-chou 97
Ting-pien chun 97
Tiruchera 105
Tirunaraiyur 105
Tiruvakkarai 105
Tiruvarur 105
Tiruvedikudi 105
Tiruvenkadu 105
Tiruvidaimaradur 105
Titicaca, Lake 16, 17
Tivoli 55
Tlaxcala 18
Tlemcen 113
Tlingit 26, 26
Todaiji monastery (Nara) 100, 101

Toji (Heian) 101
Tokaido 100
Tokolor 113
Toledo 58, 76, 83
Toltecs 18–19
Tomi 63, 65
Tonga 109
Tonggye 99
Tonggyong 99
Tonle Sap 102
Topiltzin 19
Topoc maze 23
Toro 117
Tortona 55
Torzhok 53
Tosando 100
Toul 55
Toulon 55
Toulouse 36, 49, 49, 50, 58, 60
Touques 51
Touraine 49
Tours 36, 49, 50
Trajan's Gate 64
Trani 55
Transoxiana 67, 78
Trebizond 53, 63, 65
Trelleborg 38
Trent 42, 55
Treviso 55
Trichinopoly 105
Trier 36, 50, 55
Trifels 55
Trinity 35
Triohuvanam 105
Tripoli 66, 70, 72, 82
Tripolis 63, 65
Trivento 55
trogon bird 19
tsetse fly 110
Trondheim 39
Tropic of Cancer 82, 89
Troesmis 63, 65
trogon bird 19
tsetse fly 110
Tsung-ko 92, 97, 93, 96
Tuam 89
Tuareg 109, 113
Tuat 113
Tughril 71
Tula (Tollan) 18, 18, 18–19
Tulum 18
Tumasik (Singapore) 107
Tumen 99
Tunacunhee 21
Tunai 53
T'ung-hua 94
Tung-p'ing 89
Tung-sheng chou 97
Tunis 70, 73, 82
Turin 36, 55, 58, 61
Turkmenistan 78
Turks 71, 71, 72, 73, 78–9, 82
Tusayan 23
Tuscany 55
Tuzigoot 23
Tyana 63, 65
Tyne 42
Tyrus 63

Uelen 28
Uganda 116–17
Uhtred 47
Uighurs 79, 89, 92
Uitkomst 129
Ulm 55
Ulster 44, 45
Umayyad Emirate 71, 72, 82
Umayyads 66, 76, 113
umiaks 28
Umnak Island 28
Una Vida 22

Unalakleet 28
Ungava Bay 30
Unguja Ukuu 117
Ungwana 117
Upper Burgundy 35
Upper Lorraine 55
Uppsala 35, 39
Urgench 72, 73, 79
Utrecht 55
Uvinza 117
Uzbekistan 78

Vadakkalathur 105
Valence 55
Valencia 76
Valois 49
Varangians 38, 64
Varna 53, 61
Vastergarna 39
Vedaranyam 105
Velankanni 105
Vellar 105
Venice 35, 36, 55, 58, 61, 62, 62, 73
Veracruz 18
Vercelli 55
Verdun 55, 58
Vermandois 49
Verona 55, 62
Veszprem 61
Vexin 49, 51
Viborg 39
Vicenza 55
Vich 50, 76
Vie 51
Vienna 55
Vienne 36, 49, 50, 55
Vietnam 84–5, 88, 102
Viga-Glum 41
Vijaya (Binh Dinh) 102
Vijayanagar 105
Vikings 13, 14, 32, 38–9
   England 38, 42–3
   France 51
   Greenland 29, 40–41
   Iceland 40–41
   Ireland 44
   Russia 38, 52–3
   Scotland 47
   Vinland 30–31
   western voyages 30
Viminacium 63, 65
Vinland 30–31
Viracocha 17
Virunum 62
Vishnu 107
Vistula 39, 61
Viviers 55
Vizcaya 76
Vladimir (Volodimir) 52–3, 54, 64, 65
Volga 53, 79
Volga Bulgars 53
Völuspa 41
Vridhachalam 105
Vyatichians 53
Vyner, Robert 129

Wadan (Ouadane) 113
Wade–Giles Romanization system 90
Wagadu 114
Walakpa 28
Walata 113
Walnut Canyon 23
Wami 117
Wangara 113–14
Wang Kon (T'aejo) 98
Wapanuckel 21
War Dyabi 115
War of the Irish, The 47
Wardell 24
Wargla 113
Wari (Huari) empire 16, 17
Washita 25
Waterford 44, 45

weapons, in China 90–91
Webb, Jim 129
Weeden Island 21
Wei-chou 97
Wei-ming 97
Weissenburg 55
Wembere 117
Werlto's Rincón 22
Wessex 35, 42, 42
Wessilli 58
West Coast (America) 26–7
West Frankish Kingdom (see France)
Western Capital (Liao) 94
Western Settlement 30, 40, 41
western voyages 30
Wexford 44, 45
whaling 28
White Bay 30
Wichita Indians 25
Wijiji 22
William, Duke of Normandy 43
William the Pious 37
Winchester 42, 43
Wonoboyo 107
Woollandale 129
Worms 55, 58, 59
Wright 21
Wu-chou 94
Wu-la-hai fortress 97
Wupatki 23
Würzburg 55

Xanten 58
Xicalanco 18
Xinjiang 96
Xochicalco 18

Yagul 18
Yalu 99
Yamama 67
Yamato 101
Yangchow 90
Yanggwang 99
Yangtze River 85, 89, 89, 91
Yarmuk 67
Yaroslav 53
Yasodhapura (Angkor) 102–3
Yellow River 85, 96
Yemen 67
Yen-an fu 97
Yen-chou 97
Ye-shes-'od 93
Yezd 81
Yiddish 59
Yin-chou 94, 97
Yin-chuan 96
Ying-ch'ang 89
Ying-chou 94
Ying-li 97
Yin-shan Mtn 97
York 35, 36, 42, 42, 47, 61
Yoruba 109
Yu Chou 94
Yucatán 19
Yunnan 88
Yunus, Ali ibn- 75

Zabulistan 81
Zadokites 83
Zaghawa 112
Zagros Mountains 81
Zagwe 118, 119
Zahrawi, Abu al-Qasim al- (Abulcasis) 76
Zaka 129
Zamora 76, 77
Zanj 72, 116
Zanzibar 116
Zarqali, al- (Arzachel) 76
zebu cattle 116 Zeila 119
Zenata Morocco 75
Zimbabwe 120–21
Zirids 75
Zoe 57
Zurich 55